The
Self-revelation
of God

The Self-revelation of God

by

J. KENNETH KUNTZ

THE WESTMINSTER PRESS
Philadelphia

LIBRARY OF CONGRESS CATALOG CARD NO. 67-10270

Published by The Westminster Press®
Philadelphia, Pennsylvania

PRINTED IN THE UNITED STATES OF AMERICA

To Ruth

Contents

Preface

It is by conscious design that the title of this book cannot claim for itself esotericism, cleverness, or modernity. The title is simply descriptive. But what is it that is being described? Although the present study has its own theological orientation, it cannot introduce itself as a contribution to the enterprises of systematic theology. Nor does it record a spiritual pilgrimage experienced by the author. Rather, the subject at hand is the self-manifestation of God to the Hebrew people of the Old Testament.

Throughout her history, Israel understood herself to be a *called* people. In situations that were anything but secure, she believed that she was being addressed by the deity who chose to disclose himself to her in immediate encounter. Clearly, the God of the Old Testament has long been understood by Biblical interpreters as a God who acts. Equally important, however, the events in Israel's history that were evoked and shaped by the deity were events that did not happen wordlessly. The varied Old Testament traditions persist in presenting the deity as one who speaks, and Israel as a people who *hears*. This divine speaking and self-manifestation was formalized within Israel's written literature and thereby was preserved as a precious possession.

This volume had its genesis in a dissertation for the Th.D. degree received in 1963 from Union Theological Seminary in New York City. Its title was " An Examination of Theophany in the Old Testament with Special Reference to Theophanic Contexts in the Psalter." Special attention was given to Yahweh's disclosure of himself to Israel at Mt. Sinai (Ex., chs. 19 to 24) and to the memory and representation of that event within The Book of Psalms. Although these concerns also prevail in the present volume, two new chapters have been added — Chapter IV treats the subject of theophany as it bears upon Israel's patriarchs, and Chapter V considers the prophets as the recipients of theophanic manifestation.

Both in presentation and in scope, the book is less technical than was the dissertation. For the sake of simplicity, the amount of Hebrew has been considerably reduced, and for the sake of economy, it has been transliterated. While all translations are my own, it has seemed advisable to have all verse numbers correspond with those in the Revised Standard Version. The scholar will indeed know how to cope with this problem, and the layman, for whom this study is also intended, need not care. In the writing of this book, I have tried to keep in the back of my mind — but not too far back — a functioning image of the scholar and the layman. The scholar image has motivated me to keep the compromises few in number, and the layman image has pressed upon me the urgency to make it bearable and interesting.

Special attention should be given here to one study on theophany which came into my possession somewhat late for rigorous use. This is the stimulating monograph by Jörg Jeremias titled *Theophanie: Die Geschichte einer alttestamentlichen Gattung*.[1] A thorough review of Jeremias' study is not possible here,[2] but half a dozen comparative observations of a basic sort may be in order. First, the Jeremias volume is a highly technical work and, as its subtitle suggests, it is from first to last intent upon carefully recovering and fully comprehending a theophanic literary form (*Gattung*). Although the present study in its own way quests after form, it is equally concerned with various theological facets that are an integral part of the Israelite understanding of revelation. Second, both Jeremias and I appreciate the importance of Ancient Near Eastern analogies for the study of Old Testament theophany, but Jeremias

[1] (Neukirchen-Vluyn: Neukirchener Verlag, 1965).

[2] A favorable review by Roland E. Murphy, O. Carm., has appeared in *JBL*, Vol. 85 (1966), pp. 107 f. Somewhat less supportive is the note in *ZAW*, Vol. 78 (1966), p. 119.

has drawn upon them more fully. Indeed, he avers that the second member of the original two-membered Old Testament theophanic *Gattung* that he posits, namely, " the tumult of nature," was taken up by Israel from the religious ideology of her neighbors. Third, Jeremias has made a much sharper distinction between the prose and poetic forms of theophanic depiction than the present volume has deemed necessary. In fact it is scarcely an exaggeration to say that in his treatment only the poetic forms are given a hearing. This consuming interest in Hebrew poetry is the natural outcome of Jeremias' assumption that Israel's theophanic *Gattung* in its purest state is to be detected in the original text of Judg. 5:4-5 within the Song of Deborah. Since I have come independently at the *Gattung* through such a *prose* text as Gen. 26:23-25, it is only natural that our assessment of the roles that prose and poetry play in Biblical theophany should differ.

Fourth, Yahweh's self-disclosures to the patriarchs in The Book of Genesis are completely ignored by Jeremias as having no bearing upon the subject at hand. I have devoted a full chapter to these theophanies in Genesis and have based many of my form-critical observations upon the texts involved. Fifth, in his attempt to delineate the *Sitz im Leben* (life setting) of the Old Testament theophanic form, Jeremias argues that the answer does not lie amid hypothetical proceedings of the ongoing Jerusalem cult, but rather in the context of victory celebration in song over the successful wars of Yahweh in the pre-monarchy period. Although one must work in the shadows, I am not convinced that the original spontaneity of the theophany cannot be dramatically and successfully actualized in the established cult at Jerusalem in the time of the monarchy. In short, Jeremias judges the scholarly reconstructions of the recent past on this matter to be quite unsound. With admittedly some qualification, my own approach tends to endorse them. Sixth, Jeremias has taken a vast number of Old Testament passages into account, yet I believe my own study, which focuses upon somewhat fewer pericopes, to be more exegetical in tone since it moves more freely between form-critical and interpretive issues.

One further observation, however, is to my way of thinking more vital than any of the preceding. Jeremias and I differ most radically in the kind of language we expect to find in Old Testament theophany. According to Jeremias, it is the task of theophanic passages to present with striking richness *descriptions* of (1) Yahweh's coming and (2) the terrestrial and mortal reactions to that coming. While I wish to be open to the significance of the descriptive element, I value as even more central to Old Testament theophany *the witness to the actuality of divine speaking*. If the theophany is one crucial way in which the Old Testament deals with divine revelation, then it would appear to be normative, if not necessary, that the divine *word* is basic to this theophanic medium of revelation. The following opinion of Gerhard von Rad presents the matter forcefully: "With an Old Testament theophany everything depends upon the pronouncement: the phenomena which accompany it are always merely accessories."[3] If not in all, then still in quite a number of Old Testament texts which may properly be designated as theophanic, Yahweh draws near for the manifest purpose of speaking.

Here, then, is sufficient illustration that Jeremias' treatment of theophany in the Old Testament and my own differ in range, focus, and result. I am convinced, however, that at many points Jeremias has given us an illuminating study, and we may wish that his and other volumes in the Wissenschaftliche Monographien zum Alten und Neuen Testament series will eventually appear in English translation.

Many have assisted in the preparation of this book, although only a few may be mentioned outright. First I would name my Old Testament professors at Union Theological Seminary, James Muilenburg, Samuel L. Terrien, and George M. Landes, who were the perpetual source of instruction and inspiration during my graduate study, and who all made their separate contributions to my understanding of Biblical theophany. I gratefully acknowledge the financial assistance provided me by the Wellesley College faculty research fund that permitted the excellent typing of approximately half of the final manuscript by Mrs. Donald Childs of Wellesley. Then Roland W. Tapp of The Westminster Press has proved helpful on many

[3] *Old Testament Theology*, tr. by D. M. G. Stalker (Harper & Row, Publishers, Inc., 1965), Vol. 2, p. 19.

counts. But most of all I am indebted to my wife who typed all the dissertation, all preliminary drafts of the book, and a goodly share of the final copy. Whether it was theophany phase one, or theophany phase two, she brought to bear upon the scene not a little literary advice and much wifely support. The dedication to her can only serve as partial expression of my gratitude.

J. K. K.

Wellesley, Massachusetts

Abbreviations

ANET	*Ancient Near Eastern Texts Relating to the Old Testament*
BDB	Brown, Francis, Driver, S. R., and Briggs, Charles A., *A Hebrew and English Lexicon of the Old Testament with an Appendix Containing the Biblical Aramaic*
BKAT	Biblischer Kommentar Altes Testament
BWAT	*Beiträge zur Wissenschaft vom Alten Testament*
CBQ	*Catholic Biblical Quarterly*
EB	*Estudios Biblicos*
ET	*The Expository Times*
HAT	*Handbuch zum Alten Testament*
HDB	*The Harvard Divinity Bulletin*
HKAT	Handkommentar zum Alten Testament
HTR	*The Harvard Theological Review*
HUCA	*Hebrew Union College Annual*
IB	*The Interpreter's Bible*
ICC	The International Critical Commentary
IDB	*The Interpreter's Dictionary of the Bible*
IEJ	*Israel Exploration Journal*
JBL	*Journal of Biblical Literature*
JBR	*Journal of Bible and Religion*
JNES	*Journal of Near Eastern Studies*
JPOS	*Journal of the Palestine Oriental Society*
KB	Köhler, Ludwig, and Baumgartner, Walter, *Lexicon in Veteris Testamenti Libros*

LXX	The Septuagint
MT	Masoretic Text
NRT	*Nouvelle Revue Theologique*
OTMS	*The Old Testament and Modern Study*
RSV	Revised Standard Version of the Holy Bible
STZ	*Schweizerische Theologische Zeitschrift*
TLZ	*Theologische Literaturzeitung*
UT	*Ugaritic Textbook*
VT	*Vetus Testamentum*
VTS	Supplement to *Vetus Testamentum*
ZA	*Zeitschrift für Assyriologie und verwandte Gebiete*
ZAW	*Zeitschrift für die alttestamentliche Wissenschaft*

CHAPTER I

Intercepting Theophanic Frequencies

This book is about Biblical theophanies. More specifically, it is concerned with a rather ample selection of theophanic passages and terminologies found within the Old Testament canon. From personal experience I am aware that the word "theophany" is not necessarily a part of the vocabulary of every educated person. It does not come automatically with the liberal arts diploma. This being the case, grave risks may be run in the delayed launching of a definition. A relatively intricate definition will evolve in time, but given the direct question, "What is a theophany?" what may be seized upon as an equally direct answer that will avert some intellectual crisis of the moment?

Perhaps we may best answer by saying that a theophany is a temporal manifestation of the deity to man involving visible and audible elements that signal God's real presence. However mystifying may be the tokens of his appearing, its authenticity is in no way questioned. Now, if one were wishing simply to allude to the most common characteristic of the theophany as it is known in all of world literature and in the comprehensive history of religions, the most appropriate definition might consist of a brief construct phrase — "the appearance of a god." Yet this will not suffice here, for we are to confine our study of theophany as it is represented in, and only in, Old Testament materials.[1] And in this connection, the most

[1] Although we shall not avoid mention of extra-Biblical theophanic accounts, we do not intend to subject them to any comprehensive examination. Where parallels are especially instructive, however, they will be cited.

illuminating declaration to be made may well be that the hearing is appreciated as being as central to the theophanic event as is the seeing, if not more so. Thus our insistence at the outset that when it comes to the literature of the Old Testament, the theophanic experience is in no small measure one of audition. While in his coming, the deity is thought to provide man with visual evidence of his presence, things that the mortal eye can discern either clearly or dimly, the Hebrew was to insist that the holy God drew near in particular to open man's ear to a disclosure of his will. This much appears plainly to stand in the Old Testament within the realm of the axiomatic.

But how could man in the Old Testament be certain that God *was* present? How did Hebrew man know that he was either the favored object or the victim of theophanic encounter? Did he somehow have a penchant for such things? In his seemingly all too simple existence, did he perhaps spend so much time addressing the world about him as a " thou " that he either talked himself into such experiences or in some way evoked them for his potential edification or entertainment? Do they not make theophanies today the way they used to? If not, why not? Although questions of this sort are not easily answered, we have no right to forbid their being raised. In fact, we have no power to. We are like young Elihu in this respect — these things constrain us within and they *must* be voiced. Indeed, who of us is not aware that there are men in our time who protest that if God would truly favor them with a sure sign of his presence, if he would furnish them with just one " foolproof " argument for his existence, then they might gladly believe and affirm his presence in the things that are? And are we not also aware that this is not exactly a fresh protest on the lips of a large segment of humanity?

From his own position of faith, John Baillie provides the following answer to the problem:

> It may be that this is one of the things that even the omnipotent God cannot do; He cannot, without invading the area of free personality with which He Himself has endowed us, get any further word through to us until we first hearken diligently to the word He is already speaking. We sometimes say of a man that " one can't tell him anything ";

> but may it not be true of ourselves that God literally cannot tell us anything? At all events, if there is some voice we are hearing and not attending to, we have no right to complain that there is some further voice we are not hearing.[2]

If there is some voice—the dilemma lies in this uncertain phrase. There are men who say that God is speaking and that they are in fact hearing. There are others who admit that they do not know. Still others protest that the voice is silent or that it never existed in the first place.

As such issues have been debated over the years, the compelling phrase "reason and revelation" has often come to the fore. The former noun was made to point to man's total knowledge of God that he had obtained apart from the deity's direct intervention into human affairs. Thus came into being the reasoned arguments of the theologians and philosophers, some of the latter standing within the Judeo-Christian tradition, and some outside. The other noun, "revelation," bore the responsibility of referring to the sum of man's knowledge of God that was dependent upon some action from the deity himself. Thus appeared the words of homileticians and poets. As a favorite illustration of the latter, I should like to refer briefly to a poem of Emily Dickinson, titled "A Service of Song":

> Some keep the Sabbath going to church;
> I keep it staying at home,
> With a bobolink for a chorister,
> And an orchard for a dome.
>
> Some keep the Sabbath in surplice;
> I just wear my wings,
> And instead of tolling the bell for church,
> Our little sexton sings.
>
> God preaches,—a noted clergyman,—
> And the sermon is never long;
> So instead of getting to heaven at last,
> I'm going all along![3]

[2] From *The Idea of Revelation in Recent Thought* (Columbia University Press, 1956), pp. 142 f.

[3] From *Poems,* ed. by Mabel Loomis Todd and T. W. Higginson (Little, Brown and Company, 1890), p. 74.

Apart from Miss Dickinson's possible objections to the institutional church at the time of writing (by 1860), we may detect her apparent openness to the category of "revelation" as over against the "reason" category. God preaches, and he preaches briefly! In this respect he seems to resemble the God of Old Testament theophanies. There, too, the deity spoke, but consistently in few words. To be sure, the Abraham or Moses or Isaiah who was addressed in the theophanic encounter knew nothing of bobolinks and orchards at such times, let alone "staying at home" as the means of ensuring divine visitation, yet there is an aura of openness in both the above poem and in the theophanic episodes within the Old Testament that is notably similar. Thus when the deity calls forth, "Moses, Moses," we may expect the latter to reply, "Here am I" (e.g., Ex. 3:4).

There is, however, a basic distinction. Those persons living many years before as well as during Miss Dickinson's generation were prone to shape their thinking — both consciously and not — according to the "reason and revelation" dichotomy. With somewhat less intensity, this is likewise true of us today.[4] Yet that same situation in no way obtained for Hebrew man. Within the range of theophanic experience, Abraham was not addressed with propositions about God for the sake of his intellectual development, with detached statements concerning the true character of deity. There was in the time of Abraham — and this holds true for the times of Moses and Isaiah of Jerusalem as well — neither need nor interest in categorizing two modes of human perception, one related to reason on man's part, and the other related to revelation on God's. Not that Hebrew man steered clear of such compartmentalization — he had not established it to begin with. This reason alone, then, may justify our suggesting that as a first step in intercepting the theophanic frequencies of the Old Testament, as it were, we shall benefit from a brief consideration of the essential quality of revelation in the Old Testament. Indeed, it is to this more comprehensive reality that the theophanies there depicted belong.

[4] Twentieth-century theologians do not seem as prone to employ the contrast. Cf. James Barr, "Revelation," *Dictionary of the Bible,* ed. by James Hastings; rev. ed. by Frederick C. Grant and H. H. Rowley (Charles Scribner's Sons, 1963), p. 847; also Baillie, *op. cit.,* p. 18. Moreover, such a continental Protestant theologian as Schleiermacher in the nineteenth century sought a middle course between the reason-revelation dichotomy. Even so, this dualism has suffered a slow death.

GRASPING THE REVELATION REALITY IN THE OLD TESTAMENT

We seek here to speak of the nature and meaning of revelation in the Old Testament only in select ways that have some direct bearing upon the major subject at hand — Biblical theophanies. Clearly, any exhaustive examination would require its own book. Like Jesus and his disciples, we shall glean from but a small portion of the field, yet hopefully with less ominous consequences!

While the late H. Richard Niebuhr may not have had the Old Testament foremost in his mind when he began the writing of the final chapter of his monumental study, *The Meaning of Revelation,* his accounting of the essential nature of revelation to be found there addresses itself excellently to that human era as well as to our own:

> When we speak of revelation we mean that something has happened to us in our history which conditions all our thinking and that through this happening we are enabled to apprehend what we are, what we are suffering and doing and what our potentialities are. What is otherwise arbitrary and dumb fact becomes related, intelligible and eloquent fact through the revelatory event.[5]

Revelation is here regarded as dynamic event in this life rather than as static propositional truth to which man attains by some process of self-transcendence. Revelation is event that is attended by man who is passive although not truly inactive, for he must interpret what is presented to him, and then base his response upon it. Furthermore, revelation is event which binds into a meaningful whole those diverse elements that impinge upon man which do not appear to possess or convey meaning on their own. To speak thusly is to speak of revelation as it is known in the Old Testament, but certainly not as it is there *conveyed.* In our attempt to get at the essence of revelation, we have already become abstract in a way that is quite foreign to the tenor of the Bible. Then how does the Bible, and in particular the Old Testament, speak of revelation?

Primarily its utterances and disclosures are, from first to last, concrete. There is no abstract Hebrew noun in the Old Testament that can be suitably rendered by our English word " revelation." On the

[5] (The Macmillan Company, 1941), p. 138.

whole, the Israelite did not develop a vocabulary of abstract nouns, for he was too concerned with expressing the dynamic character of life through the inflected verb. Even the student who has had but a few hours with the Hebrew language is made aware of the fact that it is basically verbal, not nominal, in character. And while there are, to be sure, passive verbal expressions, the active and intensive ones seem to matter most. Thus whenever Hebrew man spoke of a relationship between another and himself, he depended upon the verbs to express the concreteness of the I-thou situation in its manifold forms. Whether or not the " other " was a man or the deity himself, the relationships articulated were ever infused with particularity. This means, of course, that Hebrew man was a realist. He affirmed this present life with its instincts, its dangers, and its blessings. At one moment he would be found enjoying life. At another he would be coping with it. But almost never would he be caught denying it. At most, there are but three cases of suicide in some thousand relatively packed pages of literature (see I Sam. 31:4-5; II Sam. 17:23; I Kings 16:18). Thus it is no surprise that the God of Hebrew man must also be understood as intimately related to life itself. As H. Wheeler Robinson has put it, " If such a people were to know God, it would be through the concrete experience of living, rather than by any intellectualistic construction."[6] Thus the deity was perceived by Israel as being at work in events, and his deeds in history were thought to disclose who he was.

We may press the assertion even further — the God of Israel was confessed to be the *initiator* of those events. To Hebrew man, the question, " Where shall God be found? " was quite irrelevant. The inquiry that really mattered was, " How has Yahweh chosen to disclose himself to man? " Man was thus not regarded as the one who evoked revelation. Instead, the deity was affirmed to be one who takes the initiative in constantly revealing himself to man, in part through nature, yet to a greater degree in the world of history and in the entanglements of human affairs. It was he who summoned men in their particularity. In its pages the Old Testament knows nothing of a deity who avoids the sphere of the sensuous and the

[6] From "The Theology of the Old Testament," *Record and Revelation,* ed. by Robinson (Oxford: Clarendon Press, 1938), p. 303.

seen. Indeed, the God there revealed does not despise the concreteness of man's historicity. He employs it for his own ends.

In this respect, the revelation reality in the Old Testament has been aptly expressed by Albrecht Oepke in the following manner:

> Revelation is not the impartation of supernatural knowledge or the excitement of numinous feelings. Knowledge can certainly come through revelation, and the revelation of God will be accompanied by numinous feelings. . . . But revelation is not to be identified with these. In the proper sense, it is the action of Yahweh. It is the removal of His essential concealment, His self-offering for fellowship.[7]

Through historical happenings that persistently give rise to covenants, Yahweh is affirmed to be at work in the process of self-disclosure. And this affirmation is based upon an even more fundamental statement of faith, that Yahweh is constantly active in this world, guiding it according to his purposes. Revelation in the Old Testament, then, has clearly to do with the *activity* of Yahweh.

But that revelation is at least one thing else. It is unmistakably personal. It suggests relationship and communion. Yahweh is the " thou " who addresses those whom he confronts as " thous " themselves. Such revelation does not move from subject to object, but from subject to subject. One mind and will discloses itself to another. C. F. D. Moule cogently maintains that " it is himself that God reveals, or his actions, his righteousness, his wrath, rather than statements about himself." [8] In Old Testament revelation, the deity as person approaches man who is necessarily involved in the web of his own personality. In this process, God's holiness is not dissipated. His thoughts and ways are ever celebrated by Biblical faith as being higher than man's. Yet in the unfolding revelation, the deity makes himself known to man as person. Israel would not have been able to abide the thought that her God was, in the final analysis, an impersonal force or fundamental cosmic law. She knew him as a person because she found herself in communion with him. In her

[7] From an article on *kaluptō* in *Theological Dictionary of the New Testament,* ed. by Gerhard Kittel, tr. by Geoffrey W. Bromiley (Wm. B. Eerdmans Publishing Co., 1965), Vol. 3, p. 573.

[8] From " Revelation," *IDB,* ed. by George A. Buttrick *et al.* (Abingdon Press, 1962), Vol. 4, p. 55.

literature she claimed that she had heard him say, "I am Yahweh," and perhaps she was to insist upon the personal aspect of revelation in no small measure because in her response to his self-disclosure, she confronted herself as a person in some new light. In short, life appeared to the Hebrew as that realistic. Given this situation, the apparatus of revelation could scarcely have been otherwise.

Isolating Problems and Approaches

In our best moments we may give something less than a warm welcome to those who invent problems and draft methodological statements for the sheer joy of doing so. To recognize this very human reaction, however, does not exempt us from some responsibility in addressing ourselves at the outset to those circumstances which directly bear upon the Old Testament depiction of divine self-disclosure. Hence, a brief word on problem and method is in order.

We may begin by conceding that one cannot engage in Old Testament study for long without encountering occasional references to passages that are described as theophanic in character, or to terminologies that are explained as products of theophanic ideology or reflection. If some of these references may be regarded as very much on the fringes of a particular discussion, not all of them may legitimately be given such a cavalier dismissal. This is notably the case with commentaries and articles written by numerous scholars who now readily accept the presuppositions and employ the methodologies of form criticism. Few of these critics, however, have actually set down in writing what they understand to be the character, structure, and language of the theophany in the Old Testament. Although many and varied passages have been identified by commentators as theophanic, few attempts have been made to formulate lucidly a definition of the theophany and to treat comprehensively its character in the light of representative examples drawn from Old Testament literature.

Although a detailed report on the history of previous discussions of Old Testament theophanies would promise to verge all too readily on the lethal, perhaps two paragraphs containing quite selective commentary will be of use as orientation to some of the concerns of our present study. We must admit that relatively few examinations have focused directly upon the Old Testament theophany as such. In his epoch-making commentary on The Book of Genesis,[9] first published in 1901, Hermann Gunkel did take the patriarchal theophanies into account and introduce relevant parallel phenomena from the literatures of the Ancient Near East known at that time. Since the responsibilities of any Genesis commentator are understandably legion, Gunkel scarcely could have been expected to scrutinize fully the patriarchal theophanic episodes there recorded. Julian Morgenstern, in 1911, appears to have been the first critic to have issued an extensive treatment of the subject.[10] This equally lengthy and interesting essay made quite evident Morgenstern's capacity to read carefully and critically the theophanic texts of the Old Testament. His preoccupation with the theophanies enumerated in the Pentateuch, however, necessarily led to a slighting of other extremely important Old Testament theophanic accounts and allusions. Further, Morgenstern completed this study before the procedures of form criticism had significantly penetrated Biblical study. He thus ignored those issues customarily highlighted by this approach and consequently was not cognizant of the important, if problematic, role of theophanic disclosure in the cultic *Sitz im Leben* of ancient Israel.

Thanks to an expanding number of theologies of the Old Testament that have been published in the last decade or so, allusions to theophanic narratives and language are becoming more common. Yet a careful and sustained study of relevant texts has, on the whole,

[9] *Genesis* (6te Auflage, HKAT; Göttingen: Vandenhoeck & Ruprecht, 1964). Before Gunkel, an interest in Old Testament theophanies was sometimes evident, but the studies published were either regrettably inadequate or bizarre. While theophanies were examined by the early church fathers, their treatments were severely restricted by an apologetic approach. Thus Benedict Kominiak, *The Theophanies of the Old Testament in the Writings of St. Justin* (The Catholic University of America Press, 1948), p. vii, writes of the situation in St. Justin's works in which he discovers the earliest evidence of an endeavor to make acceptable to the Jews the doctrine of Christ's divinity through the argument that it is the second divine person who operates in the Old Testament theophanies and is legitimately to be identified with the angel of Yahweh.

[10] "Biblical Theophanies," *ZA*, Vol. 25 (1911), pp. 139–193; Vol. 28 (1913), pp. 15–60.

proved to be the exception rather than the rule. Moreover, the phenomena isolated therein are not thought to have been adequately interpreted. Gerhard von Rad openly admits that "the large number of descriptions of theophanies, and in particular their comparative similarity, is not as yet satisfactorily explained."[11] This is not to suggest that we find ourselves to be debt free from previous investigations, but it is rather to say simply that a thorough treatment of the Old Testament theophany is still lacking. The present study will go only part way in meeting this need, for a genuinely comprehensive handling of the subject would demand an extensive tome. Still, a form-critical examination of crucial and representative examples of theophany in the Old Testament may justifiably be expected within the boundaries of the present undertaking, and in the process some void will have been filled.

Along with other matters of Old Testament research that one might call to mind, the subject of theophany in the Old Testament appears, both to our joy and to our dismay, as a complex issue. There is much to the theophanic apparatus in its totality, for the materials relating to this area are diverse and the subordinate considerations soliciting our attention are many. Setting aside for the moment the question as to whether or not Israel actually possessed a theophanic *Gattung* (literary form) as such, we can see that any general perusal of theophanic passages within the Old Testament canon will inevitably lead us to the conclusion that they show no predilection for occurring within a single literary context. Theophanic events are embedded into narrative accounts and poetic compositions alike, and there is, to be sure, considerable variation within these two comprehensive categories.

Moreover, for at least three reasons, theophanic texts cannot be studied in some hypothetical vacuum. First, the theophany meshes

[11] From *Old Testament Theology*, tr. by D. M. G. Stalker (Harper & Brothers, 1962), Vol. 1, p. 366, n. 23. Owing to their differences in approach to the problem, we may suspect that von Rad would not emend this statement radically in the light of the recent appearance of the study by Jörg Jeremias referred to at some length in our preface, *Theophanie: Die Geschichte einer alttestamentlichen Gattung*. Von Rad's own approach is evident from his judgment that the accounts of Biblical theophanies constitute the most vital aspect of "an Old Testament aesthetic." Jeremias, *op. cit.*, p. 25, calls this judgment into question.

closely with other Old Testament motifs. For example, it is not uncommon for theophanic encounters to take place in the vicinity of the Ark of the Covenant or on the site of the Tent of Meeting. Such environments cannot be ignored, since they serve to convey more fully the nature of the theophanic disclosure at hand. Secondly, the theophanic appearance of the deity in the Old Testament belongs inextricably to the comprehensive sweep of God's revelation to his people *in history,* whether that revelation be disclosed to one Hebrew or to many. The interpreter is thus called upon to be aware of pertinent historical considerations without fabricating quasi-historical conjectures that soar beyond the available evidence. Thirdly, it is normative for Old Testament theophanic passages to be simply one part of the larger literary units in question.[12] Not all of the Sinaitic pericope, Ex., chs. 19 to 24, has to do with a theophany. Especially in the Psalter, a theophanic description may be confined to a few verses of a given psalm, and thereby comprise merely a fraction of the total composition.

Given this maze of complexity, however, there are avenues of meaningful escape. While there is no single question that can be voiced at every turn, especially in our treatment of individual literary units, we shall need to be governed by a form-critical method that persistently asks, "What kind of material do we have here?"[13] Beyond this, we may suggest that the form-critical effort in which we shall engage will require that we (1) delineate precisely the extent of the relevant literary compositions; (2) discern the various contexts in which the passages are found; (3) examine critically the

[12] This is particularly true of theophanic descriptions present in Hebrew poetry. Seldom does the theophany involve the whole poem. Claus Westermann, *The Praise of God in the Psalms,* tr. by Keith R. Crim (John Knox Press, 1965), p. 96, quite properly claims this for only Ps. 114, which he observes has been united with Ps. 115 in the LXX, and Ps. 29, which has been modified.

[13] That the form-critical approach with its stress upon the specific literary units and their *Sitz im Leben* is indispensable scarcely need be argued today. Cf. James Muilenburg, "Old Testament Scholarship: Fifty Years in Retrospect," *JBR,* Vol. 28 (1960), pp. 178 f.; "Modern Issues in Biblical Studies: The Gains of Form Criticism in Old Testament Studies," *ET,* Vol. 71 (1960), pp. 229–233; and Aubrey R. Johnson, "The Psalms," *OTMS,* ed. by H. H. Rowley (Oxford: Clarendon Press, 1951), pp. 162–209, and his introductory comment to *Sacral Kingship in Ancient Israel* (Cardiff: University of Wales Press, 1955), p. iii.

texts themselves; and (4) consider the possible cultic utilization of the pericopes so as to determine, insofar as is possible, the *Sitz im Leben* of the theophany within the cultic life of Israel. So much for problem and program.

If this is to be our method of total operation, two preliminary matters must straightway concern us. In interrogatory dress they may be presented in the following manner: What will be our definition of the theophany in the Old Testament? Is a literary type, that is, a regularly employed *Gattung,* discernible behind the theophany as preserved by Israelite tradition, and if so, what is its essential character, how did it develop, and what mutations took place in the process? The answers to these vital questions will take up the remainder of the present chapter and the next. Not only are these inquiries basic to any serious study of Old Testament theophany, but their less than obvious answers will influence the treatment of specific Old Testament materials in the remaining chapters of the present study.

Extracting a Definition

The heading above is deliberate. It is not our intention to posit some formal definition of theophany in the Old Testament at the outset, and then proceed to explain carefully, yet somewhat flatly, all the terms employed in that statement. Rather, as a hopefully more dynamic way of getting at the matter, a full definition will be *extracted* at the end of the chapter after we have had an opportunity of tasting several theophanic passages firsthand, confronting a few relevant etymological facts, and enumerating in some detail those characteristics which appear to be most dominant in theophanic depiction within the Old Testament. Since as a means of introduction, the etymological task is only equipped to constitute the small dormer window approach to the landscape, we shall first avail ourselves of a more spacious picture window perspective through the immediate confrontation of a few brief Old Testament texts that are acknowledged by the vast majority of concerned scholars as being clearly theophanic in character. The texts speak well for themselves. They stand erect on their own, and much can be gained from their careful reading. A few examples will thus be set forth here without exegetical comment so that the reader may encounter on his own, for his edification but no less for his enjoyment, something of the nature and diversity of theophanic representation. In short, the inductive possibilities are not to be underrated!

First, two short theophanic passages from The Book of Genesis, one dealing with Abraham, the other with Isaac:[14]

> And Abram traversed the land to the place at Shechem, to the oak of Moreh. And the Canaanites were then in the land. Then Yahweh appeared to Abram and said, "To your descendants I will give this land." And he built there an altar to Yahweh, who had appeared to him. (Gen. 12:6-7, J.)

> From there [Rehoboth] he [Isaac] went up to Beersheba. And Yahweh appeared to him the same night and said, "I am the God of Abraham your father; fear not, for I am with you, and I will bless you, and multiply your descendants for my servant Abraham's sake." And he built an altar there and called upon the name of Yahweh, and pitched his tent there; and there Isaac's servants dug a well. (Gen. 26:23-25, J.)

Next, a portion of the account of Yahweh's theophanic call to Moses presented early in The Book of Exodus:

> Now Moses was tending the flock of his father-in-law, Jethro, the priest of Midian; and he led the flock to the west side of the wilderness, and came to the mountain of God, to Horeb. And the angel of Yahweh appeared to him in a flame of fire out of the midst of the bush; and he looked, and behold, the bush burned with fire, but the bush was not consumed. So Moses said, "I will turn aside now, and see this great sight, why the bush is not burnt." When Yahweh saw that he turned aside to see, God called to him out of the midst of the bush and said, "Moses, Moses!" And he said, "Here am I." He said, "Do not draw near; take off your sandals from your feet, for the place on which you are standing is holy ground." And he said, "I am the God of your father, the God of Abraham, the God of Isaac, and the God of Jacob." Now Moses hid his face; for he was afraid to look upon God. (Ex. 3:1-6, JE.)

[14] Unless otherwise indicated, the Old Testament quotations appearing in this study are in my own translation. Any congruence with the established published translations is quite accidental although scarcely avoidable at every turn.

Finally, two brief selections from the prophetic literature — the opening verses depicting Yahweh's initial self-disclosure to Isaiah of Jerusalem and the concluding verses of the inaugural phase of Ezekiel's encounter with theophanic event and prophetic call:

> In the year of the death of King Uzziah, I [Isaiah] saw the Lord seated upon a throne, high and lifted up, with his train filling the Temple. The seraphim stood above him; each one having six wings: with two he covered his face, and with two he covered his feet, and with two he flew. And one called to the other and said,
>
> "Holy, holy, holy, is Yahweh of hosts;
> the whole earth is full of his glory."
>
> And the foundations of the thresholds shook at the voice of him who called, and the house was filled with smoke. Then said I,
>
> "Woe is me! for I am undone;
> for I am a man of unclean lips,
> And I dwell in the midst of a people of unclean lips;
> For my eyes have seen the king,
> Yahweh of hosts!"
>
> (Isa. 6:1-5.)

> Like the appearance of the bow that is in the cloud on the day of rain, thus was the appearance of the brightness round about. Such was the appearance of the likeness of the glory of Yahweh. And when I [Ezekiel] saw it, I fell upon my face, and I heard a voice of someone speaking. He said to me, "Son of man, stand upon your feet, and I will speak with you." (Ezek. 1:28 to 2:1.)

Having confronted a limited selection of Old Testament theophanic episodes head on, and exposed ourselves to their interests, vocabulary, and styles, we turn now to the business of etymology, a task that promises to invite meaningful, if not comprehensive, comment. Clearly, there is no Hebrew equivalent for our English word "theophany."[15] The term is Greek in origin — *theophaneia.* The Greek noun is defined by Liddell and Scott as a "vision of

[15] A Niph'al form of *r'h,* such as *nir'ā,* perhaps comes closest. The word for "theophany" in German, French, and Latin is *Theophanie, théophanie,* and *theophania* respectively. See the discussion of Rolf Rendtorff, "'Offenbarung' im Alten Testament," *TLZ,* Vol. 85 (1960), col. 833.

God." In their brief account of the word, they refer to the festival at Delphi, where the statues of Apollo and other deities were revealed to the congregation there assembled. The Greek word, a compound, consists of a noun, *theos* (God), and a verb, *phainein* (to appear). Although the noun refers exclusively to a god, the verb bears many nuances. Among the active renderings listed by Liddell and Scott are to "bring to light, cause to appear," "make known, reveal, disclose," "show forth, display in action," and "give light, shine," and among the passive are to "come to light, appear," and "be manifest."[16] As for the English noun compound, "theophany," which has been accepted into our own vocabulary, the following definition appears in *Webster's Third New International Dictionary of the English Language, Unabridged:* "A physical presentation or personal manifestation of a deity to an individual: a brief appearance of Deity."[17] If this constitutes the basic etymological background, what is the meaning of the word when appropriated as a *terminus technicus* for the appearance of God in the Old Testament?

The term refers, of course, to the regular but unpredicted disclosure of the God of Israel to his people, be they one or many. A study of various theophanic pericopes discloses that this self-manifestation of the deity in the Old Testament possesses several identifiable characteristics. To begin, *the theophany is appallingly real.* The words of W. Robertson Smith written many years ago still ring clear today, that while we find it difficult to imagine the visible disclosure of the deity as an actual event, "all primitive peoples believe in frequent theophanies, or at least in frequent occasions of personal contact between men and superhuman powers."[18] It would be ludicrous to imagine the wandering Aramean Abraham sitting in his tent at day's end discoursing to others in his "household" on the death of God. He *knew* God was not dead. His experiences could not have taught him otherwise. Whatever be the precise nature of the theophanic experience, and whether or not Johannes Lindblom is on the right

[16] *A Greek-English Lexicon* (9th ed., Oxford: Clarendon Press, 1940), pp. 792, 1912 f.

[17] Philip Babcock Gove, editor in chief (G. & C. Merriam Company, 1961), p. 2371.

[18] From *The Religion of the Semites* (Meridian Books, The Meridian Library, 1957; first published in 1889), p. 119.

track in depicting the theophany as "hallucinatory,"[19] it was nevertheless respected as utterly real. This is discernible behind such statements in the Biblical narrative as the following which depict Jacob at Bethel, the Israelites at Sinai, and Ezekiel by the river Chebar at the time of his call:

> And he [Jacob] said, "How awesome is this place! This is none other than the house of God, and this is the gate of heaven." (Gen. 28:17.)

> When all the people perceived the thunderings, and the lightning flashes, and the sound of the horn, and the mountain smoking, the people were afraid and trembled. So they stood afar off. (Ex. 20:18.)

> And when I [Ezekiel] saw it, I fell upon my face, and I heard a voice of someone speaking. (Ezek. 1:28.)

In a world encompassed by mysterious and unknown phenomena, the theophanic manifestation of God may not have been a rare event. And whatever the attendant psychological conditions of the theophany in holy places might have been, Hebrew man, as Ancient Near Eastern man, possessed a mythopoeic mentality that was amenable to the supermundane disclosure initiated by the deity. We need not doubt that the happening registered itself within his experience as awesomely authentic. It *was* and it mattered.

As a second characteristic, we may speak explicitly of something that has already been alluded to in our assertion that theophany is "unpredicted disclosure": *the theophany in the Old Testament is initiated by, and only by, the deity himself.*[20] Never is man represented as one who evokes a theophanic encounter. True, he may visit a par-

[19] "Theophanies in Holy Places in Hebrew Religion," *HUCA,* Vol. 32 (1961), p. 106. Lindblom claims there that theophanies in sites of special sanctity were "hallucinatory experiences with many analogies at all stages of human life. A good deal of the biblical reports may be legendary, some of them may even have been transmitted as pure cult legends, but this does not nullify the fact that experiences of this kind may really have occurred. To those who had such experiences the reality of Yahweh's presence and appearance in person was of course beyond all doubt." One may justifiably have reservations as to the propriety of his expression, "hallucinatory experiences." Yet Lindblom's emphasis upon the actuality of such encounters is well taken.

[20] On this consideration as a whole, note the treatments of Ludwig Köhler, *Old Testament Theology,* tr. by A. S. Todd (The Westminster Press, 1957), p. 103, and H. H. Rowley, *The Faith of Israel* (The Westminster Press, 1956), p. 23.

ticular locale reputed for its sanctity in the hope that he may be favored by divine self-disclosure; yet we shall follow Ludwig Köhler here and maintain that no human technique, be it prayer, sacrifice, or some other enterprise, possesses such efficacy that its use thereby guarantees the divine manifestation.[21] Rather, the initiative must proceed from the deity himself. A certain ridicule may be detected in Hos. 12:4, where the prophet refers to the deity which Jacob had *actively* discovered (" at Bethel he found him "). Because theophanic revelation is realized by divine initiative alone, it is normative for the encounter to begin, " and Yahweh appeared " (*wayyērā' Yahweh*), not " he/they caused Yahweh to appear." Whatever man is to learn of the self-disclosure of the deity is knowledge divinely initiated,[22] and there is no hard-and-fast principle respecting the *time* of God's appearing. The particular season for the divine apparition is established by, and only by, divine pleasure. In short, at God's will he appears.

We have already hit upon another characteristic: *the theophany is manifested as a temporal event.* It is not a permanent reality, but rather it is a momentary encounter that takes place at only particular times.[23] Theophany is transient happening. Many theophanic accounts contain only a minimum of detail, but the self-disclosure of the deity does possess a beginning and a conclusion. We may think of a relatively uneventful moment prior to the advent of the theophany, which is followed by the awful impingement of theophanic encounter itself, and that, in turn, by a moment which is distinctively subsequent to the moment of revelation. While the impact of the divine disclosure may remain conspicuously present after the full duration of the divine apparition has been spent, this does not deny that the theophanic act, which has made its way into both history and nature, is now complete. In this respect, the cumulative witness of the various Biblical theophanies supports the basic assertion of H. Wheeler Robinson that " the theophany is a transient manifesta-

[21] *Old Testament Theology,* p. 103.

[22] See P. van Imschoot, *Theology of the Old Testament,* Vol. 1, *God,* tr. by Kathryn Sullivan and Fidelis Buck (Desclée Co., Inc., 1965), p. 134.

[23] By its lead position in the article alone, the temporality of the theophany is emphasized by Hermann Gunkel, "Theophanie," *Die Religion in Geschichte und Gegenwart* (2te Auflage, Tübingen: J. C. B. Mohr, 1931), Vol. 5, col. 1130. See also E. O. James, *The Ancient Gods* (G. P. Putnam's Sons, 1960), p. 251.

tion of deity, and, as such, to be distinguished from the continuous revelation of Him in all Nature."[24] Thus the word "intensity" belongs more to our descriptive vocabulary of Old Testament theophany than does the word "continuance."

Moreover, temporality and intensity are characteristic to some extent of the mediation of Yahweh's cultic presence in the theophany as it was rehearsed in the cult. At such times there appears to have been a moment of special meaning and intensity as well as the moments of anticipation and reaction which respectively preceded and followed it. The climax of the theophanic encounter was most likely achieved with the mediation of the divine name (cf. "Be still, and know that I am God" [Ps. 46:10]; "Yahweh, your God, am I" [Ps. 50:7]; "I am Yahweh your God" [Ps. 81:10]).

Now the effects of the theophany upon the life of one who attends the apparition of the deity may seem to be permanent indeed. The description of the theophanic experience of Isaiah of Jerusalem in the Temple, at the time of his call to prophetism in 742 B.C., as presented in Isa., ch. 6, may effectively discourage any interpreter from suggesting that the impact of that encounter failed to remain with the prophet throughout his lengthy career. Yet the language of Isa., ch. 6, does lead one to infer that the event itself was compressed into a particular interval of time. It was God's temporal disclosure of himself. This seems to hold true for all other theophanic passages as well.

We further discover that frequently, although there are exceptions, *theophanic accounts are arranged so as to represent the absolute sovereignty of the deity over the universe, and the corresponding convulsion of nature in reaction to his self-manifestation.* Israel's Lord who comes to her in theophanic meeting is confessed to be in full control of nature. Sudden theophanic irruption is followed by cosmic resonance, for here stands the divine intervention of one who is sovereign over the multiplicity of settings in which he appears. At times, Yahweh seems particularly disposed to draw near amid nature's most terrifying elements.[25] The realms of nature that are se-

[24] From *Inspiration and Revelation in the Old Testament* (Oxford: Clarendon Press, 1946), p. 39.

[25] Thus the upheaval of nature is vividly portrayed in prose in the Sinai narrative (especially in Ex. 19:16-19; 20:18-21; and Deut. 5:22-27), which, we believe, has ex-

cure in their regular rhythm of times and seasons never constitute the Biblical background for theophanic disclosure. Rather, Yahweh's appearing is linked with the earthquake, with fire and lightning, with the disruptive and catastrophic natural phenomena that men are destined to encounter in this life. Such manifestations were thought to be particularly appropriate for expressing both divine power and mystery. In the terrorizing, suddenly destructive elements of nature the majesty of God was writ large in such manner that Hebrew man could not help reading it.[26] Thus the Old Testament reports that Yahweh came in a thick cloud in order to speak to Moses (Ex. 19:9). Sinai was completely wrapped in smoke when Yahweh descended upon it in fire (Ex. 19:18). Amid a flame that miraculously did not consume the bush, divine manifestation confronted Moses (Ex. 3:2). Yahweh and Moses held their conversation in thunder in the process of which Moses received divine instruction (Ex. 19:19). When Yahweh left his distant habitation and arrived to help Israel in battle against the Canaanite foe, the earth quaked, and the heavens energetically emitted water (Judg. 5:4). Even the whirlwind was thought to manifest the deity (Job 38:1), and he was perceived at work in the severest of storms (Ps. 18:7 ff.). Israel's poets affirmed that from his celestial dwelling God rode down to earth in his cosmic chariot of war (Hab. 3:8), and that beneath his treading, mountains melted and valleys were cleft (Micah 1:4). Thus Yahweh is frequently and closely related to the unmanageable and unmeasured aspects of the natural order (or shall we say "disorder"?). Yet whatever be the natural elements employed, never is there an *identification* of nature and Yahweh. Natural phenomena constitute the accompanying elements of his appearance. They intensify his coming; they do not yield his essence.

Israel did not interpret this convulsion of nature as event pure and simple. It must also be recognized as a literary creation reflecting Is-

erted a marked influence upon many of the poetically depicted theophanies, especially those in The Book of Psalms. The fundamental difference here between Jeremias' approach and our own will be taken up early in Chapter VI.

[26] A well-documented summary is presented by Walther Eichrodt, *Theologie des Alten Testaments* (Teil 2/3, 4te Auflage; Göttingen: Vandenhoeck & Ruprecht, 1961), pp. 1 f., in which he records the manifold appearances of the deity in disruptive natural phenomena.

rael's poetic imagination whereby she set down in vivid and expressive metaphor the dynamic sweep of Yahweh's revelation. The manifold responses of the cosmos thus described were not understood by Israel as the unavoidable reactions of nature to impinging blind force. Rather, Israel saw in them the reflex of the natural order in response to the special terrestrial visitations of the one she knew as sovereign deity, the one whom she had met and continued to meet as Lord of history. According to the Hebrew eye of faith, nature could not idly stand untouched in the face of theophanic impingement.[27] Thus the universe itself appears perturbed at God's coming, and in the whole process, natural and historical realities are intricately and delicately linked, for in his appearance Yahweh is thought to realize his purposes of venting his wrath against Israel's enemies and of acting dramatically as Israel's deliverer.

As such the theophanies in the Old Testament betray both the "irresistible intervention" of Yahweh in favor of his people and the obligation deeply felt by Israel to submit to the will of the author of that intervention. Perhaps it is not too much to say in this connection that the faith which Israel articulated presented itself as her own response to a deity that she was given to know via theophanic meeting. Obviously these theophanic formulations of the mythopoeic mind, with their persistent employment of natural imagery, make impossible our isolation and identification of each of the phenomena involved in some pallid yet analytical manner. Even so, the reverberations of nature are no less real and significant in the theophany. They are not idle poetic dressing. Rather, they exist as one essential characteristic of the whole.

Also it is typical for Old Testament theophanies to be designed to recount the self-disclosure of the deity in a fluid and an intentionally allusive manner. Much is deliberately left unexpressed. This is not the mark of some woefully haphazard and incomplete reporting of the divine apparition, but rather it is the conscious intent of Israel's

[27] See Evode Beaucamp, "La Théophanie du Psaume 50 (49)," *NRT*, Vol. 81 (1959), p. 910, for an excellent statement here. To be sure, this was not uniquely a Hebraic point of view. Jeremias, *op. cit.*, pp. 73–90, demonstrates in detail that in many respects Israel shared here in the common thinking of her neighbors (his summary, pp. 88–90, is especially recommended).

narrators and poets. The Old Testament offers very few details as to the inauguration of the theophany, and even fewer concerning its termination.[28] At the close of the theophany in Gen., ch. 17, which belongs to the Priestly stratum of the Pentateuch, there appears only the simple statement, " As soon as he had finished talking with him, God went up from Abraham " (v. 22), and the theophany to Moses in Ex. 3:1 to 4:17, which contains both Yahwistic and Elohistic materials, ends with the words of Yahweh, whereupon v. 18, which inaugurates a new episode, begins, " And Moses went and returned to Jethro." Yet in Yahweh's disclosure of himself to Isaiah in the Temple in Isa., ch. 6, nothing is said concerning the manner in which the encounter ends. One interpreter wonders whether Isaiah even noticed! [29]

Deliberate fluidity and vagueness may be seen in other respects as well. A perusal of Old Testament theophanic passages shows that there is no consistent *form* of the deity's appearance. The theophanic description may mention in a most fluid manner one or more of the divinely appointed instruments through which the deity might be represented. Traditionally identified by Biblical theologians as four in number, the *ḵābōd* (glory), *mal'āḵ* (messenger or angel), *pānīm* (face), and *šēm* (name), we have in these vehicles, which are technically known as *theologoumena,*[30] the " representations " or " presentations " of the deity as he draws near to man in his real yet never fully revealed nature. We shall say more about these later. The point

[28] Köhler's assertion, *Old Testament Theology,* p. 103, that the reader does not discover how the theophanies close is too extreme. Indeed, the narratives may not supply extensive detail as to *how* the theophanic visitation ends, but Köhler's unqualified statement suggesting that theophanic narratives customarily break off in uncomfortable abruption flies in the face of most evidence. The particulars about the end of the apparition may be sparse, yet admitting the fluid and suggestive character of theophanic descriptions, they do not as a whole appear to be torsos. We would agree, however, with Köhler's implication that the theophanic accounts may have been more detailed in their genesis.

[29] Köhler, *Old Testament Theology,* p. 103.

[30] Grammatically to be identified as a Greek neuter present passive participle of the root infinitive *theologein,* meaning " to discourse on the gods, talk about God," as noted in *Webster's Third New International Dictionary,* p. 2371. The plural form, *theologoumena,* is rendered in the 1875 ed. of Liddell and Scott, *op. cit.,* as " inquiries into the divine nature," and in the 1940 ed. as " discourses about the gods," pp. 696 and 790 respectively.

to be made here is that these rather frequent representations are in no way fossilized. Rather, fluidity governs. This is especially the case where the "angel of Yahweh" (*mal'aḵ Yahweh*) or "angel of God" (*mal'aḵ 'ᵉlōhīm*) is concerned. Whereas the narrative will begin with accent upon the appearance and speaking of this divine agent, in a few verses the focus may pass imperceptibly to the special word or *hieros logos* of the deity himself, that divinely uttered statement which embodies the very reason for God's self-disclosure at all. The effect is such that if one were to raise the question, "Did God appear?" the answer immediately forthcoming would be, "Certainly," and yet if one were to press on and ask, "Really?" the most conceivable answer might be, "Well, I guess not." There is no such thing as ready diagnosis. Hence, an impressionistic portrayal rather than a concrete graph consistently emerges in the Old Testament as the means of depicting God's coming. More is invariably implied than overtly articulated. And here lie both problem and fascination.

Another characteristic of Biblical theophanies, one that points to the imperfect state of the revelation imparted, joins up with the preceding comment. In short, *the theophany is limited to a partial disclosure of the deity*. The hiddenness of God does not exclusively relate to his sublime status far above the stage of human life; the hiddenness applies equally to his divine presence *in* the world.[31] During the awesome process of self-disclosure, the deity is enveloped by mystery which remains impenetrable. The secrets of his essential being are never threatened. Now the Hebrew, who nowhere appears frustrated by this state of affairs, did not call into question the genuine character or reality of God's appearances in the world. Nor may we suggest that the Semitic mentality was amenable to affirming that Yahweh had two distinct natures, one hidden, the other revealed. Indeed, the self-disclosures of Israel's God are not fraught with an unresolved tension between the hidden and the revealed. In the theophany, whether it be in the original event itself or in its cultic reenactment, Yahweh's presence is quite real.

Yet the divine sovereignty is never dissipated; a divine reticence or holding back is regularly observable. Thus in the theophanic event

[31] Bernhard W. Anderson, "Old Testament View of God," *IDB*, Vol. 2, p. 419, presents a good discussion of this point.

narrated by the Yahwist in Ex. 33:12-23, only one aspect of the deity is revealed. In answer to Moses' request that Yahweh's ways be manifested to him (v. 13), the deity announces: "And when my glory passes by, I will put you in the crevice of the rock, and I will cover you with my hand until I have passed by. I will then take away my hand, and you shall see my back; but my face shall not be seen" (vs. 22-23). In this intensely anthropomorphic narrative, we may detect an overt preoccupation with the fact that God's self-disclosure, by its very nature, must essentially remain beyond the range of human sight.

Frequently the presence of one or more of the theologoumena in theophanic pericopes provides ample evidence for maintaining that the writers involved (and in many cases, the previous oral speakers of these narratives) are consciously seeking, as it were, to protect the deity from human gaze. Thus the glory, angel/messenger, face, or name may assume a prominent position here. Such revelatory media assure that the divine self-disclosure will remain from first to last an effective abridgment of the true essence of one who, while coming near, is wholly other. Yet even apart from these narratives with their somewhat indirect representations of God, the fractional extent of divine manifestation is assumed. Thus in the sophisticated theophany of The Book of Job (chs. 38 to 42), the Joban poet affirms that the divine essence remains hidden. This theophanic depiction, as artistic as it is extensive, appears fundamentally to be dedicated to a celebration of the sheer mystery of deity.[32] In fact, never does a theophanic account presume that divine essence either has been, or can be, immediately grasped by mortal man. The person of the deity is never depicted. Rather, what description there is focuses upon the accompanying details. Thus in Ex. 24:10 the nature of the firmament is hinted, "and there was under his feet a flagstone of sapphire as it were, the very heaven for clearness," and in Isa. 6:1, 3, the emphasis falls respectively upon the hem of the divine garment and Yahweh's glory.

Nevertheless, in the theophany there *is* a partial self-manifestation of God, and the way in which that is mediated leads to a further

[32] See William Lillie, "The Religious Significance of the Theophany in the Book of Job," *ET*, Vol. 68 (1957), pp. 356 f.

generalization: with perhaps one exception, *the theophany is concerned with both visual and audible aspects of divine manifestation.* Something is said about the manner of God's apparition, and something else is confessed as to the actuality or content of his speaking. Both the optic and auditory organs of man are sensitized as he stands by — in something less than a self-assured posture — to perceive the disclosure with eye *and* ear.[33] The visual element truly exists. In her traditions, ancient Israel set forth her belief that Yahweh had both the innate capacity and active will to permit himself to be seen by man at specific moments.[34] Such occasions were taken to be exceptional in character. They were beyond the usual manner whereby God assured Israel of his guiding presence. Yet if the form of God is represented in the theophanic narrative as perceived, it is never described in specifics. Rather, as has already been suggested, theophanic descriptions have a way of focusing upon the peripheral aspects of God's visibility. Clearly, the Yahwist's account of Moses, Aaron, Nadab, Abihu, and the seventy elders of Israel (Ex. 24:1-2, 9-11), already referred to in the previous paragraph, constitutes an apt illustration in this respect. Any divine word whatever is wanting. This is quite conspicuously the only Old Testament theophany that is silent from start to finish.[35]

Normally, in the unfolding of the theophanic encounter, the act of seeing passes subtly into the act of hearing. In that imperceptible

[33] Both activities are important here. Although that of hearing may be regarded as the more significant, we are aware of the extensive and varied use of light imagery in the theophanies of the Old Testament, which, of course, assumes man's *optic* reception. Johannes Hempel, "Die Lichtsymbolik im Alten Testament," *Studium Generale,* Vol. 13 (1960), p. 353, maintains that in ancient Israel "the contact with reality through the eye was valued as being as important and efficacious (*wirkungskraftig*) as that mediated through the ear." Still there is a reticence in Biblical theophanies to describe what is seen.

[34] *Nir'ā,* the Niph'al form of the verb, *r'h,* "to appear," is frequently used in this connection.

[35] Here we take issue with G. Henton Davies' statement, "Theophany," *IDB,* Vol. 4, p. 620, that Ex. 24:9-11 is "a theophany and not an audition." These two nouns cannot adequately represent mutually exclusive categories which do not exist in the first place as far as the Old Testament is concerned. Although "theophany" does not etymologically imply anything more than what can be seen, those passages of the Old Testament which we label theophanic incorporate both visual and auditory components.

change, the visual element seems to vanish while the audible reality vividly remains. The words that are spoken are impressed upon the memory of the Hebrew whose orientation to reality is peculiarly auditory.[36] Biblical theophanies persist as the best means of reminding us of the importance of the ear as the finest organ of perception for Hebrew man. Also in such passages the actuality of the divinely spoken word is highlighted. Whatever be the visual aspects of the theophany, it was in the *hearing* that Abraham obtained the promise that he would indeed become the father of countless descendants (Gen. 15:5), that Moses received the command to lead his people out from the throes of Egyptian bondage (Ex. 3:10), and that Isaiah of Jerusalem acquired the call to deliver an ominous message to his people (Isa. 6:9-12). The special word, the *hieros logos,* of the theophany is addressed to a particular situation in which the communicating " I " of the deity confronts the awaiting " thou " of Israel engaged in the divine encounter. And in the midst of her historical particularity, Israel is called upon to respond. Through her auditory sensitivity, Israel listens, and presently her listening is to pass, again imperceptibly, into obedience.[37] In many Biblical theophanies, nothing is represented as more essential in the confrontation than the divine proclamation and human audition of words that issue from the sovereign yet intervening deity.

It is also characteristic of the Biblical theophany to be related to a particular place. Just as by virtue of its temporality there is some specification of time in the account of theophanic event, so is there normally a designation of the scene in which it unfolds. And the settings of divine self-disclosure are many, for Israel held that her God was not bound to one cultic locale which precluded his self-manifestation anywhere else. As the sovereign Lord over nature and his-

[36] Cf. Thorleif Boman, *Hebrew Thought Compared with Greek,* tr. by Jules L. Moreau (The Westminster Press, 1960), p. 206, and James Muilenburg, " The Biblical View of Time," *HTR,* Vol. 54 (1961), pp. 239 f. The significance of the auditory element in the Old Testament as the supreme vehicle for imparting the real can scarcely be exaggerated.

[37] The treatment by Erwin W. Straus, " Aesthesiology and Hallucinations," in *Existence,* ed. by Rollo May, Ernest Angel, and Henri F. Ellenberger (Basic Books, 1958), p. 159, on the close connection between hearing and obedience in language is suggestive (so *hören* becomes *gehorchen* in German; *akouein* becomes *hupakouein* in Greek; *audire* becomes *ob-oedire* in Latin).

tory, he was free to select the scene of his appearing. The Hebrew understood Yahweh to be sovereign over the cosmic forces which he directed but with which he was not to be identified. Yahweh's usual habitat was in the heavens. From there, however, he might "come down" (the verb root *yrd* being commonly employed here) to manifest himself locally upon the lofty mountain of Sinai (Ex. 19:18), at the door of the Tent of Meeting (Ex. 33:9), at a local sanctuary (Gen. 18:1 [*yrd* lacking]), or in any other locale that he might choose.

In particular, the deity appears in places which have been, or are presently being, sanctified by his presence.[38] Thus he instructs Moses, "Do not draw near; take off your sandals from your feet, for the place on which you are standing is holy ground." (Ex. 3:5.) Holy places are regarded as those precisely favored from time to time by God's theophanic presence.[39] There a determinate area of space is hallowed. This is particularly vivid in the Yahwistic stratum of the Sinai narrative in which Moses is commanded, "And you shall set bounds for the people round about saying, 'See to it that you do not ascend the mountain or touch its border; whoever touches the mountain shall be put to death'" (Ex. 19:12). That special area which is

[38] Walther Eichrodt, *Theology of the Old Testament,* Vol. 1, tr. by J. A. Baker (The Old Testament Library, The Westminster Press, 1961), p. 272, observes that in the earliest narrative strata, the sanctity that is predicated to the theophanic site (Ex. 3:5; 19:23; Josh. 5:15) or to the people confronted by their holy God (Ex. 19:6, 10, 14; Num. 11:18; Josh. 3:5; 7:13) is a derived holiness emanating from the deity himself.

[39] See the instructive article by Lindblom, *loc. cit.,* pp. 91–106. Paul Volz, *Mose: Ein Beitrag zur Untersuchung über die Ursprünge der israelitischen Religion* (Tübingen: J. C. B. Mohr, 1907), pp. 42 f., not only stresses God's revelation at holy places, but observes that his self-manifestation is limited to ancient holy sanctuaries. This may indeed correspond with the evidence of The Book of Genesis, but it is contradicted by the inaugural vision of Isaiah of Jerusalem, where it is said of Yahweh, "the whole earth is full of his glory [*ḳābōd*]" (Isa. 6:3), and by the eschatologically oriented theophanic vision of Second Isaiah where "all flesh" (Isa. 40:5) shall encounter the "glory of Yahweh." Second Isaiah presupposes a world theophany. See the study of Ludwig Köhler, *Deuterojesaja (Jesaja 40–55) stilkritisch untersucht* (Giessen: A. Töpelmann, 1923), pp. 124-127. Moreover, in Genesis the deity is not alone confined to self-manifestations in the few locales already noted for their sanctity. Rather, the sheer disclosure of the deity may make an entirely new spot acceptable to the Hebrew as a legitimate cultic place where he may await signs of divine presence.

pregnant with the holy presence of the deity is set apart, and its cultic sanctity is to be respected in lieu of death itself. Here is indeed a graphic witness to the real attachment of God's self-manifestation with specific and sanctified space.

At last we turn our attention to two other characteristics of Old Testament theophanies — fear and form. The present brevity should not suggest that these are matters of rather dismal significance. Rather, both will be the special objects of form-critical concentration in the chapter that follows. Concerning the fear element, *the theophany is inclined to link the approaching nearness of the deity with a response of fear and dread that is induced in man who attends it.* In the theophany, the God of Israel draws near as one whose ways are supremely holy and utterly mysterious. Man is overawed by the self-manifestation of the *mysterium tremendum.* The mystery of God's holiness is as unfathomable as it is terrifying. As man directly witnesses God's self-disclosure in the theophany, he cannot penetrate the mysterious aura of divine holiness, much less stand up to its frightening demeanor. Terrified by the august events unfolding immediately before him, Biblical man hides his face (so Moses in Ex. 3:6 and Elijah in I Kings 19:13), falls faceward toward the ground (so Abraham in Gen. 17:3 and Ezekiel in Ezek. 1:28), or utters a word of awful exposure (so Isaiah of Jerusalem in Isa. 6:5, "Woe is me! for I am undone") or dismay (so Jacob in Gen. 28:17, "How awesome is this place!").[40] Yet the terror he experiences is not alone negative in quality. It may be at the same time a realization that the deity is now about to intervene in the concreteness of history for the salvation of his people.[41] In either event, however, the experience that Hebrew man undergoes in theophanic encounter fills him with sheer awe. As a mortal, he is duly unnerved. He cannot control the event. He can only reverently attend it and await its consequence.

[40] It should be noted in passing that these examples surely call into question Jeremias' assertion (*op. cit.,* p. 106) that the motif of human fright plays a quite insignificant role in theophanies that stand outside the Sinai tradition.

[41] An observation suggested by Samuel L. Terrien, "Fear," *IDB,* Vol. 2, pp. 257 f., where he says of Moses that he is afraid to look at God, yet his "negative fear is compounded with a positive emotion at the disclosure of the name of Yahweh and of the divine purpose in history" (p. 258).

Regarding arrangement, we need only to say here that, on the whole, *the theophany is structured according to a definite literary form*. It is no exaggeration to aver that without an awareness of this fact, the preceding observations lose their significance. Certainly the particularities of the theophany are not linked together in any haphazard manner. Often the various sequential aspects of the theophany are ordered after a particular pattern that is especially designed in its quasi-formality to reflect both the majesty of divine self-disclosure and its effects upon man who observes and is grasped by the event. Especially when it comes to Yahweh's manifestation of himself in the Pentateuch, we see that the various narrators display a predilection for the following procedure. They first mention, although on occasion ever so tersely, the fact of the deity's appearance. Then they refer to God's disclosure of his name through a phrase of self-asseveration (e.g., " I am Yahweh "). Finally, they cite both his consoling word aimed at overcoming man's response of fear and dread, and a special word addressed to the concrete occasion — the *hieros logos*. And at times the way in which the theophany concludes is also portrayed. To imply that every theophany unfolds in exactly this manner or that all these items are always present and evident to the same extent would be less than accurate. Moreover, the Old Testament theophanies depicted in Hebrew poetry, which in some respects are the most crucial of all, appear to be liberated to a varying degree from the above-mentioned structure.[42] Yet even there several of the formal components are present in full or in part.

[42] According to Jeremias, *op. cit.*, pp. 7-16 and *passim*, the theophanic form is surely *poetic* in character and owes its genesis to the original form of Judg. 5:4-5 in the Song of Deborah " out of which the forms of *all* other theophanic descriptions of the Old Testament have developed " (p. 7, italics mine). Thus Jeremias might be expected to assess the pattern that has just been presented and will be discussed at greater length in the next chapter as a marked deviation from the original. On the other hand, it appears to me that the unfolding of many Old Testament theophanic passages is not such as to suggest to even the most sensitive reader that the form of Judg. 5:4-5 lies somewhere lurking behind. Perhaps in time two separate forms will have to be posited, each of which is discernible in many but by no means all instances. At present, however, this cannot be suggested with complete confidence as *the* felicitous solution. In any event, a recent reading of Jeremias has not convinced me that the quest for a literary form about to be undertaken here should be abandoned.

So much for our attempted characterization of theophany in the Old Testament. In the process we have claimed the theophany to be:

1. Appallingly real.
2. Initiated by, and only by, the deity himself.
3. Manifested as a temporal event.
4. Arranged so as to represent the absolute sovereignty of deity over the universe, and the corresponding convulsion of nature in reaction to his self-manifestation.
5. Designed to recount the self-disclosure of the deity in a fluid and an intentionally allusive manner.
6. Limited to a partial disclosure of the deity.
7. Concerned with both visual and audible aspects of divine manifestation.
8. Related to a particular place.
9. Inclined to link the approaching nearness of the deity with a response of fear and dread that is induced in man who attends it.
10. Structured generally according to a definite literary form.

From these considerations, we are now prepared to posit a definition. Although it will not prove to be the single key for solving all the problems that we shall subsequently encounter, it is intended to treat the Old Testament materials fairly and appreciatively. The theophany, then, may be defined as *a temporal, partial, and intentionally allusive self-disclosure initiated by the sovereign deity at a particular place, the reality of which evokes the convulsion of nature and the fear and dread of man, and whose unfolding emphasizes visual and audible aspects generally according to a recognized literary form.* Bearing this in mind as a preliminary yet relevant consideration, and realizing that not all theophanic passages in the Bible are equipped to substantiate every component in this definition, and that some are qualified to do even more, we may turn now to an examination of the form of theophanic disclosure in Old Testament literature.

After these things the word of Yahweh came to Abram in a vision, "Fear not, Abram, I am your shield; your reward shall be very great." But Abram said, "O Lord, Yahweh, what wilt thou give me, for I remain childless, and the heir of my house is Eliezer of Damascus? " And Abram said, " Behold, thou hast not given me any posterity, and lo, my household slave will be my heir." And behold, the word of Yahweh came to him, " This one shall not be your heir, but he who comes forth from you, he shall be your heir." And he took him outside and said, " Now look up toward the heavens and count the stars, if you are able to count them." And he said to him, " Thus shall your descendants be." And he believed in Yahweh, and he imputed it to him as righteousness. (Gen. 15:1-6, mainly E.)

CHAPTER II

The Form of Theophanic Disclosure in Old Testament Literature

That the depiction of theophanic encounter in the Old Testament normally follows a recognizable literary form was one of our basic assertions in the preceding chapter about theophany in general. We suggested there that although the Hebrews were not rigid in their utilization of a literary form, neither did they gather the facts and impressions of divine self-disclosure in some haphazard manner. At present we are concerned to examine this situation much more closely than a single paragraph has permitted in order that we may determine the specific dimensions of the form or forms employed. Moreover, we shall wish to discover whether or not a prevailing theophanic form actually does exist in the Old Testament. If the existence of such a form can be demonstrated, we shall further wish to take note of the manner in which form *and* content are blended into an expressive whole.[1]

Sustained argument is quite unnecessary for establishing the significance of these considerations. Let it be understood from the outset, however, that we neither view this critical enterprise as an excursus solely grounded upon aesthetics nor recommend moving on

[1] We say "form *and* content" in support of Sigmund Mowinckel's contention that the two go together: "There exists no form without a content, and no content without a form" (*The Psalms in Israel's Worship,* tr. by D. R. Ap-Thomas [Abingdon Press, 1962], Vol. 1, p. 25). What he states there concerning The Psalms applies to an even wider range of Israelite literature: "Good art means a work in which there is unity of content and aim on the one hand, and of form and style on the other — where the form serves and adequately expresses the content, makes it living and allows it to appear with its full weight and to exhibit its real character."

immediately to the concerns of the next chapter. Rather, we regard the study of formal criteria and their application as an indispensable and appropriate means for gaining an understanding of the very essence of theophany as Israel confronted it and depicted it in her traditions.[2] Although it would not do to present this quest for theophanic form as *the* Mars mission in current Old Testament study, it is true that scholars have not paid it much close attention.[3] If they have ably scrutinized one theophanic element, they have hesitated from considering the literary pattern or patterns of theophanic disclosure as a whole.[4] Form-critical judgments about theophanies have been rather sparse. That the Old Testament presents more than one prevailing emphasis in theophanic discourse should be recognized, yet form-critical observations concerning structure, key words, and repetitions have been neither frequently nor rigorously voiced. Thus in order to engage in a feasible discussion of the form of Old Testament theophanic disclosure, we intend at this juncture to suggest briefly a suitable program for form-critical investigation. Having

[2] The following insight provided by Muilenburg, "Modern Issues in Biblical Studies," p. 232, merits thoughtful consideration: "Careful literary analysis and rhetorical articulation often disclose in a startling way the interior fabric of the thought."

[3] The following, however, have given the matter some consideration: Hermann Gunkel in *Genesis* (HKAT) and *Die Psalmen* (HKAT, Göttingen: Vandenhoeck & Ruprecht, 1926); Ludwig Köhler in his *Old Testament Theology*, *Deuterojesaja*, and "Die Offenbarungsformel 'Fürchte dich nicht!' im Alten Testament," *STZ*, Vol. 36 (1919), pp. 33–39; Artur Weiser in *The Psalms, A Commentary*, tr. by Herbert Hartwell (The Old Testament Library, The Westminster Press, 1962); and Claus Westermann in *The Praise of God in the Psalms*. Moreover, Jörg Jeremias, *Theophanie*, has given the matter very close attention, but his study and the present volume often verge in quite different directions.

[4] Of the scholars mentioned in the preceding note, Jeremias and Westermann deserve to be exempted from this criticism. Westermann has sought to establish a stratification of Old Testament theophany according to its content and terminology (see his chart, "The Epiphany of God," *The Praise of God in the Psalms*, pp. 94 f.). Yet his cannot be called a truly comprehensive effort. Only the theophanies of Hab. 3:3-15; Judg. 5:4-5; and Ps. 18:7-15 have been subjected to any detailed analysis. He briefly introduces a few other theophanic passages into his argument (pp. 93 ff.), but many are omitted. While we would not freely join Weiser (*The Psalms, A Commentary*, p. 38, n. 2) in his criticism of Westermann's schematic presentation, we do aver that the latter has offered us a form analysis that is applicable to only a minimum number of Old Testament theophanies. It cannot be appropriated at all effectively to theophanic descriptions that dominate Old Testament narrative.

made that suggestion, we shall then follow that program to see where it takes us.

Programming the Investigation

Israel has her own way of discourse in the Old Testament. She is careful to put things "just right," although never at the outrageous expense of a complete loss of spontaneity. Tenaciously she holds the conviction that particular occasions, by their very nature, evoke particular patterns of speech. Thus, often the discerning reader of the Old Testament will observe that Israel is as concerned with *how* she says something as she is with *what* she says. Israel does not bequeath to the world a book of etiquette, but in her discourse she consistently shows that, in her opinion, propriety counts. In short, her patterns of speech and patterns of thought are, from the outset, closely interrelated. When this vital aspect of Israelite mentality is grasped and appreciated by the modern critic, then the quest for literary forms assumes a central position within the total task of Biblical interpretation.[5] To lay bare literary form, then, is to travel a good measure of the distance that is required for an understanding of the faith itself that is articulated.

This is, to be sure, not the place to enter into a lengthy digression on the nature and task of *Gattungsforschung* (form criticism). It is important, however, to declare what we believe to be the *objects* of form-critical inquiry as these specifically pertain to our own investigation of a possible theophanic literary form, or *Gattung*. These may be best stated as five distinct yet related tasks that are expected of the discerning eye, sensitive ear, and critical mind as they carefully respond to the literary material at hand. Form criticism, then, challenges the student of the Bible:

[5] If this subject has received all too little attention, one of its most able supporters is James Muilenburg, whose classroom teaching, seminar leadership, and scholarly writing have exerted their influence upon the writer. For the establishment of some of the methodological bases mentioned in this chapter, he is, in particular, indebted to Muilenburg's form-critical discussions in two works: "Introduction and Exegesis to Isaiah, Chs. 40–66," *IB,* ed. by George A. Buttrick *et al.* (Abingdon Press, 1956), Vol. 5, pp. 386–393 and *passim,* and *The Way of Israel* (Harper & Brothers, 1961), pp. 18 ff.

1. To establish the scope of the literary unit in question.
2. To detect the movement within the material belonging to that unit.
3. To perceive the extensiveness and frequency of expression of major motifs and elements.
4. To notice the specific ordering of the constituents.
5. To observe any recurrence of motif and/or expression that emerges from a comparison of a given literary unit with those previously examined.

Each of these tasks may be briefly explained. First, the determination of the scope of the literary unit presents itself as the initial requirement. An acceptable form-critical study cannot be undertaken until one has established precisely where the composition opens and closes. These confines of the literary unit in question should be consciously acknowledged. If this step is ignored, unnecessary confusion may later result.

Secondly, within that unit, notice should be taken of the movement that transpires from beginning to end. Although casual reading and rereading may offer some clues here, the undertaking that is most useful is a rigorous examination of the verbs that are used. These are the very bearers of the action depicted.[6] Frequently the verbs lay bare the major motifs within the passage. They can further enhance one's discernment of the overall structure of the literary unit. Thus the choice, location, and frequency of the verbs employed in a given pericope are matters of concern to the form critic.

Thirdly, the extensiveness and frequency of the major motifs and elements within a passage are not to be overlooked. For example, the vast majority of theophanic pericopes may be shown to be brief literary units of compressed events, and thus there is no reason to take the appearance of a rather lengthy presentation of a given motif or action, or perhaps its repetition, as something fortuitous. A study of

[6] Concerning the speech of Biblical narrative, Muilenburg, *The Way of Israel,* p. 24, maintains: "It is completely centered in action and movement. Beginning and end are always kept firmly in mind. Everything proceeds from the opening sentence and presses forward in action to the outcome." The sense of movement does depend upon the verbs. This holds true for Biblical theophany as it appears in narrative and poetic contexts alike.

literary form in the Old Testament will demonstrate time and again that expanded references, which themselves may consist in the repetition of a given phrase, and recurring words and phrases are all the mark of conscious literary effort. They exist not so much as the inserted glosses of later hands attempting to elucidate obscurities, but rather as an original means of achieving emphasis. If this rhetorical device is not irrelevant, neither is it uninteresting. Israel's literary abilities were such that her iterative discourse neither fatigues, bores, nor distresses the reader. He may in fact enjoy the presence of recurring phraseology. Moreover, such repetition assists one in discerning the meaning of the passage and frequently points the way to the actual divisions within the literary unit. In the final analysis, form criticism values such literary intensification as a means for uncovering the dominant motifs, the structure, and the fundamental intent of a given passage or unit.[7]

Fourthly, the form-critical endeavor does not end with some judgment as to whether or not the basic constituents of a text appear singly or repeatedly. Their specific arrangement and distribution are also matters of concern. In prose and poetic compositions alike, the sequence of particular words and sentences merits close study. The form-critical inquiry seeks to discover the manner in which the phrases of a passage fall one upon the other as well as the position of key words within those passages. Moreover, particular notice is to be made of the initial and the concluding element within the composition being examined, for the discourse employed there often bears a decidedly heavier burden of meaning. However, the ordering of the constituents *between* the two extremes is also significant, especially when the disposition of the words and phrases in one literary unit parallel or diverge from those of another.

Finally, the last-mentioned aspect of the form-critical endeavor focuses upon the recognition of motifs and literary expressions that are

[7] See James Muilenburg's solemn and well-taken warning against the unintelligent deletion of words and phrases as mere repetition in "A Study in Hebrew Rhetoric: Repetition and Style," *VTS*, Vol. 1 (1953), pp. 97–111. See also Johs. Pedersen, *Israel: Its Life and Culture, I–II* (London: Oxford University Press, 1926), p. 123; Cyrus H. Gordon, *UT* (Rome: Pontificum Institutum Biblicum, 1965), pp. 131–137; and John Hastings Patton, *Canaanite Parallels in the Book of Psalms* (The Johns Hopkins Press, 1944), p. 6.

shared by *two or more* related compositions. Indeed, for the sake of our own inquiry, if an external design or internal structure within a basic theophanic *Gattung* is to be discerned, this will be best achieved through a strict examination and comparison of the arrangement of formal elements within several theophanic compositions. Moreover, it is through a scrutiny of the exact ordering of the formal elements and a notice of which components persist and which appear only spasmodically that it will be possible to judge whether there is a development, dissipation, or deliberate rejection of the *Gattung* in the history of its actual Israelite usage.

So much, then, for programming the investigation. Still a word of caution is in order. The tasks here described may be separated and identified. Yet we have averred that they are related. Indeed, they are interrelated. And thus they require some measure of imagination on the part of those who engage in form criticism. For this reason, we cannot content ourselves with running an " x " number of passages through a " y " number of paces. Rather, the tasks as they have been set forth here may suitably inform us concerning what questions we should raise, and in the asking of questions and the rendering of answers, we may find that we have all the while conducted a responsible form-critical investigation.

UNCOVERING THE THEOPHANIC " GATTUNG "

We are in search of a literary form within Israel's literature that may appropriately be identified as Israel's theophanic *Gattung,* and we believe that we shall be able to assert its actuality, provided we can discover within Israel's literature sufficient evidence that points the way. Although nothing may be offered as sheer proof, if we are able to discover the persistence of particular sequences of elements within Old Testament theophanic passages, we might then find ourselves in a position in which we might make some rather definite statements about theophany and literary form.

Because the theophanic *Gattung* is more likely to impress us with its reality if it can be intelligently felt rather than abstractly verified, we submit that it may be best uncovered by means of a series of assertions about the dominant literary aspects of actual theophanic texts. While we shall not examine the texts *seriatim,* we shall constantly refer to them for purposes of illustration. Keeping the various form-critical concerns just presented uppermost in mind, we shall be asking in short, "What is there that persists in the Old Testament theophanic literature?" The answer should bring us close to the literary form we seek.

We may notice, first, that in Biblical theophany there is usually a combination of descriptive statement and direct conversation. The former tells, sometimes most incompletely, how the confrontation between the deity and one or more human beings transpired; the latter discloses the words of teaching and exhortation of the deity as well as the words whereby Israel or a single member of God's elect responded. Most of the speaking, perhaps both the first and the last word, may be voiced by the deity or his representative,[8] but speech is always accompanied by phrases cast in the third person. To be sure, the *what,* rather than the *how,* of speaking stands out as the dominant interest of the author (and speaker within the oral traditions) of the narrative. Nevertheless, whether it be the common brief allusion to the actuality of speaking or something more graphic, some descriptive terms appear. These are found most often, although not exclusively, at the beginning of the theophanic pericope. Thus we read in Gen. 12:1a simply, "Now Yahweh said to Abram," and in v. 7 the slightly more specific phrase, "Then Yahweh *appeared* [*wayyērā'*] to Abram and said . . ." Gen., ch. 15, opens with the description, "After these things the word of Yahweh came to Abram in a vision"; the Yahwistic theophany in Gen., ch. 28, commences in v. 13a with, "And lo, Yahweh *stood* [*niṣṣāb*] beside him and said . . ."; and in Judg. 6:11 there is a more vividly construed description that begins, "Now the angel of Yahweh came and sat under the oak. . . ." The theophany may also terminate with observations in the third person. This is true for Gen. 12:7b, "And he [Abraham] built there an altar to Yahweh, who had appeared to him," or Gen. 17:22, "As soon as he had finished talking with him, God went up from Abraham," or Ex. 4:18a, "And Moses went and

[8] Thus the theophanies in Gen., chs. 15; 17; Ex. 3:1 to 4:17; Judg. 6:11-24; I Kings 19:9-18; and Jer. 1:4-10. At times all of the speech within a theophany is divine speech: cf. Gen. 21:15-19; 26:23-25; Ex. 6:2-9.

returned to Jethro. . . ." Some description, however terse, generally appears to be a constant in Biblical theophanic presentation.

An appreciably greater emphasis, however, is placed upon the conversation between divine and human parties, or in some cases, upon the sublime and decisive divine monologue that unfolds. Several noteworthy elements emerge here. Occasionally the deity or his *mal'āḵ* (messenger/angel) addresses by name the one who attends the theophany. The name may be once uttered as part of the question directed to the one addressed: "*Hagar,* maid of Sarai, from where have you come and where are you going?" (Gen. 16:8),[9] or "What are you doing here, *Elijah?*" (I Kings 19:13). It may stand alone as the stirring word of salutation; thus in Gen. 22:1, God calls forth "Abraham," and in Gen. 31:11, the *mal'aḵ 'elōhīm* (messenger/angel of God) addresses the patriarch in a dream with the brisk utterance, "Jacob." Sometimes the name is evoked twice — "Abraham, Abraham" (Gen. 22:11), "Jacob, Jacob" (Gen. 46:2), and "Moses, Moses" (Ex. 3:4). Whether the name is spoken just once or repeated, however, the response of the one addressed is conspicuously the same: "Here am I," or more literally, "Behold me" (*hinnēnī*). Through this formal element we are given an impression of the stance of expectation that belongs to the mortal who is marvelously called by name.

Yet we discover in Old Testament theophanies that not only is the name of the one which is uttered by the deity or his representative (the *mal'āḵ*) a solemn indication that he is known by the God who intervenes in history, but by delivering his own name, there is an intentional self-giving on the part of the deity. At Bethel, Jacob heard the self-asseveration, "I am Yahweh [*'anī Yahweh*], the God of Abraham your father and the God of Isaac" (Gen. 28:13). Abraham was given to hear the deity proclaim simply, "I am El Shaddai" (*'anī-'ēl šadday,* Gen. 17:1), and to attend the more elaborate self-asseveration, "I am Yahweh who [*'anī Yahweh 'ašer*] brought you out from Ur of the Chaldeans to give to you this land as a possession" (Gen. 15:7), where divine name and divine purpose were inextricably linked. In theophanic encounter at Horeb, Moses

[9] So also in the Elohist's account of the theophany to Hagar in Gen. 21:17, although here the question precedes the name: "What troubles you, Hagar?"

attended the self-predication of the deity both in the phrase, "I am the God of your father [*'ānōḵī 'ᵉlōhē 'āḇīḵā*], the God of Abraham, the God of Isaac, and the God of Jacob" in Ex. 3:6, and in the self-disclosing words, "I am who I am" (*'ehᵉye[h] 'ᵃšer 'ehᵉye[h]*) in Ex. 3:14. Yahweh's giving of his name constitutes the climactic moment of the Sinai theophany (Ex. 20:2), and direct allusion is made to it in the cult theophany as the rubrics in the Psalter denote (cf., chs. 46:10; 50:7; 81:10). Although the declaration of the divine name through self-asseveration does not belong to every theophany in Israel's literature,[10] it does appear with conspicuous persistence. And on occasion the deliverance of divine name is most emphatic; thus at the beginning (v. 2), middle (v. 6), and close (v. 8) of his address to Moses in Ex., ch. 6, the deity proclaims, "I am Yahweh" (*'ᵃnī Yahweh*).

Divine speech in the theophany, however, consists of more than a conscious mention of divine and human names. Often statements of divine presence are also encountered, and these consistently disclose a gracious presence governed by a redemptive purpose, a comforting nearness that issues from divine concern. Yahweh assures Isaac at Beersheba, "for I am with you" (*ḵī-'ittḵā 'ānōḵī,* Gen. 26:24), and in answer to Moses' first protest that he cannot fulfill what is demanded of him, the deity declares, "But I will be with you" (*ḵī 'ehᵉye[h] 'immāḵ,* Ex. 3:12). In Gideon's theophanic encounter in Judg., ch. 6, there is a threefold mention of divine presence. Its reality is affirmed by the *mal'āḵ* in v. 12, questioned by Gideon in v. 13, and advanced in Yahweh's own words, "But I will be with you" (*ḵī 'ehᵉye[h] 'immāḵ*) in v. 16. Moreover, of particular interest is the assurance of divine presence in Yahweh's self-manifestation to Jacob at Bethel, for there such an affirmation is treated as the primary emphasis of the passage: "Behold, I am with you [*'ānōḵī 'immāḵ*], and will keep you wherever you go, and will bring you back to this land; for I will not leave you . . ." (Gen. 28:15). It becomes increasingly clear that the sum of these expressions is not fortuitous.

Yet the greater portion of the speaking that takes place in theophanic encounter is not found in the declaration of the name or in

[10] It is lacking, for example, in such significant theophanic disclosures as Gen. 16:7-14; 21:15-19; Judg. 6:11-24; I Kings 19:9-18; Isa., ch. 6; and Jer. 1:4-10.

the explicit assurance of divine presence, but rather in that element of divine speech which addresses itself with marked specificity to the concrete historical situation. This is a word of utmost particularity that presents itself as directly applicable to the present circumstance. As the unique word of disclosure it has been termed the *hieros logos.*[11] It may consist of a command (so the word of the *mal'ak Yahweh* to Hagar, "Return . . . submit . . . ," Gen. 16:9), a promise (so Yahweh to Abraham, "To your descendants I will give this land," Gen. 12:7), a commission to perform a deed as a divinely ordained agent (so Yahweh to Gideon, "Go in this might of yours and you shall save Israel from the hand of Midian," Judg. 6:14), or a sober monition (so Yahweh to the assembled congregation in the cult, "Offer to God a sacrifice of thanksgiving, / and pay your vows to the Most High," Ps. 50:14). In each theophanic disclosure, the emphases and internal structure of this portion of divine speech will vary; yet through a study of the *hieroi logoi,* it will become increasingly clear that, despite their variation in length, each uniquely issued divine discourse may be judged as one recognizable formal component in Old Testament theophany.

One other aspect that persists in Israel's literary depiction of theophany concerns man's fear. This is ordinarily embodied in the direct divine utterance, "Fear not!" Thus the first word of divine speech that Abraham hears in Gen. 15:1 is "Fear not!" (*'al-tīrā'*), and once Yahweh identifies himself in his theophanic disclosure to Isaac at Beersheba, he speaks the same word of assurance, "Fear not!" (*'al-tīrā',* Gen. 26:24). In the theophany of Judg., ch. 6, Yahweh's utterance aimed at quelling Gideon's fright presents itself as a consoling word directed to this vigorous one of Manasseh in response to the latter's appalling realization that he has seen the *mal'ak Yahweh* face to face. It is the second of three highly compressed sentences of divine assurance: "Peace be to you / Fear not! [*'al-tīrā'*], / You shall not die" (v. 23). The formula, "Fear not!" occurs repeatedly as part of the divine address in theophany. It stands as an indication that it is the divine will that man's fear abate, and further as a wit-

[11] So Muilenburg, "Isaiah," *IB,* Vol. 5, p. 390, *The Way of Israel,* p. 32, and "The Speech of Theophany," *HDB,* Vol. 28 (1964), pp. 37 f., 44; see also Weiser, *The Psalms, A Commentary,* p. 27.

ness to the dread that overtakes man when confronted by a theophanic visitation of the deity.

We notice, however, that as an identifiable formal criterion within the theophany, the reference to fear does not always appear in the divine rubric, " Fear not! " Israel avoided stereotypes here. Thus in some theophanic accounts there may be a well-wrought expression of paralyzing fear on the part of one confronted by the *mysterium tremendum,* but an absence of any specific exhortation from the deity against fear. For example, in Isaiah's inaugural theophanic experience, we read:

> Woe is me! [*'ōy-lī*] for I am undone;
> for I am a man of unclean lips,
> And I dwell in the midst of a people of unclean lips;
> For my eyes have seen the king,
> Yahweh of hosts!
> (Isa. 6:5.)

Clearly, the prophet is fearful, but the " Fear not! " formula has been replaced, as it were, by an act of sanctification (vs. 6-7). Another variation may be recognized in the third-person allusion to fear on the part of the narrator. Thus in the theophanic call of Moses, the prophet does not declare that he is afraid. Neither does the deity speak out assuredly, " Fear not! " Instead, a descriptive notation is made within the course of the encounter: " Now Moses hid his face; for he was afraid to look upon God " (Ex. 3:6). Human fear, then, seems to be mentioned regularly in theophanic passages, but the manner of its expression varies.

Although the illustrative material is far from depleted, this may suffice to show that we have come upon several elements that persist in Israel's expression of the theophany — third-person description, the divine utterance of the name of the one confronted with the theophany and that one's response, the self-asseveration of the deity, the assuring word of divine presence, the disclosure of historical particularity, and allusion to fear on the part of one who attends such awesome self-manifestation.

But does the evidence adequately argue for the existence of a theophanic *Gattung* in Israelite literature? We believe that it does, but we had best understand what kind of literary form it was. Its lines were no doubt clearly drawn, yet as is true of all of Israel's forms of discourse, it did not evolve into a stereotype that might overbearingly impose itself upon her narrators and poets. The form was no doubt taken seriously, but it did not enslave the speech of those who used it. As a form, it never existed as a petrified possession. It was not static. Rather, possibly from its origin, it seems to have been friendly toward additions. At base, the theophanic *Gattung* appears to have allowed for the creation of compressed narrative. Description was brief and the *hieros logos* was not much longer. Nevertheless, the components within the *Gattung* were variables, quite adaptable to the particular historical situation to which a given theophany referred and to its proper depiction.

Apparently that *Gattung* had its birth at some point during the oral stage of Israel's traditions, which continued alongside her period of literary output. As the oral traditions were written, collected, and redacted, the theophanic *Gattung* seems to have been disturbed. At times the theophanic account is all too brief for us to suppose that it is completely extant in its present written form. On other occasions, it appears to have been enlarged. Thus the question inevitably arises, "Do we have within the fixed written traditions of the Old Testament any example of the theophanic *Gattung* in its pure unembellished form, or must we content ourselves with only a hypothetical construct?"

Realizing that one swallow does not make a summer, we are inclined to find in Gen. 26:23-25 (J) the theophanic *Gattung* in its clearest actualization. While rooted within a specific temporal and geographical context, the theophany as here presented incorporates with all its brevity those formal elements dominant within the Old Testament theophany at large. The passage reads as follows:

> 23 From there [Rehoboth] he [Isaac] went up to Beersheba. 24 And Yahweh appeared to him the same night and said, "I am the God of Abraham your father; fear not, for I am with you, and I will bless you, and multiply your descendants for my servant Abraham's sake." 25 And he built an altar there and called upon the name of Yahweh, and pitched his tent there; and there Isaac's servants dug a well.

In it the following formal elements are to be discerned: We encounter in vs. 23-24a a brief description prefacing the theophanic confrontation proper and indicating the fact of Yahweh's self-disclosure and speaking. Then early in v. 24 we meet the self-asseveration of the deity. Also in v. 24 we witness the divine word aimed at quelling human anxiety. Later in v. 24 we confront the assuring word of gracious divine presence relating to the preceding element and introduced here by the common Hebrew particle *kī* (for). Then we note that the remaining portion of divine utterance in v. 24 may justifiably be designated as the *hieros logos* that is addressed to Isaac's particular situation. Finally, in v. 25a we read a descriptive third-person statement concerning Isaac's response to theophanic confrontation.

These formal elements within the theophanic *Gattung* as they are illustrated by this Genesis passage may be heightened through the following form-critical outline:

1. *Introductory description:*	23 From there he went up to Beer-sheba. 24 And Yahweh appeared to him the same night and said,
2. *Divine self-asseveration:*	"I am the God of Abraham your father;
3. *Quelling of human fear:*	Fear not,
4. *Assertion of gracious divine presence:*	For I am with you,
5. *"Hieros logos":*	And I will bless you, and multiply your descendants for my servant Abraham's sake."
6. *Concluding description:*	25 And he built an altar there and called upon the name of Yahweh. . . .

Here we may be facing the theophanic *Gattung* in its pristine expression. Yet we should realize that this *Gattung,* as Israel knew it, could both contract and expand. On the one hand, not all six of these elements are present in many theophanic passages. On the other, expansion was also possible. Narrative description could be lengthened and not alone confined to the opening and terminating portions of the pericope. The *hieros logos* could be enlarged and the verbal response of the mortal witnessing the divine disclosure entered into the record. Because this *Gattung* was not rigid, such a pattern as the following was within the realm of probability:

1. An introductory description in the third person.
2. The deity's utterance of the name of the one whom he confronts.
3. The brief, expectant response of the mortal addressed.
4. The deity's self-asseveration.
5. His quelling of human fear.
6. The assertion assuring his gracious presence.
7. The *hieros logos* addressed to the particular situation.
8. An inquiry or protest by the mortal addressed.
9. A continuation of the *hieros logos* with perhaps some repetition of elements 4, 5, and/or 6, possibly along with some phrases repeated from 7.
10. A concluding description.

This pattern is our own hypothetical construction, but it serves to emphasize the fluid state that existed in the actual utilization of the theophanic *Gattung* within the Old Testament. To no small degree, Israel's narrators, poets, and redactors were free to add or drop basic formal constituents. Yet in its complete, pure, and unembellished state, the theophanic *Gattung* may have presented itself in the manner previously described and illustrated by Gen. 26:23-25.

Scrutinizing the "Gattung" Components

In the process of uncovering a theophanic literary form within the literature of the Old Testament, we have, to be sure, offered some word of identification for each of its various components. Up to this point, however, we have not had the opportunity of inspecting a very full range of the possibilities that are within their reach, or to put it in another way, we have not yet been in a position to appreciate the full burden of their responsibility, much of which is overtly theological in nature. In order that this might be realized, we propose now to examine the six components of our theophanic *Gattung* with somewhat closer scrutiny.

1. *Introductory description.* This formal element of the theophanic *Gattung* appears as a briefly executed but necessary means of initiating the narrative of theophanic encounter. It is essentially verbal in character with any one of several verbs being employed. Thus it is said of the deity: "then he appeared to . . . and said" (*wayyērā' Yahweh 'el . . . wayy'ōmer,* Gen. 12:7), or "and lo . . . he stood beside him and said" (*wᵉhinnē[h] . . . niṣṣāb 'ālāw wayy'ōmar,* Gen. 28:13), or "the word of Yahweh came to . . ." (*hāyā dᵉbar-Yahweh 'el . . . ,* Gen. 15:1).[12] These descriptions are most often framed in third-person discourse (*Erform*), but they are also attested in the first person (*Ichform*): "And the word of Yahweh came to me, saying . . ." (so Jer. 1:4). Although in some actual sense of the term, the third-person introductory description may consider the "how" of the theophanic experience—by saying that the divine word was encountered in a dream or through a vision,[13] the first-person description employed by the prophet in the recounting of his own theophanic experience is decidedly more immediate and personal. Isa., ch. 6; Jer., ch. 1; and Ezek., ch. 1, all serve to make this evident.

The opening descriptive element of theophanic discourse is deliberately terse and is perhaps marked as much by what it tries to withhold as it is by what it purports. Ordinarily no effort is made to describe the form of the deity's appearance, for the narrator knows that he would have to cope with the ineffable.[14] What is essentially reported is the fact that a divine word is about to be addressed to the one attending theophanic encounter. No attempt, however, is made

[12] Gerhard von Rad, *Genesis, A Commentary,* tr. by John H. Marks (The Old Testament Library, The Westminster Press, 1961), p. 178, observing that the formula is "foreign to the Hexateuch and frequent in the prophetic literature," accepts this as a tradition necessarily perpetrated as a prophetic call.

[13] E.g., Gen. 31:11 and 15:1 respectively.

[14] Hence the exceptional nature of the description in the theophany narrated in Ezek., ch. 1. James Barr, "Theophany and Anthropomorphism in the Old Testament," *VTS,* Vol. 7 (1960), p. 32, maintains that "in many cases the describing of the theophanic appearance is less important than the registering of the words spoken; or perhaps more probably, . . . the recording of the appearance in detail was felt by writers often to be too serious and difficult to attempt except in special cases."

to capture the reader's *sustained* attention here, since the introductory description exists as a preface that directs the reader to the decisive verbal engagement to follow.

2. *Divine self-asseveration.* Since it is through this significant formal element that the deity emphatically identifies himself with his first-person " I " to the one whom he has elected to confront in theophany as the second-person " thou," both the significance and structure of the divine self-asseveration merit our attention. Designated by Walther Zimmerli as the *Selbstvorstellungsformel,*[15] the self-asseveration, theologically speaking, constitutes a supreme act of self-giving by the deity which in turn provides a firm basis for that relationship between deity and mortal which ensues from theophanic encounter.[16] As an Ancient Near Eastern phenomenon attested outside the Old Testament canon,[17] the self-asseveration was respected by Israel as a poignant and recurring disclosure of the incomparable

[15] "Ich bin Jahwe," *Geschichte und Altes Testament* (Beiträge zur historischen Theologie, No. 16, Tübingen: J. C. B. Mohr, 1953), p. 182.

[16] That the oft-repeated antiphon, "I am Yahweh your God," indicates a *binding relationship* between God and people is clear from the way in which it is employed in the Holiness Code (Lev., chs. 17 to 26). In this connection, Muilenburg, *The Way of Israel,* p. 22, avers: "Statute follows upon statute, but they are established and given authority by the climactic word: '*I am Yahweh your God.*' The repetitions are not merely stylistic; they are meant to call Israel to remembering and to hearing, to acknowledgment and to faith."

[17] Self-asseverations appearing in Egyptian and Akkadian materials may be noted through the translations of John A. Wilson and Robert H. Pfeiffer respectively in *ANET,* ed. by James B. Pritchard (2d ed., Princeton University Press, 1955). On the "Sphinx Stela," the words of the god within the Sphinx, Harmakhis, to Thutmose IV include, "I am thy father, Harmakhis-Khepri-Re-Atum," p. 449. In the "Oracles concerning Esarhaddon," pp. 449 f., the repeated "I am Ishtar of Arbela" asseveration (with slight variations) is accompanied in the text by two more lengthy locutions, "I am the great divine lady, I am the goddess Ishtar of Arbela, who will destroy your enemies from before your feet," and "Your gracious leader am I, who unto protracted days, everlasting years have fixed your throne under the wide heavens . . . ," and also by "I am the god Nabu, lord of the tablet stylus. . . ." Wilhelm Schubart, "Die religiöse Haltung des frühen Hellenismus," *Der alte Orient,* Vol. 35, No. 2 (Leipzig: J. C. Hinrichs, 1937), p. 27, n. 1, includes the text of the Isis Hymn in which divine first-person affirmations abound. Further comment on Ancient Near Eastern divine self-asseverations may be found in Sigmund Mowinckel, "The Name of the God of Moses," *HUCA,* Vol. 32 (1961), p. 123, and Charles G. Cumming, *The Assyrian and Hebrew Hymns of Praise* (Columbia University Press, 1934), p. 87.

transcendence of her sovereign Lord. In the occasional but regular theophanic disclosures she experienced, the self-introduction of Yahweh became for Israel an awesome reminder that she was faced by one who voluntarily shrugged off his incognito and allowed himself to be known. Having thus been graciously favored, Israel could now call upon the name of Yahweh (cf. Gen. 12:8; 26:25). For this people, the self-asseveration statement of theophany established the relationship between worshiper and the one worshiped. It bound divine subject and mortal object into a historically concrete association involving divine promise and saving intent, on the one hand, and Israel's accountability on the other.

Both the significance and actual literary expression of the first-person affirmations of the deity may be further realized through an examination of the various formulae which this theophanic component assumes. One of these is, to use Eduard Norden's terminology, the *egō eimi* (" I am ") type.[18] Thus the deity proclaims his name to Abraham in Gen. 17:1 as " I am El Shaddai " (*'ᵃnī-'ēl šadday*), and to Moses in Ex. 6:2, 6, and 8, as " I am Yahweh " (*'ᵃnī Yahweh*). The self-asseveration, while pure and simple, is fraught with meaning. Through even the most succinct divine self-predication, the mortal attending a given theophanic disclosure was given to know the identity of the one who intervened into his time and space.[19] A slightly longer self-introduction, with the personal pronoun appearing at the end of the locution, occurs in the original form of Ps. 50:7 with " Yahweh, your God, am I " (*Yahweh 'ᵉlōhe[y]ḵā 'ānōḵī*). Upon hearing this divine first-person utterance with its detectable covenantal nuance, the pious in the cult might know that they stood before divine presence. Moreover, the emphatic form of the personal pronoun and the suffixed form of the divine name constitute two re-

[18] *Agnostos Theos: Untersuchungen zur formengeschichte religiöser Rede* (Leipzig/Berlin: B. G. Tuebner, 1913), pp. 186–188.

[19] We refrain from an excursus into the rich meaning that Israel found in the simple self-asseveration, " I am Yahweh." The studies of Zimmerli, *loc. cit.*, pp. 179–209, and Karl Elliger, " Ich bin der Herr — euer Gott," *Theologie als Glaubenswagnis* (Hamburg: Furche-Verlag, 1954), pp. 9–34, deserve careful study although much of their effort is given to an examination of nontheophanic contexts. In our consideration of the divine self-predication in the Sinaitic theophany in the next chapter, we shall have occasion to refer more extensively to their contributions.

minders that might move the cult to focus upon the particular self-asseveration disclosed in the Sinai theophany that is here reflected in the psalm (so Ex. 20:2 with "I am Yahweh your God, who . . . ," [*'ānōḵī Yahweh 'ᵉlōhe(y)ḵā 'ᵃšer* . . .]).

Other variations of the divine self-asseveration occur. Once the *mal'aḵ 'ᵉlōhīm* (messenger/angel of God) addresses Jacob with, "I am the God of Bethel" (*'ānōḵī hā'ēl bēt-'ēl,* Gen. 31:13). This form incorporates the name of a cultic place where the patriarch had previously been visited by a theophany (Gen. 28:10-22). In self-proclamation the deity voluntarily relates himself to antecedent event. Rolf Rendtorff avers that in this manner of mentioning the divine name, where prior cultic events or names of ancestors are recalled, the entire history of God's direction resounded.[20] This applies in yet another formulation, in the first-person pronouncements of the deity which bear the phrase "the god of your father." Thus we encounter Yahweh's word to Isaac, "I am the God of Abraham your father," in Gen. 26:24; his utterance to Jacob, "I am Yahweh, the God of Abraham your father and the God of Isaac," in Gen. 28:13; and the divine self-asseveration to Moses, "I am the God of your father, the God of Abraham, the God of Isaac, and the God of Jacob," in Ex. 3:6. In the traditions of the fathers, then, the divine name is tied with antecedent promises, events, and persons.

Then another and more elaborate form of the deity's self-introduction contains overt expression to Yahweh's prior action in Israel's history. This is the self-asseveration that is accompanied by the relative pronoun "who" (*'ᵃšer*) plus a participial clause alluding to a specific instance of Yahweh's historical intervention. This may be illustrated with reference to the full divine self-predication of the deity to Abraham in Gen. 15:7, "I am Yahweh who brought you out [*'ᵃnī Yahweh 'ᵃšer hōṣē'tīḵā*] from Ur of the Chaldeans to give to you this land as a possession," and Yahweh's self-introduction at Sinai in Ex. 20:2, "I am Yahweh your God, who brought you out of [*'ānōḵī Yahweh 'ᵉlōhe(y)ḵā 'ᵃšer hōṣē'tīḵā*] the land of Egypt . . . ," the *locus classicus* of the expanded formula.[21]

Finally, the self-asseveration of the deity reaches both its most em-

20 "'Offenbarung' im Alten Testament," col. 835.

21 So Elliger, *loc. cit.*, p. 32.

bellished and moving formulation in the oracles of Second Isaiah. With considerable freedom, the author meshes first- and third-person discourse,[22] thereby assuring a liberation of the divine formula of self-asseveration from any possible rigidity accruing from imposing formal limits. To illustrate, in Isa. 44:24-28b, the prophet-poet initiates the divine pronouncement with the familiar "I am Yahweh" (*'ānōḵī Yahweh*), understandably drops any explicit mention of the rather unpoetic relative pronoun "who" (*'ăšer*), and at once introduces the first of a *dozen* participial and finite forms whereby Yahweh's specific deeds in human life and history are celebrated! Clearly, in these Old Testament formulations of varying length and style, the self-giving of the divine name is integrally connected with the divine promise and intervention that is part of the total *Heilsgeschichte* (sacred history) to which Israel continually bore witness. The divine self-asseveration that we meet in Biblical theophany, then, is no idle disclosure.

3. *Quelling of human fear.* In Old Testament theophanies, the sudden appearance of the deity is depicted again and again as an event that evokes a keen sense of fright in the individual or group[23] attending such august disclosure. It is, no more, no less, the necessary correlative to divine holiness.[24] That a mortal is perturbed by the immediacy of divine presence is not uniquely an Israelite reaction to the theophany. Not only does the injunction "Fear not!" appear as a formal component within New Testament theophanies,[25] but it is a pronounced element in the Akkadian oracles and located there at crucial points in the divine discourse.[26] If this divine admonition en-

[22] Cf. Köhler, *Deuterojesaja,* pp. 121 f., and his thorough examination of ch. 40:22-25 as an authentic self-predication cast in the third person.

[23] Cf. Ex. 20:18-21 (group); Isa. 6:5 and Ezek. 1:28 (individual).

[24] Cf. Eichrodt, *Theologie des Alten Testaments,* Teil 2/3, pp. 184 ff.; Th. C. Vriezen, *An Outline of Old Testament Theology* (Oxford: Basil Blackwell, 1958), p. 135; and Johannes Hempel, *Gott und Mensch im Alten Testament,* 2te Auflage (Stuttgart: W. Kohlhammer, 1936), pp. 4 ff.

[25] See Luke's Gospel with the admonition against fear uttered by the angel of Yahweh to the shepherds in ch. 2:10 as well as the utterances of the angel Gabriel to Zechariah in ch. 1:13 and to Mary in ch. 1:30.

[26] In the "Oracles concerning Esarhaddon," *ANET,* pp. 449 f., the divine command, "Fear not!" occurs seven times. It is well spaced throughout, appearing first in the opening clause, "[Esarhad]don, king of the countries, fear not!" The same

joyed widespread use in the Ancient Near East, it is in Israel's traditions that it dominated in a special sense. From the simple theophanies of Genesis to the more sophisticated theophanic speech of Second Isaiah, which employs the "priestly oracle of salvation,"[27] the efficacious utterance of this formula communicated most clearly the deity's concern for the one he had chosen to address as "thou" in special meeting. With the subduing of fear on the part of the individual or people listening to this yet prefatory component of divine speech, the way was cleared for the deity's subsequent speaking in the redemptive yet compelling *hieros logos* which could now be eagerly attended.

This theophanic component also enjoys several formulations and these have been subjected to a rigorous form-critical examination by Ludwig Köhler.[28] Of the five types of expression he mentions, four relate to theophanic contexts. The first of these formulations, which Köhler avers is the most ancient, is the simple "Fear not!" formula (*'al-tīrā'* or one of its variants) with or without a word of direct address. Thus in the theophanic context of Isa. 44:2c we meet, "Fear not, O Jacob, my servant." The direct utterance of divine assurance and a personal address (even if extended) are the single components here. But apart from this example and Daniel's vision of Gabriel in Dan. 10:15-19, this form does not occur in Biblical theophany. Köhler also cites a more complex form which contains, in addition to the direct summons to courage, an independent motivation clause. This is the stylistic situation in the theophany of Gen., ch. 15, where the opening portion of the divine speech runs, "Fear not, Abram, *I am your shield*" (v. 1). Similarly, Isa. 41:14 in part reads, "Fear not, . . . *I will help you.*" The injunction of the deity and the motivation upon which fearlessness is to be grounded appear asyndetically side by side. As a third variation, Köhler identifies a formulation that consists of the usual "Fear not!" admonition plus a

utterance occurs as the initial element in the "Oracle of Ninlil concerning Ashurbanipal" (*ANET*, p. 451) and is thrice repeated near its close. Moreover, the first word of Ishtar to the king in "An Oracular Dream concerning Ashurbanipal" (*ANET*, p. 451) is "Fear not!"

[27] Cf. the study of Joachim Begrich, "Das priesterliche Heilsorakel," *ZAW*, Vol. 52 (1934), pp. 81–92, in which he focuses upon the "Fear not" formulation.

[28] "Die Offenbarungsformel 'Fürchte dich nicht!' im Alten Testament."

question which in its sheer asking seeks to substantiate why one should not be frightened. This rarely employed type occurs in theophanic speech in Isa. 44:8: "Fear not, nor be afraid, / have I not told you from of old and made it known?"

But it is Köhler's fourth type that is especially relevant to theophany. Here, in contrast to the second formulation, the "Fear not!" injunction is followed by a substantiation or motive clause which is formally introduced by the deictic *ḵī* (for) particle.[29] In the Elohistic account of the theophany to Hagar, the *mal'aḵ 'elōhīm* (messenger/angel of God) addresses the Egyptian maid, "Fear not, *for* God has heard the voice of the lad" (Gen. 21:17). Moreover, in the Yahwistic narrative of the deity's appearance to Isaac at Beersheba, a portion of the divine speech reads, "fear not, *for* I am with you" (Gen. 26:24). Thus through a variety of stylistic forms, we discern that the quelling of human fear is vividly and emphatically enjoined in theophanic encounter. With stylistic diversity and theological suggestiveness, this formal element implies again and again that in his self-disclosure, the deity draws near not to perturb creation but rather to act in man's behalf.

4. *Assertion of gracious divine presence.* A word of assurance is part of the total pattern of divine speaking in the theophany, and this word most often promises in one way or another Yahweh's gracious dwelling with his people. The Holy One of Israel openly resolves to abide with those before whom he has chosen to appear. In the phrase "I will be with you," a meaningful and decisive relationship between God and people is declared as established.[30] The helping proximity of the deity is pledged. Again, the explicit statement of divine presence in the theophany is not solely an Israelite possession. It belongs to Egyptian and Akkadian oracles as well.[31] Nevertheless,

[29] *Ibid.*, pp. 36 f. Cf. James Muilenburg, "The Linguistic and Rhetorical Usages of the Particle *ḵī* in the Old Testament," *HUCA*, Vol. 32 (1961), p. 158.

[30] The comments of George A. F. Knight, *A Christian Theology of the Old Testament* (John Knox Press, 1959), p. 56, on the diverse significance of this phrase for Israel's very existence are helpful.

[31] See *ANET*, pp. 449 and 450. In the former instance, the "Sphinx Stela" bears this word of Harmakhis that came to Thut-mose IV: "Behold, I am with thee; I am thy guide." In the latter, Esarhaddon receives the assurance from Ishtar of Arbela, "I have not abandoned you," which interestingly parallels the situation in many Old Testament theophanies since it follows upon the injunction, "Fear not!"

Israel knew such promises in a peculiar sense.

Ordinarily the affirmation of divine immediacy was part of a longer declaration in which the deity promised his support. Thus in Gen. 26:24, the proclamation "for I am with you" is directly followed by "and I will bless you, and multiply your seed for my servant Abraham's sake." In Gen. 28:15 the formal expressions of the helping nearness of the deity are piled one upon the other, as we have already observed. This component of the theophany may exist as the first element of divine discourse (so Judg. 6:12) or appear much later as the deity's assuring response to some protest voiced by the mortal before whom he has come and summoned for a special task (so Ex. 3:12 and Jer. 1:8). In either case, however, we may discern in this component one further piece of evidence that in theophanic meeting the deity is intent upon extending himself to those before whom he appears. Israel understood Yahweh's coming as an act of grace, an act that showed quite clearly that he did not abhor the concreteness of his creation.

5. "*Hieros logos.*" This element of the theophany may be characterized as the unique word of the deity addressed to the particularity of time and place within which the recipient stands. It is, in all cases, the new element disclosed. On the basis of its dominance in the theophany, Millar Burrows aptly observes, "God appears in order to speak." [32] In contrast to the notably general utterances delivered by the gods and goddesses in the Akkadian oracles, the *hieros logos* of Israel's Lord embodied in the Old Testament theophanies consistently bears upon the specific.[33] There Yahweh's word is ever particular and ever aimed toward concrete situations. Its presentation, then, varies a great deal from theophany to theophany. This observation applies to its length,[34] but even more to its content and

[32] From *An Outline of Biblical Theology* (The Westminster Press, 1946), p. 28.

[33] Morris Jastrow, *The Religion of Babylonia and Assyria* (Ginn and Company, 1898), pp. 343 f., refers to the impressive yet quite general phrases of Assyrian oracles. An examination of the Akkadian oracles in *ANET,* pp. 449–451, will confirm Jastrow's assertion.

[34] E.g., cf. the very brief *hieros logos* that Yahweh delivers to Abraham in Gen. 12:7, "To your descendants I will give this land" (four words in Hebrew plus the sign of the accusative), and the lengthy oracles in Second Isaiah set in theophanic style.

phrasing. Such diversity precludes extensive form-critical comment here, but our interpretation of various Biblical theophanies is liable to err if we do not appreciate the significant role borne by this component. In short, the *hieros logos* in each theophany stands as the crucial word wherein lies *the very purpose of divine self-disclosure.*

6. *Concluding description.* If most theophanic accounts in the Old Testament may be expected to open with a brief yet discernible descriptive element, most may be expected to end similarly. In the theophanic disclosure of the deity to Abraham briefly narrated by the Yahwist in Gen. 12:7, the account which commences with "Then Yahweh appeared to Abram and said . . . ," will imminently close with "And he built there an altar to Yahweh, who had appeared to him" (see also Gen. 26:25). In the Priestly account of the institution of circumcision, which is depicted as being established through the medium of theophanic meeting (Gen. 17:1-22), the confrontation terminates quite discreetly: "As soon as he had finished talking with him, God went up from Abraham" (v. 22). The theophany has ended and the remainder of the chapter describes Abraham's entering upon the circumcision of self and household. The theophany may also draw to a close with a combination of third-person description and spoken statement: "When Jacob awoke from his sleep he said, 'Surely Yahweh is in this place; and I did not know it!'" (Gen. 28:16).

The concluding description, however, is characteristically a terse element. Granting that the Yahwistic and Elohistic accounts of Yahweh's theophany to Moses in Ex. 3:1 to 4:17 are not extant in their entirety, we may still observe that the disclosure that opens with not a little elaboration formally closes with ch. 4:17, and is immediately followed by the simple comment, "And Moses went and returned to Jethro" (ch. 4:18). Then there are passages in which this element is altogether lacking. In Gen. 31:10-13, with Jacob's report of his theophanic experience to his wives, the *hieros logos* of the *mal'āḵ* is the last-mentioned component. Moreover, in the account of his Temple vision, Isaiah concludes with divine speech itself. Despite its occasional absence in theophanic narrative, a concluding descriptive statement does appear to have been an integral part of Israel's theophanic *Gattung.*

TAKING NOTE OF THE ACTUAL USE OF THE THEOPHANIC "GATTUNG"

One important form-critical consideration remains. As an inquiry it may be expressed as follows: "How was Israel's theophanic *Gattung* actually employed?" We have stated at the outset of this chapter that the Hebrews were not rigid in their utilization of a literary form. Is this perhaps a facile way of glossing over the fact that they were genuinely much less enthusiastic about following literary forms than are some scholars today in trying to uncover them? A lack of space does not permit a full answer to that question, but there are several assertions that can be made briefly.[35]

It should be clear from the preceding discussion that Israel took her forms of speaking quite seriously. In the various Biblical examples that have been quoted, it is obvious that the phrases are too calculated, too symmetrical, too smoothly drawn to permit us the conclusion that in their discourse Israel's narrators, poets, and redactors were indifferent to formal matters. We are also aware, however, that the Biblical illustrations used in this chapter have shown that the various components of the theophanic *Gattung* were employed with some variation. In Israel, the imagination was not an unheard-of force. Taking the long view, then, we would have to say that the *Gattung* we have discovered in the Old Testament is more readily recognized in narrative pericopes than in poetic passages. Moreover, it is better illustrated in the Pentateuch than elsewhere in the Old Testament. We cannot marshal all the evidence here, for that would require our scrutinizing every theophanic unit within the Old Testament canon. We shall, however, take note of the actual employment of the *Gattung* in those theophanic passages which we are now about to examine more directly. Thus both explicitly and implicitly, we shall be regularly checking the evidence against our present findings.

[35] The writer's doctoral dissertation, "An Examination of Theophany in the Old Testament with Special Reference to Theophanic Contexts in the Psalter" (Union Theological Seminary, 1963), pp. 68–77, enters more fully into these matters by engaging in a form-critical examination of some twenty theophanic passages drawn from various sections of the Old Testament. Special note is taken there of the presence or absence of the various components of the theophanic *Gattung* proposed. The conclusions reached are essentially included in this brief section.

Meanwhile, we may submit that in Israel's traditions and literature it appears clear to us that a theophanic *Gattung* did enjoy an existence and a rather rigorous use. In it were prescribed the formal ways of speaking of theophanic disclosure. But the description of divine confrontation was always open to fluid and spontaneous expression. The visual and audible phenomena that ensued were never subjected to the narrow requirements of fossilized formulations incapable of expansion, change, and development. Particularly in the poetic expressions of the theophany, through mythical imagery and expanded phraseology, the theophanic description was emancipated from the stricter canons of Pentateuchal discourse. Nevertheless, the original theophanic *Gattung,* toward which we believe we have drawn near, does present itself in Israel's literature as one of her own and well utilized possessions.

CHAPTER III

The Theophany on Sinai

Israel's traditions consistently represented theophanic disclosure as unfolding within a *crucial* historical moment. It is through a theophany, for example, that divine call and promise are issued to Abraham, that Moses is confronted by the terrifying prospects of leading his people, and that the divine summons to the prophetic office is delivered to Isaiah and Jeremiah.[1] In each instance, the theophanic encounter is presented as constituting a most decisive moment in the life of the individual involved. If one Biblical theophany, however, were to be regarded as the preeminent theophanic disclosure of the God of Israel, it would be the theophany to the people — and especially to Moses — on Mt. Sinai.[2] Here is the theophany par excellence. On the basis of its vivid presentation in Ex., chs. 19 to 24, the numerous allusions to it within the Old Testament, and the influence it has exerted upon subsequent theophanic descriptions, the Sinaitic theophany was understandably respected by Israel as an act of unique and unsurpassed revelation.

[1] Cf. Gen. 12:1-4a, 6-8 (J); 15:1-21 (JE); 17:1-22 (P); Ex. 3:1 to 4:17 (JE); 6:2-9 (P); Isa. 6:1-12; Jer. 1:4-10.

[2] Also referred to in the Old Testament as Mt. Horeb. Martin Noth, *The History of Israel,* tr. by Peter R. Ackroyd (2d ed., Harper & Brothers, 1960), pp. 128 f., maintains that "the juxtaposition of these two names and their interrelationship is a complete mystery; and only one point is clear, namely that the name 'Sinai' is the older of the two in the tradition that has come down to us." In *Überlieferungsgeschichtliche Studien,* Teil I (Tübingen: Max Niemeyer, 1957), p. 29, Noth claims that the name "Horeb" is a secondary element in the Pentateuchal narratives. Should the E traditions antedate those of J, which is not impossible, this assertion would be called into question.

Through this crucial self-disclosure, the people were granted an opportunity of perceiving the divine essence and will in an unprecedented and unrepeated manner. On the one hand, the theophany on Sinai was dynamically reappropriated by later generations through their cultic observances that transformed past moment into present reality. On such occasions, the reenactment of the anterior event in question was truly vivid and effective. Repeated reenactment led to the inevitable conventionalization of the language about the Sinaitic revelation. Those who participated in this cultic worship of the deity adopted that language with increasing fervor. In short, the cult kept the Sinaitic event alive in the Israelite conscience. On the other hand, the seeing, hearing, and speaking that transpired in the Sinaitic theophany per se ever must have been esteemed as belonging to a *sui generis* event so consequential in its depth and scope that one could say of it that it was at this moment that Yahweh became the God of Israel, and Israel the people of Yahweh. The fixation of cultic practice was incapable of altering that.

The basic question to be posed in this chapter may be phrased as follows: " How did Israel remember and interpret the theophany accorded her on Mt. Sinai? " Any adequate answer will require, to be sure, a literary inspection and theological evaluation of those traditions embodied in the Elohistic, Yahwistic, and Priestly Pentateuchal strata that comprise Ex., chs. 19 to 24.

At the outset, we would grant that not even the earliest of these traditions, namely, those which have been incorporated into the J and E narratives, can be understood as exactly representing a historical happening as sheer event. The traditional picture of the Sinaitic revelation cannot be subjected to simple factual analysis. Martin Buber was right in his judgment that " we are no longer in a position to replace that immense image by actual data." [3] Both the volcanic and storm traditions here presented may themselves be secondary methods of depicting the historical theophany.[4] Moreover, the materials

[3] *Moses: The Revelation and the Covenant* (Harper & Brothers, Torchbook edition, 1958), p. 111.

[4] Martin Noth, *Exodus, A Commentary,* tr. by J. S. Bowden (The Old Testament Library, The Westminster Press, 1962), p. 160, cogently avers that " we cannot obtain any completely reliable reference to the situation of Sinai even from the existence of the volcano-tradition."

of Ex., chs. 19 to 24, are primarily cultic in character, and must be understood as such. Still, Israel's literary depiction of the Sinai experience in Ex., chs. 19 to 24, is not to be judged solely as a product of cultic *invention*. On the contrary, Biblical interpreters have rightly discerned a historical nucleus in the Sinaitic theophany and covenant ceremony. Although Gerhard von Rad is most careful to point out the cultic nature of the material here transmitted by the Elohist, he does not doubt the "historical rootage" of the original event.[5]

The very ordering of the various incidents at Sinai by both the J and E strata attests the effective influence of the cult. In this connection we may cite the preparatory ceremonies of purification, the anticipated advance toward God at the sound of the horn (*šōpār*), the deity's significant disclosure of his nature and will, and the sealing of the covenant by sacrificial rite. If the cult has enjoyed unusual power in shaping the traditions it has transmitted, if it appears to be the agent that *conditions* the concrete expression of much of Israel's literature, it is also to be understood as a *conditioned* agent. The Israelite cult characteristically remembers and meditates upon historical actuality. Its responses are contingent upon anterior event. The refraction and reworking of the historical tradition within the cult, which is inevitable, neither intends nor accomplishes some wholesale perversion of the underlying historical experience. Thus we may rightly assume that the theophanic encounter, and the act of covenant making, which is an integral part of the total Sinaitic event, did in fact occur in "historically conditioned forms." [6]

Now we are primarily interested in examining the several ways in which Israel recalled and comprehended the Sinaitic theophany. Although we shall ignore almost entirely the legislative detail of these chapters, with the Decalogue (Ex. 20:1-17) and the Book of the Covenant (Ex. 20:22 to 23:33), most all of chs. 19 and 24 along with portions of ch. 20 will be scrutinized. Both the detailed prelude to the

[5] So *The Problem of the Hexateuch and Other Essays,* tr. by E. W. Trueman Dicken (McGraw-Hill Book Company, Inc., 1966), pp. 28 f.

[6] A phrase borrowed from Noth, *The History of Israel,* p. 134. He claims, "There is no doubt that the Sinai tradition, the basic substance of which is quite unique and unrelated to any other phenomenon in the history of religion, derived from an actual event," p. 128. Cf. John Bright, *A History of Israel* (The Westminster Press, 1959), p. 115, where a defense for the historical veracity of the Sinaitic tradition is presented in bolder language.

theophany, with the deity's instructions to Moses and the prevailing interest in ceremonial purification, and the sacrificial ceremonies that seal the covenant that immediately follow the theophany merit our attention. Moreover, there are elements within Ex., chs. 33 to 34, that necessitate brief consideration, but we shall not attempt in the process any extensive crisscrossing of the materials.[7] Nor shall we present detailed arguments in defense of our identification of the Pentateuchal strata. Since the differentiation of the strata within Ex., chs. 19 to 24, is quite difficult, any adequately defended presentation would require a tedious excursus that would do little to advance the real interests of this study. Also that exercise has already been attempted by many commentators whose relatively coordinate results are readily available.[8] The well-informed reader will note without difficulty that our own assumptions rather consistently stand within the rank and file of scholarly consensus. Thus for reasons that shall not be presented here, we take the literary stratification of Ex., chs. 19 to 24, to run as follows: Ex. 19:2b-8, 10-11a, 14-17, 19; 20:18-21, 1-17; 20:22 to 23:33; 24:3-8, 12-15a, 18b, belong to the Elohistic; 19:9a, 11b-13, 18 (secondarily vs. 20-25); 24:1-2, 9-11, to the Yahwistic; and 19:1-2a; 24:15b-18a, to the Priestly Sinaitic narrative.

The Elohistic Theophanic Narrative

Since the Elohistic account of the Sinaitic theophany is by far the dominant one in these chapters, it deserves primary and rather extensive consideration. Six different elements may be discerned: (1) the invitation to the people and their response (ch. 19:2b-8),

[7] As does Murray Newman in his rearrangement of Ex., chs. 19 to 24; 33 to 34, in *The People of the Covenant* (Abingdon Press, 1962). In order to set forth two separate and complete J and E covenant traditions, Newman has found it necessary to change the verse order rather extensively in his establishment of "The Jahwist's Version of the Covenant" (pp. 42–46). If we are here presented with a very plausible construct, it is still hypothetical.

[8] Cf., *inter alios,* J. Estlin Carpenter and G. Harford-Battersby, *The Hexateuch According to the Revised Version,* Vol. 2 (Longmans, Green, & Co., Inc., 1900); S. R. Driver, *The Book of Exodus* (Cambridge University Press, 1911); Otto Eissfeldt, *Hexateuch-Synopse* (Leipzig: J. C. Hinrichs, 1922); W. O. E. Oesterley and Theodore H. Robinson, *An Introduction to the Books of the Old Testament* (London: S.P.C.K., 1934); Walter Beyerlin, *Origins and History of the Oldest Sinaitic Traditions,* tr. by S. Rudman (Oxford: Basil Blackwell, 1965); Noth, *Exodus* (1962); G. Ernest Wright, "Book of Exodus," *IDB* (1962), Vol. 2, pp. 188–197; and Newman, *op. cit.* (1962).

(2) the sanctification of the people (ch. 19:10-11a, 14-15), (3) the appearance of the deity (ch. 19:16-17, 19), (4) the fear of the people and their request that Moses mediate (ch. 20:18-21), (5) the self-asseveration of the deity and proclamation of his will (ch. 20:1-17 [with chs. 20:22 to 23:33 subsequently added]), and (6) the establishment and sealing of the covenant (ch. 24:3-8). We propose to inspect each in turn.

1. *The invitation to the people and their response* (*Ex. 19:2b-8*)

> 2b Israel encamped there in front of the mountain. 3 And Moses went up to God and Yahweh called to him from the mountain, saying, "Thus you shall say to the house of Jacob, and tell the children of Israel, 4 'You have seen what I did to the Egyptians, and how I bore you on eagles' wings and brought you to myself. 5 Now therefore, if you will indeed obey my voice and keep my covenant, then you shall be my special possession among all peoples; for all the earth is mine, 6 and you shall be to me a kingdom of priests and a holy nation.' These are the words that you shall speak to the children of Israel."
>
> 7 Then Moses came and called for the elders of the people, and he set before them all these words that Yahweh had commanded him. 8 And all the people answered together and said, "All that Yahweh has spoken we will do." Moses then reported the words of the people to Yahweh.

The narrative opens with a notation that the people have arrived at a mountain whose identity is assumed as known. Having led the people to the site of his call, to the locale where the deity presumably dwells, Moses now advances nearer to God, who is apparently enthroned upon the mountain.[9] The statement that the deity called to Moses "from the mountain" suggests, however, that Moses did not ascend immediately to the summit. In any event, that Moses should hear the divine message of invitation and convey it to the people is the sole purpose of Yahweh's speaking here.[10] The language

[9] The LXX subdues the anthropomorphic tone of v. 3a by reading, "unto the *mountain* of God."

[10] The very wording of the invitation establishes quite effectively Moses' role as messenger. Clearly, the use of three distinct Hebrew roots for speaking (*'mr* and *ngd* in v. 3b, and *dbr* in v. 6b) and the emphatic "children of Israel" (also vs. 3b and 6b) may be understood as contributing elements here.

and studied structure within the message itself present a notable contrast with the flow of narrative that precedes and follows.[11] The first and last lines of the invitation commence with a conscious mention of the second-person plural pronoun (*'attem*). In v. 4, which contains the opening phrases of Yahweh's invitation, we meet a tricolon that speaks for the reality and power of anterior divine accomplishment that has favored this people now encamped at Sinai. In v. 5 we discover a second tricolon with its word of obligation and promise which is formally introduced by the emphatic "now therefore" (*w*^{e}*'attā*). Moreover, the immediacy of the imminent encounter is enhanced by a stylistic consciousness that is evident in the repeated use of the first- and second-person pronouns in vs. 4-6.

That message given to Moses which he is then to convey to the people forms an indispensable portion of the prelude to Yahweh's appearing. Prior to theophanic meeting, Israel is called to *witness* Yahweh's historical deeds in her behalf, and to *decide* whether her response will be one of obedience or disobedience. Her decision is to be made in the light of the possibility of her being chosen as Yahweh's special possession if she obeys, and in recognition of divine sovereignty ("for all the earth is mine," v. 5b). Witness prefaces decision, for it is Yahweh who has taken the initiative in graciously and effectively delivering Israel from the Egyptian yoke. The narrative thus assumes that those who attend the theophany are also those who have previously witnessed Yahweh's mighty deeds in the exodus.[12] In a most crucial moment, Israel beheld the defeat of the Egyp-

[11] Cf. James Muilenburg, "The Form and Structure of the Covenantal Formulations," *VT*, Vol. 9 (1959), p. 354, who comments: "This style is familiar to us from the similar phraseology of the Mari royal texts and the Hittite treaties. It is the characteristic speech of the messenger. . . . It is probable that the style and form of the whole unit have their origin in royal discourse."

[12] On the basis of Ex. 19:4, it seems to us at least reasonable to conclude that, owing to the efficacy of the Israelite cult, the Exodus and Sinai motifs were deliberately linked at a very early age. Von Rad, in particular, has argued for a rather lengthy independence of these motifs prior to their literary juxtaposition. He has heightened the distinction by judging the Exodus tradition to be "redemptive history," but the Sinai tradition to be "apodeictic law" (so *The Problem of the Hexateuch and Other Essays*, pp. 18 f.). On the other hand, Artur Weiser, *The Old Testament: Its Formation and Development*, tr. by Dorothea M. Barton (Association Press, 1961), pp. 88 ff., contends that the linking of the traditions betrays cultic activity rather than some literary stroke on the part of the Yahwist, and he is able to

tians. She thereby experienced divine deliverance. The marvelous character of her rescue is conveyed by metaphor — " I bore you on eagles' wings." Whether we side with Driver that the figure aptly calls to mind " the swiftness, the security, and the affectionate care with which the deliverance from Egypt had been effected," [13] or with Buber that the image by its very nature cannot be adequately comprehended by the modern reader,[14] certainly *for Israel* the metaphor was most significant and could be readily grasped as a graphic indication of Yahweh's historical intervention which was, after all, the very ground for Israel's being where she was at the present moment, a moment that was calling her to decision. She was now standing at that place where Yahweh could declare, " I brought you to myself " (v. 4b).

But Israel is not to be solely concerned with those past events which have shaped the existential present. There is in the divine summons an eager expectation for obedience that will be manifested by Israel's present word of commitment and substantiated by her future life of covenantal loyalty. The divine promise is *conditional* in character.[15] Yahweh is not setting forth unconditional pledges.

---

adduce many Old Testament passages that connect the Sinai and Exodus-Conquest traditions without showing any literary dependence whatever upon the Yahwist.

Whether or not the Sinai theme is an isolated Biblical tradition constitutes one of the current storm centers of Old Testament scholarship. Although we do not propose to delve into the issues that separate such scholars as von Rad and Noth from Wright, Bright, Weiser, and Beyerlin, we are inclined to believe that, both in terms of style and effect, Ex. 19:4 may indeed attest a quite early conjoining of the Sinai and Exodus traditions. The issue, of course, is most complex. In addition to the works cited above, the reader is referred to von Rad, *Genesis,* p. 20; and Noth, *Überlieferungsgeschichte des Pentateuch* (2te Auflage, Stuttgart: W. Kohlhammer, 1948), p. 65; *Exodus,* p. 11; *The History of Israel,* pp. 128, 133, and *passim,* who wish to keep the two traditions separate, and to Wright, " Cult and History: A Study of a Current Problem in Old Testament Interpretation," *Interpretation,* Vol. 16 (1962), p. 17; " Book of Exodus," *IDB,* Vol. 2, p. 195; Bright, *Early Israel in Recent History Writing* (Studies in Biblical Theology, No. 19; London: SCM Press, Ltd., 1956), pp. 105 f.; *A History of Israel,* p. 115; and Beyerlin, *op. cit.,* pp. 69 f., who argue for their original unity. A brief but useful article by Philip B. Harner, " Exodus, Sinai, and Hittite Prologues," *JBL,* Vol. 85 (1966), pp. 233–236, may also be consulted. To be sure, our listing attempts to be representative, not exhaustive.

[13] *The Book of Exodus,* p. 170.

[14] *Op. cit.,* p. 102.

[15] The conditional aspect is *grammatically* emphasized in v. 5a with its use of the

Rather, he declares that *if Israel will indeed obey,* her continuing relation with the God who has brought her to Sinai will be marked by special immediacy.

Now in the Elohist's account, Yahweh will not enter into the theophanic act itself until Israel has had the opportunity of hearing some word from Moses about the covenantal promise that Yahweh graciously extends to her. Basically that promise is ontological. It expresses what Israel will become if she observes the terms of the covenant that is initiated by the one who is to approach her in theophanic meeting. First, she will become Yahweh's "special possession" (*s*ᵉ*gullā,* v. 5b), the valued property of the one who has chosen her for himself. Six of the eight appearances of this noun in the Hebrew Old Testament are located in metaphorical descriptions of Israel's relation with the deity.[16] The metaphorical use of this noun in The Book of Deuteronomy is especially apt in affirming that Israel is a holy and special treasure of Yahweh who has been specially chosen from all peoples who inhabit the earth and from whom is expected an obedience to Yahweh's commandments. Obligation and election are intimately linked. The covenantal promise, then, is conveyed by a second expression, "kingdom of priests" (*mamleḵet ḵōh*ᵃ*nīm,* v. 6a). A mutuality of obligation and privilege are also denoted here. Israel is charged to live in the service of her Lord; in turn, Israel will be in position at all times to delight in the right of access to Yahweh. Through a third expression, "a holy nation" (*gōy qādōš,* v. 6a), which recurs in Deut. 7:6; 14:2; and 26:19 in the form "a holy people" (*'am qādōš*), Israel plainly has the choice of becoming an exclusive people set apart from the world at large for both privilege and responsible obedience to divine command.

Moses' reporting the words of Yahweh to the elders, the willing response of all the people, and Moses' informing Yahweh of the people's pledge of obedience constitute the interests of vs. 7-8. At first glance, the words of the people may seem strange, since the deity has

---

infinitive absolute (*šāmoă'*), which immediately follows the introductory particle *'im,* and immediately precedes the finite verb *tišm*ᵉ*'ū.* See Friedrich H. W. Gesenius, *Hebrew Grammar,* ed. and enlarged by E. Kautzsch, and revised by A. E. Cowley (Oxford: Clarendon Press, 1910); #113-o, pp. 342 f.

[16] Cf. Ex. 19:5; Deut. 7:6; 14:2; 26:18; Ps. 135:4; and Mal. 3:17.

yet to communicate his commandments through the theophany. But if we may entertain a stylized development in the Elohist's account, the words will no longer impress us as being awkward. Moreover, this communication of Yahweh's purpose to the people by Moses, who is their mediator, and the statement of the people's readiness both emerge as the natural subsequent phases of the full unfolding of theophanic narrative. Yahweh has expressed to Moses his desire that the people obey his voice and keep his covenant (v. 5). Moses conveys the message, and the people respond directly, " all that Yahweh has spoken we will do." We need not assume that the people are expressing their willingness to obey a series of commandments that has already been given them and talk ourselves into shifting these two verses to another position in the text. Rather, we may interpret Israel's speaking here as an expression of her ready consent to what the deity has, through Moses, already declared thus far and her keen interest in what he will disclose in the anticipated theophanic meeting.

2. *The sanctification of the people (Ex. 19:10-11a, 14-15)*

> 10 And Yahweh said to Moses, " Go to the people and sanctify them today and tomorrow, and let them wash their garments, 11a and be ready by the third day." 14 Then Moses went down from the mountain to the people, and he sanctified the people; and they washed their garments. 15 And he said to the people, " Be ready by the third day; do not approach a woman."

Although Yahweh's invitation to Israel to enter into a covenantal relationship with him has been extended to, and accepted by, the people, the anticipated theophany does not take place at once. One important phase of the prelude has run its course, but another remains. The people are to be sanctified. Again the phrasing of the narrative is to be taken seriously. An emphasis upon the sanctification of the people and the requisite distance between God and people is achieved through a conscious repetition of phrases. Moreover, in the divine decree to Moses, the reader's attention is directed to three verbs that follow one upon the other — " and thou shalt sanctify them " (*w^{e}qiddaštām,* v. 10), " and let them wash " (*w^{e}kibb^{e}sū,* v. 10), " and let them be ready " (*w*^{e}*hāyū n*^{e}*ḳōnīm,* v. 11). In the report of vs. 14-15 that Moses executed these divine orders aimed at the appropriate consecration of the people, precisely the same verbs in that same sequence are employed. An admonition does occur in Moses' speech to the people, however, that is not part of the preceding speech of the deity to Moses — " do not approach a woman " (v. 15). Martin Noth is justified in his assertion that the " lame " expression of this regulation justifies our identifying it as an addition.[17] Indeed, Noth has the formal structure of these verses on his side.

As a whole, this portion of the E Sinai pericope attests the danger and temporality of the Sinaitic theophany. The perilous holiness of the mountain is to be resolutely respected. This locale of impending divine self-disclosure requires of its visitors a preparatory discipline of a particular sort. Of equal importance is the fact that theophanic meeting will take place at a definite moment, at a fixed time following the interval of preparation. Obviously the subsequent and outspoken cultic point of view permeates the narrative.[18] The efficacy of a given event in the Israelite cult depended much upon its execution at the proper moment. The event was not to be evoked prematurely. Rather, it was to be anticipated through correctly instituted cultic preparation. Thus the received tradition of the theophany to which the Elohist had access is plainly a cultic tradition. But whether the theophanic event here depicted be thought of as original happening in later dress or as cultic reenactment, its temporality is accentuated by several specific words for time. " Today " (*hayyōm*) " and tomorrow " (*ūmāḥār*) the people are to engage in purificatory ritual (v. 10) that will prepare them for the appearance of the deity on " the third day " (*layyōm hašš*^{e}*līšī,* v. 11). They are to anticipate Yahweh's coming at the *designated* time, not at some uncertain moment late or soon. The people's declaration of volitional readiness with respect to the covenant is to be matched by ceremonial readiness with respect to theophanic engagement.

[17] *Exodus,* p. 158. See also Beyerlin, *op. cit.,* p. 7. However, J. Coert Rylaarsdam, " Introduction and Exegesis to the Book of Exodus," *IB,* Vol. 1, p. 976, argues that the prescription for continence existed in early Israel and here refers to I Sam. 21:4-6.

[18] Cf. Beyerlin, *op. cit.,* p. 140; and Helmer Ringgren, *Israelite Religion,* tr. by David E. Green (Fortress Press, 1966), pp. 35, 71.

The awaited encounter between the holy deity and the people understandably presupposes a basic distinction between God and man that is ceremonially honored through ritual undertakings. The Pi'el forms of the Hebrew root *qdš*, " to consecrate, sanctify," in vs. 10 and 14 ably denote the transformation of the people from ritual uncleanness to a condition of sanctity that alone will enable them to approach the deity in theophanic meeting.[19] That the clothing of the people is to be washed is surely another projection of the cult. Rylaarsdam suspects that the washing is enjoined " to neutralize the garment of those who will come into the presence of the holy." [20] Thus a more immediate relation with the deity is guaranteed than would otherwise be possible. In sum, the ritual preparation of the people is looked upon as a vital prerequisite to theophanic encounter. There is no hint of the casual in these verses. Indubitably, the entire situation is marked by an ominous tone.

3. *The appearance of the deity* (*Ex. 19:16-17, 19*)

> 16 And on the third day when it was morning, there were thunders and lightnings and a thick cloud upon the mountain, and the blast of a very loud horn, so that all the people who were in the camp trembled. 17 Then Moses brought forth the people from the camp to meet God, and they took their stand at the foot of the mountain. 19 And when the blast of the horn grew louder and louder, Moses spoke, and God answered him in thunder.

These three verses along with Ex. 20:18 constitute the Elohist's description of the actual theophanic self-disclosure of the deity to the attending community. As such, they bear the awesome burden of depicting the ineffable theophany. With emphasis upon audible phenomena, the approach of the God of Sinai for theophanic encounter is depicted by the Elohist in moving terms. The narrative advances in a straightforward manner; repetition as a rhetorical device is employed sparingly, although the repeated words that do occur possess vitality. In both vs. 16b and adjacent 17a there is mention of the people encamped at Sinai who significantly participate as witnesses in

[19] See KB, pp. 825 f.; and BDB, p. 873.
[20] From *loc. cit.*, p. 975.

the theophany. Spectators though they be in part, they are deeply involved in the events at hand. Although Moses plays a unique role in the theophanic meeting, he does not witness the divine presence alone, as is the case with the theophany to Moses in Ex. 3:1 to 4:17. Moreover, near the extremities of this literary unit, attention is called to the thunder and the blast of the horn (Ex. 19:16 and 19) which grants a particularity to the *audible* dimension that is uppermost in the Elohist's mind. Notwithstanding such duplication, each verse has its own function. The time, the concrete theophanic phenomena, and the fear of the people are especially communicated in v. 16, the expectant stance of the people is reported in v. 17, and the antiphon between Moses and God is the subject of v. 19. Whether or not the reality depicted here is meteorological in fact or metaphorical in description is not the major issue.[21] The crucial character of the encounter, however, merits closer inspection.

After designating the actual moment of theophanic meeting, v. 16 lists the audible and visual elements that induced a trembling in the people who were to witness the appearance of the deity. The audible phenomena, " thunders " and " the blast of a very loud horn," appear in first and last position as the more important manifestations that surround the somewhat less essential visual phenomena, " lightnings " and " a thick cloud."

Mention of thunder, lightning, and the accompanying cloud con-

[21] For its able representation of present-day scholarship, the following statement by Rylaarsdam, *loc. cit.,* p. 977, is cited: " It seems impossible to decide definitely whether this description is based on an actual recollection of meteorologic conditions at Sinai or represents a literary portrayal in metaphors that were considered appropriate to a theophany. Inasmuch as these are widely used stock metaphors, and inasmuch as this account, at least in its written form, must be several centuries removed from the event, the latter seems much more probable." We cannot agree with the methodological principle of W. J. Phythian-Adams, " The Volcanic Phenomena of the Exodus," *JPOS,* Vol. 12 (1932), pp. 89 ff., that the volcanic character of Sinai can be established simply by drawing parallels between the description in Ex., ch. 19, and eyewitness reports of volcanic eruptions of the present day. The fact that Sinai cannot be located with certainty complicates the problem, since it precludes any decisive criterion for determining whether it is the volcanic eruption or the severe mountain storm that lies most directly behind Ex., ch. 19, or whether both influence in equal measure. Especially in the E stratum we need not presuppose the existence of volcanic phenomena. Moreover, we must ever be sensitive to the presence of metaphorical and cultic language in this chapter.

vey most naturally the image of a storm with which Yahweh is associated. In its plural form (*qōlōt*), the Hebrew noun, *qōl,* denotes both the literal fact of thunder and the metaphorical designation of the voice of Yahweh.[22] In the former instance, the thunder may be closely related to its divine author who sends it (e.g., Ex. 9:23 and I Sam. 12:17-18). A more intimate linking of deity and storm phenomena, however, is achieved when the thunder is equated with the divine voice. This is the implicit assumption of Ex. 19:16 which is made explicit by v. 19. The close association of storm phenomena with the approaching nearness of the deity in his august power is then reinforced in v. 16 through mention of lightning and the thick storm cloud at rest upon the mountain. The Hebrew noun *ʿānān,* rendered most often as " cloud," frequently designates a *theophanic* cloud apparatus.[23] But in contrast with the downward movement of the cloud which is presupposed in Ex. 34:5 (J), " And Yahweh *descended* in the cloud," Ex. 19:16 understands the cloud as a permanent apparatus. This, of course, accords with the dominant assumption in the E stratum that the mountain is the seat of *continuous* divine residence, with the cloud regularly enveloping the deity in his mysterious seclusion, and protecting him from mortal gaze.[24]

In the E stratum, however, theophanic visitation is further proclaimed through a conspicuous cultic element, the sound of the horn (*šōpār*), that has been infused into the Sinai tradition. Not only does v. 16 refer to the presence of the blast of the horn which precedes and evokes the assembling of the people at the foot of the mountain, but v. 19 discloses the manner in which Israel heard the horn amid theophanic encounter: " And when the blast of the horn grew louder and louder, Moses spoke, and God answered him in thunder." While there is much that is vague and unexpressed, especially any indication of the one who blows the *šōpār,* a cultic utilization of the Sinai tradition has clearly made itself felt in the E account.

[22] See KB, p. 831, and BDB, pp. 876 f.

[23] E.g., Ex. 13:21-22; 14:20; 16:10; 19:9; 24:15; 34:5; Num. 10:34; 11:25; 14:14; Deut. 1:33; 4:11; 5:22; I Kings 8:10-11; II Chron. 5:13-14; Isa. 4:5; Ezek. 1:4; 10:3-4; Ps. 97:2.

[24] For further statement on the frequent and quite complete association of Yahweh and storm phenomena, see J. L. McKenzie, " God and Nature in the Old Testament," *CBQ,* Vol. 14 (1952), pp. 34 f.

In this connection, we would agree with Walter Beyerlin that it is unjustifiable to assume that the *šôpār* has been introduced secondarily as a commentary of a later period reflecting a preferred interpretation of the narrative.[25] After referring to the cultic theophanies represented in II Sam. 6:2, 14-15; Ps. 47:5; 81:3; and 98:6 where the *šôpār* is also utilized, Beyerlin concludes that the sounding of the *šôpār* is an indigenous element within the cultic theophany of Yahweh, a feature that dominates other accompanying phenomena present in the Sinaitic theophany. Convinced of the dramatic actualization of the theophany in the cult which has exerted no small influence upon the shaping of the E Sinai account, Beyerlin maintains that the blast of the *šôpār* was specifically employed in cultic theophanies as the chosen means of indicating the divine voice. Beyerlin contends, " The epiphany of the God whom no man could look upon . . . and who remained hidden in the cloud of incense . . . could only be perceived by the cultic community in terms of such dramatic representation." [26] Clearly, the present narrative manifests a significant cultic overlay.

The response of the people is the special concern of Ex. 19:17. The first half of the verse reports *that* the people were brought forth from the camp by Moses to meet God. The second half indicates *how* that was accomplished: " and they took their stand [*wayyitᵉyaṣṣᵉbû*] at the foot of the mountain." As in v. 3, the narrative presumes that the God who calls Israel is the God who dwells upon the mountain. The fear-struck people do not assemble for meeting of their own accord but are guided to a specific place by Moses. In contrast with the rather elaborate instruction to Moses concerning the locus of theophanic meeting in the J account (ch. 19:11b-13), the Elohist's narrative contains this very brief although important designation of place. The cultic concern for the appropriate reservation of time and place for theophanic meeting is, nevertheless, exhibited in the E stratum. Indeed, in v. 17 it is buttressed by the use of the root *yṣb,* " to take one's stand," which plays a significant role in the language of Israelite worship.[27] Thus with fear and anticipation, the people now stand

[25] *Op. cit.,* pp. 135 f.

[26] *Ibid.*

[27] See Walter Harrelson, " Worship in Early Israel," *Biblical Research: Papers*

ready to witness the theophany. The conversation between Moses and the deity, designated through the frequentative use of the Hebrew imperfects *y^e^dabbēr* ("he [Moses] spoke") and *ya'^a^nennū* ("he [Yahweh] answered him"), commences immediately. The narrative does indicate, however, that the *content* of the conversation was not disclosed at that moment to the people. They only heard inarticulate noise. That they already perceived and acknowledged the awesome aspect of authentic divine presence through the repeated thunderings is confirmed, however, by the fourth phase of the Elohistic report to which we now turn.

4. *The fear of the people and their request that Moses mediate (Ex. 20:18-21)* [28]

> 18 When all the people perceived the thunderings, and the lightning flashes, and the sound of the horn, and the mountain smoking, the people were afraid and trembled. So they stood afar off, 19 and said to Moses, "You speak to us, and we will listen, but let not God speak to us, lest we die." 20 And Moses said to the people, "Fear not, for God has come in order to prove you and in order that the fear of him may be before you that you may not sin." 21 And the people stood afar off, but Moses drew near toward the dense darkness where God was.

If the witnessing, yet fearful, community can at first confront the powerful impact of theophanic meeting, it cannot continue to endure the august presence of the deity. The people manifest their anxiety by withdrawing from the prescribed place of theophanic encounter, and this in turn leads them to entreat Moses to act as their mediator (vs. 18-19). Moses attempts to quell their fear by interpreting the meaning of the theophany, whereupon he draws nearer to the deity for more immediate confrontation (vs. 20-21).

A form-critical examination of the movement present within the

---

of the Chicago Society of Biblical Research III (Amsterdam: North-Holland Publishing Co., 1958), p. 4.

[28] In taking up ch. 20:18-21 before treating ch. 20:1-17, we are supporting the contention advanced by a number of scholars that it is only in this manner that the original order of the Elohist may be uncovered. The merit of this approach can, we think, be readily recognized by a matching of this verse sequence over against the traditional order.

narrative will highlight several noteworthy features. The verses at the beginning and end of this literary unit represent third-person descriptions of the event. In v. 18 the people witness, fear, and withdraw. In v. 21 Moses advances toward the deity, although the retreat position of the people has not changed. In the intervening verses a conversation takes place between the community and Moses. In contrast to the cumbersome and somewhat perplexing words of Moses, those uttered by the people are marked by lucidity and balance. The word of fear, not the word of interpretation, is the more readily communicated. In v. 19a, Moses' future speaking to the people is linked with their eagerness to listen, while in v. 19b the deity's future speaking is linked with their thought of sure annihilation. In both instances, the auditory situation is first established; the result is then enumerated.

According to v. 18, four separate phenomena confronted *all* the people — thunder and sounding horn on the audible side, and lightning and smoke on the visual. All may be considered to be objects of *perception,* since all are related to one Hebrew participle of *r'h,* a root that commonly denotes seeing.[29] Because v. 18a in a sense provides a summary of the preceding phase of the theophany (ch. 19:16-17, 19), new elements are not numerous. Yet an explicit statement that the people did in fact perceive the theophanic phenomena, mention of the lightning flashes, and allusion to the smoking mountain have not been set forth heretofore in the E narrative.[30]

But it is what immediately follows in v. 18b that constitutes the primary interest of this section. The community that has beheld signs of the real presence of the unseen deity is clearly intimidated.[31] Fear and trembling overtake this people which lead directly to their fran-

[29] The complexity may be attributed in part to the blending of originally separate elements. Cf. *inter alios,* Noth, *Exodus,* p. 168, and Beyerlin, *op. cit.,* p. 13.

[30] Chapters 19:16 and 20:18 may offend our understanding of the natural world as we notice mention of thunder *prior* to mention of lightning. Our discussion of ch. 19:16 suggests that this might be for emphasis. In both these verses, an audible element heads the list of the theophanic phenomena attended. Moreover, as a vivid symbol of divine speaking, the thunder, as the *voice* of Yahweh, would naturally be mentioned first.

[31] On the basis of the versions (Samaritan Pentateuch, LXX, and Vulgate), the context (particularly the emphasis upon fear in v. 20), and the transmitted Hebrew consonantal text, *wayyar'* is to be read *wayyir^{e}'ū,* "and they were afraid."

tic retreat. The staggering and unsteady movement of the awestruck community is superbly conveyed by the verb *nwʿ* which is used in the Old Testament to represent the shaking and quivering of both animate and inanimate objects all of which are being overcome by some force or agent at work upon them.[32] Those who have been brought to the foot of the mountain leave of their own accord. If they depart with little dignity, they exit without delay. And now from a remote stance they implore Moses to mediate in their behalf.

The natural phenomena as a whole have served to make unmistakably real for the witnessing community the dreadful yet unseen presence of the deity. The thunder in particular has impressed itself upon the people as the divine voice that addresses them, although the specific content of divine speech has not been theirs to know. Fearing the even more formidable reality of the words that they might hear, the people request Moses to act as mediator of the *hieros logos* (Ex. 20:19). They will learn of the divine will through the only one among them who is able to assume the office of covenant and theophanic mediator. If Israel is to know the name and nature, the will and purpose of the God who has previously shown himself in her history as gracious deliverer, and who presently confronts her in divine awfulness, she must have a mediator. Moses responds favorably to the people's request by speaking to them a word of comfort and explanation (v. 20). The theophanic word, "Fear not," that is often uttered by the deity or by his divine messenger, the *mal'āḵ*, is now spoken by Moses, Yahweh's human agent. The remainder of Moses' speech is designed to communicate in some measure to the people the meaning of divine visitation. God has come in order to grant his people a direct experience of his terrible presence.[33] Hopefully they will be enlivened with a positive fear of the deity, and not enter into sin through a flagrant disregard of the divine will that is to be communicated. Moses immediately assumes the prerogatives and duties of his office by approaching the dense darkness (*ʿrāpel*) [34]

[32] While this verb is used in many different contexts, it is rooted in the theophany in Isa. 6:4 and 24:20 as well as in the passage under consideration.

[33] See Moshe Greenberg, "*Nsh* in Exodus 20:20 and the Purpose of the Sinaitic Theophany," *JBL*, Vol. 79 (1960), pp. 273–276.

[34] That this noun plays an important part in the vocabulary of the Old Testament

that surrounds the God of Sinai. He ascends as the unique representative of the people before God and the singular agent equipped by his office to convey the divine name and will to the people.

5. *The self-asseveration of the deity and proclamation of his will (Ex. 20:1-17)*

> 1 And God spoke all these words saying, 2 " I am Yahweh your God, who brought you out of the land of Egypt, out of the house of slaves. . . ."

Moses, the covenant and theophanic mediator, presently attends the proclamation of the name and nature (ch. 20:1-2), as well as the commandments (ch. 20:3-17), of Yahweh which he will in turn impart to the people at the close of the theophany (ch. 24:3). Even if Noth's " negative conclusion " should be valid, namely, that the Decalogue never persisted in the original narratives of the Sinaitic theophany, but was subsequently inserted,[35] *something* of the name, character, and will of the deity must have stood at this juncture of the theophanic tradition. The disruptive manifestations of nature and the fear of the people have marked well the actual and impinging presence of the God of Sinai. The theophanic mediator has been chosen to represent the community before the deity, to attend the divine speaking that characteristically relates to the present concrete situation, and to pass this on to the people. Thus it is not a question of whether or not some direct encounter between Moses and the deity might have taken place. Rather, the narrative requires that it *must* take place, and take place now through divine speech.

We may identify ch. 20:1-17 in its entirety as the *hieros logos* of the Sinaitic theophany. Since truncated exegetical comment on each of the Ten Commandments would prove less than useful, we shall confine our study to vs. 1-2 with its manifestation of the divine name

---

theophany is clear from its use in Deut. 4:11; 5:22; I Kings 8:12; and Ps. 18:9 [II Sam. 22:10]; 97:2.

[35] *Exodus,* pp. 154 f. We suspect that one of Noth's motives for insisting upon the supplemental character of Ex. 20:1-17 arises from his interest in keeping separate the Sinai and Exodus-Conquest traditions which have been dramatically linked through the historical reference (ch. 20:2) that immediately precedes the enumeration of the commandments.

and nature. Indeed, the ensuing commandments all assume the priority of the first-person asseveration of the theophany. They can be properly understood only in the light of the self-giving of the divine name.

The earlier elements in the divine self-asseveration, "I am Yahweh your God,"[36] resound with maximum clarity and meaning. With the sheer mention of "your God" (*'ᵉlōhe[y]ḵā*), we may discover in the self-asseveration of the deity that element which effectively binds God and people. But this bestowal of the divine name is considerably expanded by the relative clause of v. 2b — "who brought you out of the land of Egypt, out of the house of slaves." The complete self-asseveration is obviously rich in theological implication. Yahweh emphatically relates himself to a living people. He does not turn aside from the historical particularity that surrounds all humanity, but rather he moves toward it with redemptive power. Thus not only the might, holiness, and grandeur of the deity are testified here, but also his personal affection for Israel and his intent for her salvation. Without a doubt, the *locus classicus* of this "I am Yahweh who . . ." mode of divine self-asseveration lies in this verse that heads the Decalogue. That mode, however, is taken up in a variety of Old Testament passages. It is found in the H corpus of legislation in The Book of Leviticus. It is part of prophetic oracle and it is at home in the Psalter.[37] Wherever it is found, a vital aspect of the personal presence of Yahweh is set forth.

[36] Here the Hebrew has been translated in agreement with the special studies of Walther Zimmerli and Karl Elliger and in contrast to the rendering, "I, Yahweh, am your God," submitted by Albrecht Alt and Martin Noth. The pertinent materials are as follows: (1) Zimmerli, "Ich bin Jahwe," *Geschichte und Altes Testament,* pp. 179–209, especially pp. 179 f.; (2) Elliger, "Ich bin der Herr — euer Gott," *Theologie als Glaubenswagnis,* pp. 9–34; (3) Alt, "Die Ursprünge des israelitischen Rechts" (1934), *Kleine Schriften zur Geschichte des Volkes Israel* (Munich: C. H. Beck, 1953), Vol. 1, p. 329; and (4) Noth, "Die Gesetze im Pentateuch" (1940), *Gesammelte Studien zum Alten Testament* (2te Auflage, Munich: Chr. Kaiser Verlag, 1960), p. 33, n. 38. Cf. also Zimmerli, *The Law and the Prophets,* tr. by R. E. Clements (Oxford: Basil Blackwell, 1965), pp. 56 f., for his incisive examination of the divine self-asseveration of Ex. 20:2 and his isolation of a second self-asseveration in Ex. 20:5 ("for I am Yahweh your God, a jealous God") which represents a later stage of development and interpretation of the Sinai event.

[37] E.g., Lev. 18:2; 19:4, 10, 25; Isa. 43:3; 48:17; 51:15; Ezek. 20:5, 7; Ps. 50:7; 81:10.

The importance of the relative clause in v. 2 can scarcely be overstated, for it is here that the relation between God and people, which has already been established effectively by mention of " your God " (*'ᵉlōhe[y]ḵā*), is greatly intensified. Through vivid allusion to the exodus event, Israel is called to remember that the God of Sinai who now discloses himself through the words, " I am Yahweh," is the God who has already proven himself historically as the God of Israel. In the exodus event, his might and grace were amply demonstrated. And as the God of a people and sovereign over its history, it is he who comes to them in the theophany with a just claim upon his chosen, a claim that is made concrete through the promulgation of a law that Israel is summoned to obey. That law is to be grasped in the light of the provocative and full-scale unfolding of the divine name. The latter is the very nucleus of divine disclosure.

6. *The establishment and sealing of the covenant* (*Ex. 24:3-8*)

> 3 Then Moses came and told the people all the words of Yahweh and all the ordinances; and all the people answered with one voice and said, " All the words that Yahweh has spoken we will do." 4 So Moses wrote down all the words of Yahweh. . . . 7 Then he took the Book of the Covenant, and read it in the hearing of the people; and they said, " All that Yahweh has spoken we will do and obey." 8 And Moses took the blood and threw it upon the people, and he said, " Behold the blood of the covenant which Yahweh has cut with you according to all these words."

The establishment and sealing of the covenant stand as the final component in the Sinaitic narrative. Here we confront the third-person descriptive conclusion of the theophany, although it is more than that, since a significant conversation takes place between Moses and the people. Nevertheless, this is the way the theophany draws to a close. The text equally emphasizes what is physically accomplished by way of ritual and what is spoken. Thus our attention is called to the construction of an altar, the erection of twelve pillars (v. 4), the sacrifice of two types of offerings (v. 5), and especially, the distribution of the blood (vs. 6, 8). Yet the speaking and listening are also central. Moses tells the people " all the words of Yahweh " [38] to

[38] We follow Beyerlin, *op. cit.,* p. 15, in regarding the phrase, " and all the ordi-

which they pledge obedience (v. 3); he reads aloud the Book of the Covenant while the people listen, and presumably it is at the end of that reading that they pledge their submission to the divine claim upon them (v. 7); and the narrative concludes with Moses' words that call attention to the blood of the covenant as the impressive sign of covenantal unity that now exists between Yahweh and people (v. 8).

When this passage is read as the terminus of the Elohistic theophany, it acquires fresh significance. The *hieros logos* concluded at ch. 20:17, but if the people are to hear the word that Yahweh addresses to them, they must hear it through Moses, their theophanic mediator, whose ears alone have perceived the particular content of divine speech. That is plainly the assumption of ch. 24:3, where both the will of Yahweh and the oath of the people are set forth. In the midst of theophanic meeting, a law has been given. Through Moses, the people are not simply informed of the peculiar name of the God of Sinai; they are likewise taught the divine will in the specificity it has assumed through the Decalogue. To this they swear obedience. It is Moses, however, not the people, who speaks the final word. Just as the metaphor of the eagles' wings appeared near the start of the Elohist's account of the theophany (ch. 19:4) as a symbol of divine *grace,* so the blood of the binding covenant is mentioned at its close (ch. 24:8) as a sign of *obligation,* the needful complementing element in the relation between God and people. And whatever else it may do, the latter image lends dramatic support to Moses' earlier statement (ch. 20:20) as to the purpose of the deity's ominous visitation: "for God has come in order to prove you and in order that the fear of him may be before you that you may not sin."

7. *Conclusions*

Having closely traced the course of the Sinaitic theophany in the E stratum,[39] we are now ready to draw some conclusions as to its prevailing and most significant motifs.

---

nances," as a later insertion added after the Book of the Covenant (Ex. 20:22 to 23:33) had been incorporated into the E narrative.

[39] We have refrained from commenting upon Ex. 24:12-15a, 18b. Although these verses are traditionally assigned to the Elohist, the ceremony of covenant ratification, and correspondingly, the reaction of Moses and the people to the major theophany, concludes in E with ch. 24:8.

a. *The theophany is structured according to a definite order.* Prior to the theophanic encounter per se, there is an extended prelude consisting of (1) the invitation to the people and their response, and (2) measures for their purification. The advent of the deity in his theophany is then described and this is accompanied by an account of the fear invoked in the people and their authorizing Moses as their covenantal and theophanic mediator. Moses then enters directly into theophanic meeting to attend the *hieros logos* which he subsequently mediates to the people who pledge their obedience. Throughout the narrative there is an unambiguous movement involving initiative and response between the deity, Moses, and the people.

b. *The theophany involves the disclosure of the deity who dwells upon Sinai.* The God of Sinai does not " descend " (*yrd*) [40] from heaven to the mountain. Rather, he is represented as continuously inhabiting the top of the mountain, as if he were mysteriously enthroned there in his seat of residence. Immediately upon the people's arrival at the mountain, Moses ascends toward the deity who calls him " from the mountain " (ch. 19:3). After receiving the divine instructions, Moses must descend the mountain in order to reach the people below (ch. 19:14).

c. *The theophany is attended by all the people.* The cultic expression, " all the people " (*ḳol-hā'ām*), dominates in the narrative. Each of its four uses is significant. Most likely reflecting Israel's later amphictyonic association, the Elohist declares that " all the people " responded positively to Moses' preliminary mediation of the divine word (ch. 19:8). The God of Sinai disclosed himself to " all the people " who perceived the reverberations of nature (chs. 19:16; 20:18). Then Moses has the duty of proclaiming the divine name, nature, and will to " all the people " (ch. 24:3). Moreover, when simply " the people " (*hā'ām*) appears in the narrative,[41] they are indeed represented in their cultic totality.

d. *The theophany embodies both audible and visual aspects, but the former are emphasized.* Admittedly, the narrative reports that the people saw the lightning flashes (chs. 19:16; 20:18) and the heavy cloud (ch. 19:16), and that Moses drew near the darkness that

[40] The subject of the verb in ch. 19:14 where it is once used in the E Sinaitic account is Moses, not the deity.

[41] Cf. Ex. 19:7, 8, 10, 14-15, 17; 20:18, 20-21; 24:3, 5, 7-8.

enveloped the deity (ch. 20:21). Of greater significance, however, is what is heard, whether it be the thundering and the blast of the horn (chs. 19:16, 19; 20:18), or the words that are spoken by God to Moses, who in turn mediates them to the people. A climax is reached in ch. 19:19 with the loud antiphon in which Moses and the deity engage. Continuous speech is implied there. Throughout the theophanic account it is clear that the ear is assumed to be the organ of maximum perception.

e. *The theophany conveys a dominant note of fear on the part of the people.* Although the first indication that the people are terrified does not appear until ch. 19:16, where we learn that " all the people who were in the camp trembled," the motif prevails from that point until Moses enters the darkness for immediate encounter with God (ch. 20:21). Every verse in ch. 20:18-21 attests the fear-struck condition of the people. Confronted by divine awfulness, the people tremble and retreat (ch. 20:18), keeping a safe distance from the unmistakably ominous reality that confronts them.

f. *The theophany testifies to the centrality of a mediator.* While he is not specifically requested by the people to mediate for them in the early phases of the narrative, Moses in fact serves as their mediator from the outset. In one way or another, Ex. 19:3, 7-8, 14-15, 17, and 19 all depict Moses' mediatorial capacity. In ch. 20:19, however, the terrified people entreat him to serve as their mediator, and after a word with the people, Moses draws nearer the deity for direct confrontation. Through his communication of the *hieros logos* to the people (ch. 24:3) and the cultic act that follows, Moses stands as the one who alone can implement the covenant relation between God and people.

g. *The theophany stands as the self-disclosure of the deity in both his gracious and awful aspects.* The God of Sinai confronts the people as the benefactor of a group whom he now chooses for himself. In particular, chs. 19:4 and 20:2 disclose the grace of the deity who has entered into the concreteness of Israel's history for the sake of her deliverance. Moreover, the divine speech in ch. 19:5-6 holds out before Israel the rewards of covenantal fidelity. Yet awesome visual and audible indications of divine presence linked with the imperatives of the Decalogue which are imposed upon the people rigorously demonstrate the holiness of God, who commands obedience from those whom he graciously elects.

The Yahwistic Theophanic Narrative

Early in this chapter we claimed that within Ex., chs. 19 to 24, the J theophanic narrative is limited to the following verses: chs. 19:9a, 11b-13, 18 (secondarily vs. 20-25); 24:1-2, 9-11. Since the Elohist's account is the dominant narrative in these chapters, and since there is no extended sequence of narrative in the J version, we propose to confine our attention to the more noteworthy aspects within the Yahwist's account. If his handling of the Sinaitic theophany is more fragmentary, owing primarily to its losing out in the competition of subsequent redaction, it is assuredly not lacking in significance.[42]

We would first recognize that in the Yahwist's view, Sinai was the locus of three separate but related theophanic acts. In Ex., ch. 19, a general theophany is accorded to the people and has as its purpose the authentication of Mosaic leadership through the special role that he is to assume as covenant mediator (see v. 9a with Yahweh's speech to Moses). In Ex., ch. 24, another theophanic act is witnessed by Moses, Aaron, Nadab, and Abihu, along with seventy elders, and in Ex., chs. 33 to 34, there is still another, a special theophany to the distraught Moses at his own supplication. Although the last-mentioned lies beyond our present focus, the J theophanic motifs existing in the other two accounts of divine self-disclosure will be treated without our calling attention each time to the separation of the two events taking place at Sinai.

What, then, is especially characteristic of the Yahwistic depiction of theophany? First, *the J narrative shows a cult-oriented concern for the appropriate preparation for, and conduct during, theophanic meeting, and it chooses to express this along temporal and especially spatial lines.* The initial emphasis of the Yahwist's version falls upon the declaration of the deity concerning the immediate intent and ul-

[42] Admittedly a complete examination of the J Sinaitic tradition would require serious consideration of Ex., chs. 33 to 34, with its theophanic elements. Because the Yahwistic theophanic terminology is revealed quite clearly in Ex., chs. 19 to 24, however, we shall forgo any formal investigation of Ex., chs. 33 to 34.

timate purpose of his coming. In Ex. 19:9a, Yahweh's first word to Moses, " Behold, I am coming to you [sg.] in a thick cloud," which bears direct divine intent, is immediately accompanied by the second, " so that the people may hear me speaking with you, and may also believe you forever," which imparts ultimate divine purpose. Here is the formal announcement of Yahweh's resolution to enter into theophanic meeting with the man of his choice. Mention of the time of the encounter immediately follows — " on the third day " (v. 11b). The temporality of the event is grounded upon a *fixed* time that betrays the cultic point of view, and at this juncture the J and E (with ch. 19:11a) traditions coincide. But while *time* of meeting is designated prior to *place* of meeting, the latter receives a special emphasis. Yahweh instructs Moses:

> 12 And you shall set bounds for the people round about saying, " See to it that you do not ascend the mountain or touch its border; whoever touches the mountain shall be put to death; 13a no hand shall touch him, but he shall be stoned or shot; whether it be beast or man, he shall not live."

The imminent self-disclosure of the deity is expected to discharge a dangerous holiness about the mountain, that space which is singled out as the very destination of Yahweh's coming. Specific limits are established to govern the approach of the witnessing community. This preventative measure anticipates any uncontrolled curiosity about, or lack of reverence for, the one who comes. Thoughtless intrusion would pollute the sanctified enclosure and automatically invoke a sentence of death upon the offenders. In short, the people are to be warned against some indiscreet disrespect of hitherto profane space that is to become holy by virtue of the visitation of divine presence. Whether it be the Jerusalem Temple or the mountain of Yahweh's manifestation, the Hebrew faith insists that this divine presence commands the respect of mortal distance. The hallowed site of the impending theophany is thus specified, and uniquely so. In contrast to ch. 19:17 in the Elohist's narrative, where the phrase " at the foot of the mountain " indicates the space that the community is in fact to occupy for the theophanic meeting, the J account approaches the issue from the other direction, and explicitly refers to the space that is *not* to be occupied. Both the J and E narratives, however, manifest a mutual cult-oriented concern for the proper time and place of theophanic confrontation.

The sacrosanct character of the mountain also appears as a dominant concern in the theophanic event narrated by the Yahwist in Ex. 24:1-2, 9-11. A preoccupation with space is revealed by the various gradations of approach toward the deity that obtain in vs. 1-2. The community as a whole is not permitted to " ascend toward Yahweh." Aaron and his two sons, Nadab and Abihu, along with the seventy elders, may approach part way, but even they must " worship afar off " (*wᵉhištaḥᵃwītem mērāḥōq*). Only Moses is allowed direct access to Yahweh. However, in the continuation of narrative in vs. 9-11, the greater distinction does not lie between Moses, on the one hand, and Aaron, his sons and the elders, on the other, but rather between the people below and the " distinguished men of the Israelites " (*'ᵃṣīlē bᵉnē yiśrā'ēl*), the delegation that sees God and, by eating and drinking, engages in a concrete covenantal act in the face of divine presence. Although vs. 9-11 do not mesh perfectly with vs. 1-2 on this matter — perhaps because of a lacuna prior to v. 9 where Yahweh might have commanded that all who have accompanied Moses part way up the mount should now take their stand before him — the significance of the holy place as the ground of intimate theophanic meeting is either explicit or implicit throughout the J portions of Ex., ch. 24. It is by divine invitation that mortals may enter the sacral precincts of theophanic confrontation. Exodus 24:1-2, 9-11, however, is silent as to the fixed *time* of theophanic meeting. For this reason, we are attracted by Martin Noth's suggestion that the instruction in ch. 19:13b, " When the ram's horn blows, they shall come up to the mountain," persists as a fragment from a nonextant narrative that had a " factual connection " with Ex., ch. 24, where a designated group ascends the mount.[43] Consequently a temporal stress would be supplied to the narrative. The ram's horn (*yōbēl*) would signal the proper cultic time for the beginning of theophanic encounter. Thus the Yahwist is much concerned for both temporal and spatial aspects of divine self-disclosure, with the spatial element being especially ac-

[43] *Exodus*, p. 158. He is followed by Beyerlin, *op. cit.*, pp. 9, 35 f.

centuated as the focal point of instruction and narration concerning Israel's conduct before Yahweh.

Secondly, *the J account depicts Yahweh's approach for theophanic confrontation as a descent by means of the cloud vehicle from his heavenly residence to Mt. Sinai below.* Contrary to the assumption of the Elohist that the deity is continuously enthroned upon the top of the mountain, the Yahwist supposes that the heavens are the suitable abode of the deity (Ex. 24:9-10) from which he takes leave in a momentary descent for theophanic encounter. Such a downward motion is only implied in the phrase, " Behold, I am coming *to you* in a thick cloud " (ch. 19:9a), but through the J *terminus technicus,* " to descend " (*yrd*), in ch. 19:11b, 18a, and elsewhere,[44] it is expressly stated. Moses, who has heard the deity say at the time of his call to the prophetic office, " and I have *come down* to deliver them out of the hand of the Egyptians, and to bring them out of that land into a good and broad land " (Ex. 3:8, J), now learns of Yahweh's design to " come down " upon Sinai before the witnessing community (ch. 19:11b). According to J, it is Yahweh's fulfillment of intended theophanic visitation that produces the smoke phenomena that encompasses Sinai (ch. 19:18). The smoke may be regarded as the simple accompaniment of the fire in which Yahweh is said to have descended, and thus we are not constrained to seek the presence of volcanic phenomena in the passage.[45]

In ch. 19:9a, however, Yahweh has declared that he will descend in a " thick cloud " (*b*^{e}*ʿab heʿānān*). But the apparent contradiction is not real. It requires no stretch of the imagination to deduce that in the *sight* of the people, it is the cloud enveloping mysterious divine presence that is perceived. Within the cloud, however, Yahweh's unseen presence is interpreted as a fiery essence, and thus it is also the intent of the Yahwist to report that the deity descends " in fire " (v. 18a). We do not meet a harmonization of two traditions, but instead, two ways of speaking of the manner of momentary descent of

[44] Cf. Ex. 3:8; 19:20; 34:5; also Gen. 11:5; 18:21 and Num. 11:17, 25.

[45] Here we would take issue with Jeremias, *Theophanie,* p. 104, and side with Morgenstern, " Biblical Theophanies," *ZA,* Vol. 25 (1911), p. 165, n. 3, who says, " the fire can not but produce smoke as a matter of course." Morgenstern cogently regards the smoke in v. 18 as parallel to the customary cloud.

the transcendent deity, with the cloud motif being the more common of the two. Apart from its concealing Yahweh from the gaze of mortals who could not endure his immediate disclosure, it functions in J as the vehicle that facilitates Yahweh's descent for his time-bound revelation of himself.

Thirdly, *the J tradition displays a preference for the visual aspects of the theophany.* We discover quite early in the extant J narrative an unusual interest in the optic perception of the *entire* witnessing community. In ch. 19:11b, Yahweh announces to Moses that he will descend upon Sinai (presumably in the " thick cloud " mentioned in v. 9a) " in the sight of all the people." Moreover, the J material in Ex., ch. 24, closes with an account of a *select* but sizable group, seventy-four persons in all, who " beheld God " (*wayyeḥᵉzū 'et-hā'ᵉlōhīm,* v. 11b) as they partook of the covenantal meal. The verb *ḥzh* (" to see, behold ") can indeed designate the interior appropriation of a vision, but it is closely preceded in v. 10 with the verb *r'h,* which naturally points to the more objective act of vision.

Again a contrast should be drawn between the J and E approach to theophany, for the latter emphasizes the attending audible dimensions while it understates the visual as a source of theological embarrassment. In the J tradition, however, the auditory experience of the people is given scant attention. Granted, the narrative in ch. 19:9a opens with the record of what Yahweh *says* to Moses and a vital note is struck through that clause which discloses the purpose of divine visitation, ". . . so that the people may *hear* me *speaking* with you, and may also believe you forever." But this thread, strangely, is never taken up later in the narrative. The Yahwist records no subsequent conversation between the deity and Moses.[46] The only other audible component within the narrative is the displaced mention of the blowing of the ram's horn (ch. 19:13) which signals the ascent of a particular group up the mountain.

Conversely, the visual elements in J are conspicuous. In addition to what has already been mentioned, we may cite the cloud vehicle of

[46] This is an element in Ex., chs. 33 to 34. Some, perhaps much, of the original J narrative within Ex., chs. 19 to 24, has been suppressed by the redaction of the strata with its preferential treatment of E. Thus the intended divine speaking may have occurred. As the J tradition now stands, certainly it does not.

Yahweh's descent (ch. 19:9a), an object of visual perception, and similarly, the smoke that ascends " like the smoke of a kiln " (ch. 19:18), and symbolizes the unseen fire within. This accumulation of illustration, however, is not as impressive as is the concrete mention in Ex. 24:10 that the Israelite delegation ". . . saw the God of Israel " (*wayyir'ū 'ēt 'elōhē yiśrā'ēl*). To be sure, it is not the deity himself but that which surrounds him, ". . . a flagstone of sapphire as it were, the very heaven for clearness " (ch. 24:10b), that stands as the specific object of their vision. If the Yahwist thought of this act of seeing as quite real, he makes it plain that the vision that the deputation perceived consisted of the clear firmament that is below whatever unseen specific divine form might be assumed above.[47] The penetration of human vision decidedly has its limits. Still the very record of such an experience, which the Yahwist himself states is unusual because *these men lived* (the implication of ch. 24:11), together with the *lack* of reference to divine speech, does highlight in dramatic terms the pervasive and emphatic visual motif belonging at the core of the J tradition. These, then, are the noteworthy features of the J version of the Sinaitic theophany — cultic preoccupation with the time and space that theophanic encounter occupies, belief in the momentary descent of Yahweh for theophanic engagement, and an unembarrassed reference to the visual aspects of divine self-disclosure.

The Priestly Theophanic Narrative

Although the Priestly Sinaitic tradition is the first to appear in Ex., chs. 19 to 24, after two sentences that report Israel's arrival at " the wilderness of Sinai," the narrative is suspended until ch. 24:15b. At that point approximately three verses briefly depict the inauguration

[47] The LXX reads, " And they saw the *place* where the God of Israel stood." We cannot concur with the judgment of G. Buchanan Gray, " Theophany," *Encyclopaedia Biblica,* ed. by T. K. Cheyne and J. S. Black (The Macmillan Company, 1903), Vol. 4, col. 5034, that the narrator " gives no hint that what was seen was anything less than the fullness of the glory and person of the deity." Indeed, something is said concerning what is under the *feet* of the God of Israel, but this anthropomorphism does not begin to provide us with a full description of the divine image. Cf. Barr, " Theophany and Anthropomorphism," *VTS,* Vol. 7 (1960), p. 32, and Noth, *Exodus,* p. 195.

of the Sinaitic theophany (vs. 15b-18a). Following one clause of the Elohist (v. 18b) and the single P introduction to the divine speech (ch. 25:1), the lengthy *heiros logos* (chs. 25:2 to 31:17) ensues, which conveys Yahweh's directions for the institution of legitimate and sustained cultic worship. We shall, however, confine our examination to Ex. 24:15b-18a for its manner of theophanic depiction.

From Ex. 24:15b we learn that although the theophany of Yahweh will not take place immediately, a sign that assures its coming is at once evident. The cloud, which customarily envelops the glory (*ḳā-bōd*) of Yahweh, presumably descends and covers the mountain for six days. The " third day " time interval of J and E is doubled. The glory of Yahweh that dwells upon Mt. Sinai is enshrouded by the protective cloud and this alone may be seen by the people. On the seventh day, Moses is called by Yahweh " from the midst of the cloud." According to v. 18a, Moses enters at once into the cloud which appears to have covered the entire mountain, and he ascends to an undesignated destination. On the basis of vs. 16 and 18a it is clear that the encounter involves only Yahweh and Moses, one calling, the other responding. In agreement with both the J and E traditions, Moses' role is presented as unique. He stands as the special channel of divine revelation. But in contrast to those traditions, Moses is not here endowed with the office of covenant mediator. The covenant has already been cut with Abraham (Gen., ch. 17). Still Moses may be properly designated as the *theophanic mediator,* since it is he alone who is invited to attend the *hieros logos* concerning the establishment of the cult, which the P tradition takes very seriously.

In Ex. 24:17 the people also witness the theophany in some measure, for " the appearance of the glory of Yahweh " emanated momentarily at the mountain peak in their sight. The people have lingered about the cloud-covered Mt. Sinai for six days and have perceived only the cloud. On the seventh, however, their theophanic vision is significantly altered. They perceive the theologoumenon par excellence that denotes the actuality of divine presence. Through the simile, " like a devouring fire " (*ḳᵉʼēš ʼōḳelet*), this visual component of the theophany, which is availed to the witnessing community as a whole, is intensified. But that simile relates immediately to " the appearance " (*marʼē*[*h*]) of the glory of Yahweh, rather than to the glory (*ḳābōd*) itself. We note a certain safeguarding in the description.

Thus with its limited description of the Sinaitic theophany, the Priestly stratum calls our attention to (1) the period of anticipatory waiting prior to the moment of encounter, (2) the audible divine summons to Moses who alone is invited to hear the *hieros logos,* and (3) the visual manifestation to the people who may be thereby convinced that they are confronted by august divine presence.

The Combined Impact

The literary traditions which we have been examining make it obvious that Israel could not help but enthusiastically affirm the decisive character of the Sinaitic theophany. Whether in relation to storm or volcanic phenomena, the ensuing theophany of Yahweh marked the eventful disclosure of divine presence. Whether interpreted in the J and E traditions as the awesome preface to the establishment of the covenant between God and people, or in the P tradition as the prelude to detailed cultic rubric which alone might maintain the existing covenantal relation, the theophany impressed upon the witnessing community the transcendent yet demanding character of the God who came for encounter with Israel.

In our study we have attempted to emphasize the peculiar features of each literary stratum. We have seen that the Yahwist and Elohist differed both in style and theological concern, and that neither stood especially close to those interests that were to emerge later in the Priestly stratum. Also each account varies in its use of the theophanic *Gattung* advanced in the preceding chapter. The E narrative, of course, accounts for the theophany in greater detail than does either J or P. No doubt the J version was much longer prior to its redaction. We may not venture a similar conjecture for P, however, since it typically rushes hastily over the matter of *how* theophanic disclosure operates in order to concentrate upon *what* is spoken. Moreover, we have seen that Yahweh's relation to the sacred mountain is fashioned differently in each stratum as is the manner whereby his near and demanding presence is made known.

If we were to set up the J, E, and P materials in columns in order to establish precisely what the theophanic descriptions have in common, we would come up with very minimal results — a cloud, a mountain, the deity, Moses, a period of waiting, and some kind of notation on the audible and visual. This least common denominator approach cannot carry us very far. What is truly requisite to our proper appreciation of these materials is our awareness that in all three traditions, the theophany at Mt. Sinai matters, and matters much. They jointly connect this theophany with Moses whose role is unique, and with the formative years of Israel's development. Whatever their cultic connections and descriptive patterns, these narratives kept fresh in the Israelite mind the experience, and no less the lessons, of that event. The past made its sharp impact upon the present and in the process, the decisive action of God in history was graphically discerned. Because these tenaciously preserved traditions stood at the center of Israelite life and faith, what might have been pallid prose was to become existential affirmation.

CHAPTER IV

Theophanies Surrounding Israel's Patriarchs

Undoubtedly many who have been reared in the Protestant tradition will be able to recall with the author an experience that befell approximately every third Sunday in the youth department of the local church. There, with scrubbed faces and unblended voices, we joined in the singing of "In the Garden," whose words and waltz tune (technically 6/8 rhythm) we owe to C. Austin Miles. If its sentimental words make for problematic theology and its secular rhythm induces the judgment that it is not good music,[1] we may wish for its expeditious eviction from the church. Our sole reason for introducing this hymn into our study of the patriarchal theophanies lies in the three suggestive phrases from its verses — "I come to the garden alone . . ."; ". . . and the voice I hear, falling on my ear, the Son of God discloses"; "And he walks with me, and he talks with me, and he tells me I am his own." To be sure, the hymn is given to depicting the "just Jesus and me" feeling that is eagerly sought within some evangelistic forms of Protestantism. But it might be instructive to imagine how Israel's patriarchs, Abraham, Isaac, and Jacob,[2] would have reacted to these words were they to be slightly edited to refer to Yahweh himself and his engagement with man.

If the Canaanite-inhabited land of Palestine with its arid southern stretches might not overly impress Israel's patriarchs as a garden,

[1] See the instructive discussion of "The God of Hymn and Song" in Erdman Harris' *God's Image and Man's Imagination* (Charles Scribner's Sons, 1959), pp. 173–198.

[2] Because theophany does not figure in the Joseph sagas, they shall not come into consideration.

they knew that they were coming and going *alone*. Of some eighteen theophanic passages that emerge in the J, E, and P strata of Gen., chs. 12 to 50, not one depicts theophanic encounter as a corporate experience involving the deity's self-disclosure to an assembled group.[3] In contrast to the Sinai event described by Ex., chs. 19 to 24, man in Gen., chs. 12 to 50, is ever alone when confronted by theophany. Again in some agreement with the hymn, the speaking that transpires constitutes the most essential component of theophanic engagement. The deity persistently addresses each patriarch in the concreteness of his own situation, and in effect he tells Abraham, Isaac, or Jacob that he *is* his own. The patriarchs of Genesis, however, would chafe at the hymn's concluding note, " And the joy we share as we tarry there . . . ." The Book of Genesis does not record patriarchal elation over theophanic visitation, although it does attest statements that disclose their belief in the divine promise which they have been privileged to receive in theophany — " And he [Abraham] believed in Yahweh, and he imputed it to him as righteousness " (ch. 15:6, E). We are even more certain that God and man do not *tarry* in theophanic meeting. On the whole, these theophanies in Genesis are frequent, intangible, and remarkably brief. Although the narratives are consistently terse, and may annoy us in their ready tendency to withhold so much, they often speak by implication, and here too we are led to think that theophanic encounter for the patriarchs was momentary. God and man did not linger in a hypothetical spiritual embrace. Perhaps the theophanies in Gen., chs. 12 to 50, and Miles' " In the Garden " enjoy their closest affinity, then, in their joint assumption that the divine impinges upon human existence, that this impingement lacks great formality, and that it is ever an " I-thou " encounter.

[3] This number is difficult to ascertain. The following passages in Gen., chs. 12 to 50, however, appear to be theophanic: 12:1-4a, 6-8 (J); 13:14-18 (J); 15:1-21 (JE); 16:7-14 (J); 17:1-22 (P); 18:1-16 (J); 18:22-33 (J); 20:3-7 (E); 21:15-19 (E); 22:1-3, 9-19 (E); 26:1-6 (J); 26:23-25 (J); 28:10-22 (JE); 31:3, 10-13, 24 (JE); 32:1-2 (E); 32:22-32 (J); 35:9-13, 15 (P); 46:1-5 (E). Approximately half will be directly examined in this chapter.

Introductory Considerations

Before the patriarchal theophanies are examined one by one, the quality of theophanic encounter that obtains in Gen., chs. 12 to 50, and the method of our inquiry should be established. To discuss that encounter at all will involve both our disentangling Pentateuchal strata and positing some statement regarding the underlying presuppositions and actual practices of patriarchal religion. Further, we shall wish to consider the manner and direction of the Genesis theophanies, although our interpretation will not in some cases involve an elucidation of every verse within the theophanic passages in question. Nor shall we protest at great length that a particular verse belongs to J or to E, for here we can build upon the work of others and acknowledge as well that Biblical scholarship in our time has shown that there are sensible limits to such investigations.[4] In a word, our pursuit will be more intensive than extensive.

Even so, some context for these theophanies must be argued. Indeed, they can scarcely be considered apart from the role they play in relation to the fundamental themes that the Yahwist, Elohist, and Priestly authors are intent upon developing. To put the matter as simply as possible, regardless of literary stratum and diversity of presentation, the J, E, and P strata alike affirm that the deity had a special purpose for the individual patriarchs, that he chose to make himself and his purpose known to them, and that he elected to mediate this divine purpose through repeated, if unanticipated, theophanic encounter. It was solely through theophanic visitation that the patriarchs learned that the deity intended that a particular people in history should receive the benefit of his concern and blessing, expand in numbers, and be augmented through the possession of a land that could presently be anticipated in promise but not realized in fact. Through the theophany, promise is initiated and renewed. This is the way Israel knew her God to operate. Certainly since the master-

[4] See E. A. Speiser, *Genesis: Introduction, Translation, and Notes* (The Anchor Bible, Vol. 1; Doubleday & Company, Inc., 1964), p. xxi, for a reasoned statement on the limits and possibilities of source criticism in the Pentateuch. Two other significant studies are C. R. North, "Pentateuchal Criticism," *OTMS,* pp. 48–83, and John Bright, "Modern Study of Old Testament Literature," *The Bible and the Ancient Near East,* ed. by G. E. Wright (Doubleday & Company, Inc., 1961), pp. 13–31.

ful study of Albrecht Alt, " Der Gott der Väter " (" The God of the Fathers "), first published in 1929, it has been stressed that the patriarchal deity voluntarily bound himself to *persons*.[5] He was notably distinct from the Canaanite deities who, dwelling in Palestine long before the patriarchs arrived there, were each bound to a particular holy place. The God of the patriarchs moved as the patriarchs themselves moved, and they in turn moved as they were instructed in the theophany to do so.

Thus we would aver that theophanies have an essential place in the patriarchal narratives. If Gen., chs. 12 to 50, is intent upon recording God's way with man, it is further dedicated to depicting man as one who is given to confront deity and who is quite susceptible to theophanic disclosure. He is at all times open to this sort of thing. A phenomenon at once social and religious in character is operating in the patriarchal era that is far distinct from what we insist upon as the suitable canons of contemporary normalcy. Cyrus H. Gordon writes, " In Hebrew society, it was not abnormal for people to experience theophanies, . . . to see divine manifestations, and converse with the apparition." [6] An absolute distinction between God and man had yet to be established. Moreover, the susceptibility to theophanic disclosure is not alone reserved for Israel's venerable patriarchs as a way of enhancing their status, for Sarah's Egyptian maid, Hagar (ch. 16:7-14, J; 21:15-19, E); the Aramean relative, Laban (ch. 31:24, E); and the (anachronistic!) Philistine king of Gerar, Abimelech (ch. 20:3-7, E) are also visited by theophany. It is partly on the ground that the relatively unimportant Hagar attends theophanic meeting that Johannes Lindblom conjectures that in antiquity such experiences must not have been uncommon in real life.[7] We are not to be misled, then, by those scholars who prefer for one reason or another to ignore Biblical theophany as it is diversely set forth in The Book of Genesis.[8] If one can handle the subject of the-

[5] " Der Gott der Väter," *Kleine Schriften zur Geschichte des Volkes Israel,* Vol. 1, pp. 1–78; note especially pp. 21 f.

[6] From *Introduction to Old Testament Times* (Ventnor Publishers, Inc., 1953), p. 106.

[7] " Theophanies in Holy Places in Hebrew Religion," *HUCA,* Vol. 32 (1961), p. 106.

[8] So Artur Weiser, who in " Zur Frage nach den Beziehungen der Psalmen zum

ophany with some thoroughness and still ignore Genesis,[9] he cannot ignore the theophany and still render a thorough treatment of Genesis.

But what of the literary tenor and its relation to religious thought and expression in Genesis as it relates to patriarchal theophanies? Just as the depiction of the theophany on Sinai in Ex., chs. 19 to 24, varied according to the interests of the J, E, and P strata involved, theophanic presentation in Gen., chs. 12 to 50, varies for precisely the same reason. Since the Genesis theophanies are abundant, we have some basis for presenting here a characterization of theophanic depiction in the three strata as it is known in Gen., chs. 12 to 50. These statements may then be borne in mind as we investigate a representative selection of Genesis passages. Of course we are concerned to offer here a word on the variation of theophanic presentation; we are not attempting a full-scale characterization of each stratum.

With his lucid, direct, and winsome style, the Yahwist of the tenth century B.C. offers in Gen., chs. 12 to 50, the most tangible picture of theophanic encounter that is available. We are not necessarily presented with a quantity of words; in fact, the contrary is more often the case. The Yahwist, however, possesses that rare gift which enables him to convey within the confines of a single verse a situation in its entirety. And in showing more concern for action than description, he draws the greater share of his reader's attention toward the characters that are involved. This applies even when one of them is divine. The earth-centered world that the late E. A. Speiser claims for J is reflected in theophanic and nontheophanic texts alike.[10] Yahweh's self-disclosure necessitates his entering into man's sphere of activity. In such a typical J phrase as, "Then Yahweh appeared

Kult: Die Darstellung der Theophanie in den Psalmen und im Festkult," *Bertholet-Festschrift* (Tübingen: J. C. B. Mohr, 1950), pp. 513–531, claims that the Genesis theophanies may be dropped owing to their secondary insertion into the Yahwistic religion (p. 515, n. 1). Presumably he means that they were not an integral part of amphictyonic Yahwism. Moreover, the recent monograph of Jeremias, *Theophanie,* in no way addresses the theophanies in Genesis.

[9] While Jeremias has been able to accomplish this, we find ourselves less prepared to defend this assertion due to our constant reference to the Genesis theophanies in the process of ascertaining the theophanic *Gattung* in the second chapter.

[10] *Op. cit.,* p. xxvii.

[*wayyērāʼ*] to Abram," in ch. 12:7, the Yahwist may be assuming a corporeal form for the deity. This conclusion seems inevitable in ch. 18 when Yahweh is linked with hungry human strangers (v. 8). Moreover, the deity stands *beside* Jacob at Bethel and declares, "I am Yahweh" (ch. 28:13). If the Yahwist is nowise embarrassed in entering into a bold anthropomorphic presentation of theophanic encounter, twice he entertains some limits. In his account of the expulsion of Hagar from Abraham's household (ch. 16:1-14), he mentions the "angel of Yahweh" (*malʼaḵ Yahweh*) no less than four times (vs. 7, 9, 10, and 11), which suggests some thought of a transcendent deity who deals with mortals through his chosen agent. Yet the Yahwist is so little inclined in this direction that the *malʼāḵ* and Yahweh himself coalesce in the narrative (vs. 10, 13).[11] J's self-imposed restrictions on anthropomorphic presentation appear to be quite minimal. Then in ch. 32:24 the Yahwist reports that Jacob wrestled all night with a man (*ʼîš*). As the J narrative concludes (v. 32), the reader has the distinct impression that Jacob's anonymous protagonist is divine — perhaps he is Yahweh! But the Yahwist is careful not to declare himself on the matter. Despite these precautions, he is clearly willing for his deity to be interpreted as one who, in the process of theophanic disclosure, sets foot on the human stage. Abstract thought about deity is neither demonstrated nor encouraged.

Since it is rightly affirmed that the Yahwist and Elohist were individual Israelites, not "committees," who lived as near contemporaries, and mutually delighted in telling a good story, at times it is understandably difficult, if not impossible, to disentangle their redacted narratives. It follows, then, that any characterization of E, be it partial or complete, is not to be erected at right angles from that of J. The latter is consistently the greater artist, but the former is to be given his due. The Yahwist can match, but not excel, the consummate skill of the Elohist in the latter's moving account of the near sacrifice of Isaac (ch. 22). This in effect calls into question Speiser's assertion that E is primarily interested in events, while in J it is per-

[11] This also holds true for Gen. 22:15-16 within a J insertion (vs. 15-18) into the (predominantly) E narrative. We shall inspect the *malʼaḵ Yahweh* more carefully at a later moment.

sons.[12] Perhaps it would be more advantageous to say that with J there is greater spontaneity and with E greater calculation. This is quite evident in the Elohist's treatment of patriarchal theophanies. He insists that the nature of a God-man encounter is something other than a man-man encounter. While he matches the Yahwist in employing the *mal'āḵ* (" the angel of God " [*mal'aḵ 'elōhīm*]) as a medium of divine revelation, he resorts to this theologoumenon more frequently. Besides invoking it in his telling of Hagar's expulsion (ch. 21:9-19), he employs it in his account of the near sacrifice of Isaac (ch. 22:11; now *mal'aḵ Yahweh* but not so originally), and he connects the *mal'āḵ* with Jacob on three distinct occasions (chs. 28:12; 31:11, and 32:1). Generally the Elohist attaches the *mal'aḵ 'elōhīm* to the heavenly sphere. In both chs. 21:17 and 22:11, the *mal'āḵ* mightily projects his voice " from heaven," and in ch. 28:12 Jacob dreams of angels moving in the vicinity of heaven itself as they tread the stairway connecting heaven and earth. Both E's God and his theophanic agent are thus isolated from the terrestrial realm.

But the Elohist is unique in utilizing a second means for upholding the distinct supermundane quality of theophanic encounter. He narrates divine self-disclosure as taking place within the context of dream or vision. The theophany to Abraham in ch. 15 begins, " After these things the word of Yahweh came to Abram in a vision " (*bammaḥᵃze*[*h*]), and in ch. 46:2 the deity is reported to have spoken to Israel (Jacob) " in visions of the night " (*bᵉmar'ōt hallaylā*). The recipients of theophanic dreams include not only the patriarch Jacob (chs. 31:10-13 and 28:12-15), but also his Aramean father-in-law Laban (ch. 31:24), and the Philistine Abimelech (ch. 20:3-7). All encounter the deity as they are engaged " in a dream " (*baḥᵃlōm*). The Elohistic theophanies in Gen., chs. 12 to 50, then, are less prone to depict divine corporeality, although there is the occasional lapse. For example, we may be taken back by E's report of the deity's action in Abraham's vision in ch. 15: " And he [the deity] took him outside and said . . ." (v. 5), but this situation is rare. Moreover, the Elohist's more extensive use of the *mal'āḵ* and his predilection for speaking of theophanic encounter as belonging to the experience of vision and dream accomplish more in safeguarding the otherness of the deity than in detracting from the vividness of theophanic representa-

[12] *Op. cit.*, p. xxxi.

tion that critics have at times implied. We would err were we to suggest, for example, that the ancient might react to his awakening from a dream by quipping, "That was unreal and irrelevant." [13] Thus E and J part company not so much according to the degree of vividness that their theophanic depictions possess, but in their respective concern for point of origin and destination. Because J wishes to state as convincingly as possible that Yahweh's arrival in theophanic encounter was quite immediate, he will do so at the cost of ignoring the deity's normal place of dwelling. But E is constantly mindful of the deity's heavenly locale and governs his expression accordingly. On the witness of theophanic narrative alone, we would concur with Speiser that if J's world is earth-bound and P's celestially fixed, E's world lies somewhere between.[14]

The Priestly stratum presents vivid contrasts to both J and E. If in date, P stands on the other side of Israel's Babylonian exile, in style and theological assumption it is likewise distant from the other two major Genesis sources. It is nominally concerned with personalities, and displays no spontaneous excitement about events. To be sure, history is everywhere predetermined, but its unfolding in engaging narrative is not the goal that Israel's postexilic priests set up for themselves. Rather, the deity's connection to Israelite society as a whole and the establishment of institutions enjoy the spotlight. It is conceivable that the priests might have brought this off without resorting to theophanic encounter at all, but this is not the case. The two patriarchal theophanies that the Priestly stratum provides, however, manifest a conspicuous disparity with J and E alike. If P stands over against J in permitting no *corporeal* self-disclosure of the deity, P is antithetical with E in not attesting that the patriarchs were theophanically visited through dreams and visions. Against both, P does not employ the *mal'āḵ* theologoumenon as a way of favoring divine transcendence. The latter in fact needs no protecting whatever since the Priestly stratum uses only very general terms for depicting theophanic encounter. In the theophany to Abraham in Gen., ch. 17, we learn only that the deity "appeared" (*wayyērā'*) and "spoke" (*wayy'ōmer*) to the patriarch (v. 1), and that when the speaking had run its almost uninterrupted course, God "went up" (*wayya'al*)

[13] Cf. Barr, "Theophany and Anthropomorphism," *VTS,* Vol. 7 (1960), p. 33.
[14] *Op. cit.,* p. xxxi.

from Abraham (v. 22). In ch. 35:9-13, 15, in a theophany to Jacob, the deity is made the subject of three verbs — " appear " (*r'h*), " bless " (*brk*), and " say " (*'mr*), but nothing specific is suggested concerning the " how " of theophanic meeting.

The divine speaking is the thing, which rigorously assumes the patriarchal readiness to listen, and listen at length. Moreover, those who are honored with a theophany are not permitted any prominence in the Priestly narrative, and this further assumes that the deity's transcendence will not be dissipated. Thus in the greater part (ch. 17:1-14) of the P theophany to Abraham, the only word that is imparted about Abraham concerns his obliging gesture in the face of divine presence (v. 3, " Then Abram fell on his face "). In v. 17 we are told of the patriarch's skepticism at the *hieros logos* that his aged wife, Sarah, will bear him a son, but this narrative openness and patriarchal aggression are never again indulged. Thus if the P stratum is willing to commit itself in asserting that in theophanic engagement with Israel's patriarchs God *speaks,* it is adverse to venture any further thought on the matter.

In the process of focusing upon the diverse manner of theophanic presentation in Gen., chs. 12 to 50, we have already become engaged in estimating patriarchal religion. Some further observation, however, is necessary. It should be noted that the religion of the patriarchs is not a static phenomenon that has partitioned for itself a locus of protective isolation. Instead it expresses itself rather spasmodically in dynamic ways which must be understood against a Canaanite polytheistic background. The Book of Genesis plainly shows that the patriarchs neither suffered from the compulsion of weekly religious observances at a favored place nor worked overtime to ward off relationship with the deity. Their religion did not lead them into lofty meditation upon the universe, but rather involved them in special moments that were vested with unusual significance. The words of H. Wheeler Robinson on ancient religion clearly apply to the patriarchal situation: " It usually begins in some definite occurrence, some surprise on the path of familiar custom, some unexplained experience." [15] Moreover, if the religion has its genesis in the unanticipated momentary event, it is furthered by similar moments in the

[15] From *The Religious Ideas of the Old Testament* (London: Gerald Duckworth & Co., Ltd., 1956), p. 102.

unknown time that lies ahead. Theophanic meeting thus assumes a dominant role in the very expression of patriarchal religion.

But this pre-Mosaic religion ever stands against the backdrop of Canaanite religion. Although the later writers have offered us a less than clear picture, the former does borrow from the latter.[16] Ugaritic texts, for example, disclose that in Canaanite religion the West-Semitic deity El headed the pantheon. Through such compound names as *'ēl 'elyōn* in Gen. 14:18-20, 22; *'ēl r°'ī* in ch. 16:13; *'ēl šadday* in chs. 17:1; 28:3; 35:11; 48:3; 49:25; and *'ēl 'ōlām* in ch. 21:33, El's presence has been preserved in the Genesis tradition. Such appellations closely resemble Ugaritic compounds.[17] In his "Der Gott der Väter," Alt accepted the *'ēl* titles as appellations of local *numina* that were bound to specific Canaanite shrines which Israel confronted upon entering Palestine and whose characterizations were gradually adapted as simple epithets for Yahweh.[18] Roland de Vaux maintains, however, that these *'ēlīm* were not various local deities, but rather "manifestations of the supreme god El" of the Ugaritic tablets.[19] F. M. Cross, Jr., concludes that "'El, 'Elyōn, Šadday, and 'Ōlām continued throughout Israel's history to be suitable names for Yahweh despite fierce animosity to Ba'l, the chief god of Syria in the first millennium, B.C."[20]

The complexity of the problems is matched only by the incomplete character of the evidence. In the present study, however, the following assertions may be allowed: (1) the patriarchs, who appear to have been neither intense polytheists nor genuine monotheists, probably did not differentiate between the various names and ideas of deity that came to them, for it is likely that they did not discern here the raw material for serious religious tension;[21] (2) Israel's patriarchs enjoyed a personal religion that evolved around an immediate

[16] For greater clarification cf. *inter alios,* Herbert G. May, "The Patriarchal Idea of God," *JBL,* Vol. 60 (1941), pp. 113–128; James Muilenburg, "The History of the Religion of Israel," *IB,* Vol. 1, pp. 296 f.; Bright, *A History of Israel,* pp. 91 f.; J. M. Holt, *The Patriarchs of Israel* (Vanderbilt University Press, 1964), pp. 127–173.

[17] Cf. May, "The Patriarchal Idea of God," p. 115; W. F. Albright, *From the Stone Age to Christianity* (The Johns Hopkins Press, 1946), p. 188.

[18] "Der Gott der Väter," p. 7.

[19] *Ancient Israel: Its Life and Institutions,* tr. by John McHugh (London: Darton, Longman & Todd, Ltd., 1961), p. 294.

[20] From "Yahweh and the God of the Patriarchs," *HTR,* Vol. 55 (1962), p. 257.

[21] Cf. Holt, *op. cit.,* p. 141.

clan deity who was distinct from, although not in competition with, the more distant and lofty West-Semitic El, and who manifested himself to them in a quite personal way through theophanic disclosure; (3) the religion that focused upon this special and more companionable patron deity was passed on to each patriarch's descendants, and thus the deity came to be known as "the God of the Fathers"; [22] (4) patriarchal religion attached a special significance to several Canaanite sanctuaries, but not without radically transforming antecedent Canaanite ideology.

This last statement requires further clarification. Albrecht Alt, some of his contemporaries, and many of his successors have held that whereas specific Palestinian sanctuaries were deemed vital to both Canaanite and patriarchal religion, in the Canaanite scheme the deity was essentially bound to a place and secondarily to persons, but in the pre-Mosaic faith, the opposite was true.[23] What mattered most in "the God of the Fathers" religion was the deity's continuing relation with a human group. As that relation was being established and strengthened through theophanic meeting, however, the patriarchs noted the sites of such encounter, doing so apparently in the belief that such space now emitted a sacred air. Just as in Ex., ch. 19, Sinai is esteemed as holy because of Yahweh's self-manifestation before the assembled people, the sanctity of Mamre and Bethel are defended respectively on the basis of theophanic disclosure to Abraham in Gen. 18:1-16 (J), and to Jacob in Gen. 28:10-22 (JE) and ch. 35:9-13, 15 (P). In fact, von Rad holds that in their original state, these narratives were cult legends.[24] Hence, many of the Genesis theophanies have been designated as "foundation theophanies" intentionally designed to legitimatize ensuing cultic activity at the sites involved. Indeed, the Yahwist frequently reports the erection of

[22] On points (2) and (3) we are especially indebted to Alt, "Der Gott der Väter," pp. 21 f., 44, and *passim*.

[23] "Der Gott der Väter," pp. 21 f. R. E. Clements, *God and Temple* (Fortress Press, 1965), p. 16, writes, "The religion of the patriarchs represents a religious personalism, whereas that of Canaan a religious materialism."

[24] *Genesis*, p. 17n. De Vaux, *op. cit.*, p. 277, indicates that Mesopotamian parallels of a sort are available — at least the deity visits his temple when it is *restored*. He suggests that "they must have done the same when they were first built." The problem lies in our not having sufficiently clear texts on the initial foundation of other Ancient Near Eastern sanctuaries.

an altar on the site of theophanic engagement (cf. ch. 12:7 at Shechem, ch. 13:18 at Hebron, and ch. 26:25 at Beersheba), and the Elohist mentions that Jacob set up a pillar at Bethel (ch. 28:18-19). But as J. M. Holt rightly points out, the Genesis narratives do not hint that the patriarchs made much actual use of these sites.[25] They seem to have been indifferent.

What matters is that the patriarchs mainly established altars on those sites where Yahweh had honored them with a theophany, and these follow the itinerary that the patriarchs pursued. Although many theophanic narratives specify the locus of Yahweh's appearing, it is still the *hieros logos* there issued that consistently acquires a position of maximum importance. Jacob may remember Bethel as Yahweh's sanctuary, but he is far more involved in the divine promise that he heard there. Moreover, that the Genesis theophanic traditions regularly represent the deity as having said, " I am with you," is impressive evidence that the patriarchal religion, which owed much to theophanic meeting for its development, was not to be dominated by the interests, and tied to the boundaries, of a few Palestinian sites.

Theophanic Confrontations with Abraham

We propose presently to examine a selection of theophanic texts, four focusing upon Abraham, two upon Isaac, and three upon Jacob. Now all three Genesis strata preserve one or more accounts of the deity's self-disclosure to Abraham. It may be argued that these are the most significant theophanies that Genesis has to offer. It was through such an experience that the patriarch knew himself to be specially chosen. Besides saying that Abraham was honored with theophany, the strata further attest that he received a vital twofold divine promise that assured an abundance of progeny and eventual possession of the land.[26] These passages shall be taken up in the order in which they appear in the text.

[25] *Op. cit.*, pp. 167–169. Much earlier, Hermann Gunkel, *The Legends of Genesis*, tr. by W. H. Carruth (Schocken Books, 1964; first published in 1901), p. 106, implied the same in assessing the Genesis sanctuary legends as having a wholly colorless character.

[26] Bright, *A History of Israel*, p. 91, suggests quite cogently, " Nothing does the seminomad desire more."

1. *Theophanic encounter at Shechem and its antecedent* (*Gen. 12:1-4a, 6-8, J*).[27] On the surface one might wonder whether Gen. 12:1 inaugurates a theophany at all. With astonishing suddenness the account begins *in medias res:* "Now Yahweh said to Abram, 'Go forth.'" There is no mention of the form of abrupt divine appearance, no identification of this man Abraham, no reference to time or place, and no hint of psychological impact. Instead, against the unpromising background of Babel where men had unsuccessfully attempted to make a name for themselves (ch. 11:4), the Yahwist is fully committed to the task of conveying the crucial word that is divinely imparted, a word that Abraham's name *will be made great* (ch. 12:2). The divine purpose in the world is to begin afresh; and without any anticipatory note, Abraham is charged to undertake a singular course that makes him a man of destiny. Although the Yahwist elaborates the promise of descendants more fully here than anywhere else — and that promise is renewed with each patriarch — it is prefaced with the barest statement possible.

The theophanic character of this event, however, may be tentatively granted on the basis of v. 7 with its phrase, "Then Yahweh appeared [*wayyērā'*] to Abram and said . . . ," and notation that in the vicinity of Shechem, Abraham built an altar "to Yahweh, who had appeared [*hannir'e*(*h*)] to him."[28] This verse introduces the other familiar aspect of divine promise, future bestowal of the land. The two promises, progeny and land, which are usually linked within one theophanic meeting, are here severed as a means of highlighting Abraham's faith; the patriarch courageously left the familiar Mesopotamian haunts with no vision whatever of what lay ahead. Yahweh said, "Go forth" and he went. Since ch. 12:1-4a and vs. 6-8 impart subsequent phases of theophanic encounter, immediate person-to-person confrontation, we may be permitted to embrace them as a meaningful whole. As such, they present the barest statement of

[27] A near universal recognition of this chapter as the work of the Yahwist makes source critical argumentation unnecessary.

[28] While J indicates that the name "Yahweh" had been used since primeval times (cf. Gen. 4:26), E and P, in Ex. 3:13 ff. and Ex. 6:3 respectively, declare that Moses was the first Israelite to know the name. Since E and P appear to be more historically trustworthy on this point, we are permitted to think of J's use of the name as anachronistic.

theophanic engagement, yet their implications are vast, as Genesis commentators have readily noted.

Rather than analyzing those vital words of Gen. 12:1-3 which weigh heavily upon Abraham, which express an unspeakable expectation that is matched only by the marvelous promise that is also discharged,[29] we shall proceed to observe those theophanic touches which mark ch. 12:6-8. Abraham arrives at " the place of Shechem," a locale nearby the city which is respected for its tree, " the oak of Moreh," whose name attests its connection with the oracular. Julian Morgenstern believes that the Canaanites, who had been long settled in this area (cf. v. 6b), regarded it as the dwelling place of a deity who often communicated to man from the tree.[30] As the locus of divine power, this proved to be an auspicious site for theophanic disclosure. Yet it is no local deity, but Yahweh himself who appears to Abraham, and thus the patriarch builds an altar to commemorate the event. For the Yahwist, the significance of this locale as a holy place (*māqōm*) lies in its being the site of Yahweh's self-revelation to Abraham, the man of his choice. It is now to be understood as Yahweh's sanctuary. He does not belong unreservedly to it, but it is implied that the converse is true. In short, this is J's account of a foundation theophany that assumes an even greater significance in its attesting Abraham's election.

2. *Theophanic encounter at Mamre/Hebron* (*Gen. 15:1-21, JE*).[31] The original Elohistic and Yahwistic theophanic accounts are to be discerned in vs. 1-6 and vs. 7-12, 17-18, respectively. The former opens with E's descriptive and circumspect statement that is theologically motivated: " After these things the *word* of Yahweh came to Abram

[29] See the recent exegesis provided by James Muilenburg, " Abraham and the Nations: Blessing and World History," *Interpretation,* Vol. 19 (1965), pp. 390–393.

[30] *The Book of Genesis: A Jewish Interpretation* (Schocken Books, 1965), p. 104.

[31] Since Gen. 13:18, Abraham has settled at Mamre. Gen., ch. 15, itself makes no explicit mention of the place of theophanic manifestation. Moreover, source analysis of this chapter is complex. While there are indications that the E stratum has its beginnings here, no proposal for disentangling J and E has been accepted as fully adequate by a consensus of scholars. We shall follow the broad lines advanced by von Rad, *Genesis,* pp. 177–184, that vs. 1-6 are basically E, vs. 7-18 are J with an insertion (vs. 13-16) that is possibly E, and vs. 19-21 are a subsequent E addition. Because of possible editorial revision, the strata cannot be solely distinguished on the basis of the divine name employed.

in a vision " (v. 1). If the theophanic confrontation that unfolds is utterly real, it is not recorded as immediate. The divine word that is succinctly imparted opens with an injunction against fear, continues in v. 1 with the divine self-asseveration, and concludes with the *hieros logos* of promise: " Fear not, Abram, I am your shield; your reward shall be very great." Each phrase represents a different form-critical component belonging to Biblical theophany. The first, " fear not," initiates the speaking-hearing contact, the second advances the name of the deity, and the third, the *hieros logos,* interprets the meaning of that name for this particular occasion.

We are informed of the patriarch's responding protest and skepticism (E's characters are also convincingly drawn) to the effect that Abraham, who is still without natural heir, can only hope in Eliezer of Damascus as an *adopted* son, thus reflecting a custom well known in patriarchal times.[32] Again the *word* addresses the patriarch (although this time the phrase " in a vision " [*bammaḥ^{a}ze(h)*] is absent), and in such a way to contradict Abraham's word: " This one shall not be your heir, but he who comes forth from you, he shall be your heir " (v. 4). Then in v. 5 the Elohist lapses into anthropomorphic language indicating that since it was night, the deity took Abraham outside his tent in order to make an analogy which we might express in the vernacular, " Like stars, like descendants, when it comes to counting them." Thus the first and last words belong to the deity. The essential promise of progeny is extended to the patriarch, and while nothing is said here about the giving of the land, this is the major motif in the *hieros logos* of the E (?) insertion (vs. 13-16) into the J paragraph. The theophanic narrative closes on v. 6 with a third-person description which commends the highly conscious Abraham, one that the apostle Paul has made famous: " And he believed in Yahweh, and he imputed it to him as righteousness." In man's response to theophanic disclosure, E is contending that it is belief, not deed, that matters.

Its lack, however, is recorded early in the J narrative that immediately follows (vs. 7-12, 17-18). In the *hieros logos* of v. 7, the patri-

[32] As attested by Hurrian (Nuzi) family legislation which differentiates between two kinds of heirs, the *aplu* (direct) and the *ewuru* (adopted). See Speiser, *op. cit.,* p. 112.

arch is told that he will possess this land of present sojourning, but in v. 8 Abraham demands concrete proof: " how am I to know that I shall possess it? " According to v. 7, the deity has volunteered his identity through the self-asseveration, " I am Yahweh who brought you out from Ur of the Chaldeans," [33] which is cast in the longer participial construction to denote the deity's gracious past action in Abraham's behalf. It is Yahweh who has led Abraham to that point in time and space that he now occupies, yet the patriarch does not receive the promise with conspicuous belief that is so incisive at the close of the E theophany (v. 6). The deity, however, does not now favor Abraham's skepticism with further elucidation. Rather, he gives him instructions for the performance of an act that is at once ceremonial and covenantal in nature.[34] Then in vs. 12 and 17-18, the descriptive tenor of theophanic meeting is intensified. It takes on an eerie cast. Rather than depicting the *conscious* Abraham as has E, J reports that the patriarch fell into a deep sleep (*tardēmā,* v. 12). In order to establish the impending covenant, Yahweh as one of the partners must in some manner pass between the pieces of animal offering. J represents this in the terse and realistic expression of v. 17, " behold, there appeared a smoking fire-pot and a burning torch." Yet the Yahwist is obviously reluctant to suggest a simple equation between Yahweh and these weird elements.

Our understanding of the text may be assisted by at least two considerations. First, a study of the Sinaitic theophany has shown that fire and smoke play a prominent role in theophanic depiction, and this also applies here. These accompanying phenomena are the vivid adjuncts of Yahweh's effective presence. Secondly, we dare not press too far in attempting to clarify the nature of these sensory elements. Von Rad justifiably warns that by imputing a reasonable explanation to them, " one loses the meaning of the whole, which is simply the gift of quite a real guarantee." [35] The Yahwist is deliberately allusive in depicting Yahweh's person. Rather, the accompanying phenomena are emphasized. They alone serve as the confirmation and

[33] Itself an indication of a new theophanic narrative.

[34] Von Rad, *Genesis,* pp. 181 f., and Speiser, *op. cit.,* p. 112, may be consulted on the ceremonial preparations of vs. 9-11.

[35] From *Genesis,* p. 183.

answer to the questioning and doubting Abraham. This is buttressed finally by Yahweh's word in v. 18 which repeats in part the *hieros logos* of v. 7, and at the same time refers explicitly to Abraham's progeny: "To your descendants I give this land." Theophany is again mated with the twofold divine promise so central to The Book of Genesis.

3. *Theophanic encounter at Mamre/Hebron in the P stratum (Gen. 17:1-22).*[36] We have already claimed for the Priestly theophanic materials a very general presentation of the *how* of theophanic disclosure, a pronounced interest in divine speaking, an absence of theologoumena, a near lack of concern for man's reaction to theophanic visitation, and a celestially centered orientation. Since a careful reading of ch. 17:1-22 will bear this out, little further comment here is needed. Apart from the general indications, "Yahweh appeared to Abram" in v. 1 and "God went up from Abraham" in v. 22, the divine self-disclosure is wholly conceived along verbal lines. This, to be sure, must not be interpreted as an indication that the P stratum is attempting to deny the reality of the theophany. Rather, the priests were content in their realization that they were dealing with the ineffable, and resolved to treat theophanic event inconcretely.

The speaking-hearing contact is initiated by the self-asseveration, "I am El Shaddai" (*'ᵃnī-'ēl šadday*), the only name according to P by which the patriarchs knew the deity.[37] Thus the P stratum joins J and E in affirming that the imparting of the divine name stands at the center of theophanic disclosure. As we might expect, P follows J (ch. 15) in connecting the theophany with the establishment of a divinely initiated covenant, but depicts the covenant act in quite another manner. In the entire account, Abraham is forceful only at one instance (Gen. 17:17-18), and this appears primarily to be a means of implementing further divine speech that resumes in v. 19. In sum, the P stratum shows that the deity has honored the man of his choice with a theophany for the sole purpose of addressing him with solemn

[36] Since Mamre/Hebron is the setting for the theophanies of Gen., chs. 15 and 18, and no further phase of journey for Abraham is hinted, we assume that P also claimed this site as the locus of his theophanic account. This chapter is unanimously attributed to P. Note that ch. 16 has influenced the use of "Yahweh" for "Elohim" in ch. 17:1.

[37] As Speiser observes, *op. cit.*, p. 124, the etymology of this name cannot be satisfactorily explained. See also Cross, *loc. cit.*, p. 244, and Holt, *op. cit.*, pp. 132 f.

discourse which in a most elaborate manner sets before the patriarch the dual promise of progeny and land.

4. *Further theophanic encounter at Mamre/Hebron (Gen. 18:1-16, J).*[38] This final theophany to Abraham, which we shall examine directly, excludes any mention of further acquisition of the land, but manifests much concern for the imminent realization of the previously promised progeny. It is presumably Yahweh who says in v. 10, " I will surely come back to you at the time for life to appear, and Sarah your wife shall have a son." And now the aged Sarah is incredulous (v. 12). Like Abraham in ch. 15, Sarah is convincingly drawn with her inevitable ear to the tent (v. 10), her question betraying absolute disbelief (v. 12), and her deliberate denial that she laughed to herself (v. 15) which is no doubt motivated out of fear of the worst sort — suddenly she realizes that she is contending with Yahweh!

An air of leisure and a relative abundance of detail as to the manner of theophanic engagement both confer an indisputable charm upon the narrative. In a way that resembles the editorially reworked P account (ch. 17:1), the J narrative opens with, " Now Yahweh appeared [*wayyērā'*] to him [Abraham]," but at this point the similarity stops! The Yahwist wishes to inform his reader at the outset that the mysterious event about to take place is one more vital theophanic manifestation of the deity himself. Thus we have a decided advantage over Abraham who realizes only gradually that he is being visited by Yahweh in theophanic meeting. The consummate narrative art of the Yahwist is delightfully manifested in the first two verses:

> 1 Now Yahweh appeared to him by the oaks of Mamre, as he was sitting at the doorway of his tent in the heat of the day. 2 He lifted up his eyes and looked, and behold, three men were standing in front of him. When he saw them, he rushed from the doorway of the tent to meet them, and he bowed to the earth.

Abraham supposes that he is suddenly being confronted by mortal visitors. In bowing before them, he does not betray any knowledge that these " three men " are divine beings. Rather in the role of host,

[38] An overwhelming majority of scholars claim these verses for J. Eissfeldt, *Hexateuch-Synopse,* pp. 27* f., disagrees and apportions them to both J and L (*Laienschrift* or lay source).

Abraham is simply engaged in the self-effacing Oriental gesture of courtesy that the situation demands. The patriarch is quickly transformed from stunned spectator to gracious, indeed extravagant, host.[39] In the phrase " my lord " in v. 3, Abraham seems to be addressing *one* of the strangers, for the rest of the verse attests singular objects — " in thy sight " (*bᵉʿēne[y]ḵā*) and " thy servant " (*ʿabdeḵā*). The consonantal Hebrew text (*'dny*) clearly allows this interpretation. Perhaps Abraham has observed in one the mark of leader — the Yahwist is not explicit on all matters. The plural of vs. 4-5 indicates, however, that the patriarch is now speaking to all three. His hospitality, the multiple signs of which are manifest through v. 8, embraces all three.

The evidences of Yahweh's presence are cumulative. In v. 9 these strangers inquire of Sarah — they even know her name; in v. 10 the decisive word of one of them that he will return and Sarah will have a son is understandably startling; in v. 13 it is revealed that one among the company (who is openly designated for the reader's benefit as Yahweh) was aware that Sarah had laughed although he could have neither seen nor heard her in any sensory manner; and in v. 14 the question is posed, " Is anything too much for Yahweh? " Once that Abraham and Sarah are made aware that Yahweh himself has visited them with his gracious yet august presence, the theophanic narrative terminates (v. 16). Now Yahweh's relationship to the " three men " is expressed by J with deliberate obscurity. An exact and full identity of Yahweh is unavowed, and the divine self-asseveration is conspicuously lacking throughout. One gains the impression that Yahweh appeared in all three guests, and that J was willing for his readers to infer that Yahweh was truly represented by men possessing both bodily features and appetite (cf. v. 8). Von Rad, who among others advances this interpretation, defends it by saying, " where the text mentions Yahweh himself it is singular (vs. 10, 13), for Yahweh is one in spite of this form of his appearing." [40] Thus if

[39] Among potential Ancient Near Eastern parallels, perhaps the closest is found in the Ugaritic material where the host Danel entertains visiting deities. See C. H. Gordon, " The Patriarchal Age," *JBR*, Vol. 21 (1953), p. 242.

[40] From *Genesis*, p. 199. See also A. R. Johnson, *The One and the Many in the Israelite Conception of God* (2d ed., Cardiff: University of Wales Press, 1961), pp. 30 f., who avers that we need not attribute this apparent confusion either to an inexact fusion of sources or to poor editorial expansion.

the Yahwist shows some reserve, he has teased our minds into wondering just what was the actual shape of divine appearance on that day to the susceptible patriarchal couple. As in Gen., ch. 15, an indefinite air and a marked realism are both achieved. The reader must leave the narrative with amazement and unanswered questions. Evidently the Yahwist intended it that way.

Theophanic Confrontations with Isaac and Jacob

The Book of Genesis testifies that Abraham was not the only patriarch to be favored by theophanic meeting and promise. Theophanic texts relating to Isaac and Jacob are also numerous, although at times they are quite brief and accomplish little more than the transfer of the promise of progeny and land from Abraham to a later patriarch. Yet if this does not open up many new avenues of divine self-disclosure, this transfer is most significant. Since the Isaac traditions are few, both theophanic disclosures to Isaac reside in ch. 26, the one chapter in Genesis that is totally given to the patriarch. The theophanies to Jacob are rather well spaced. We shall ignore their sequence established by the written text of Genesis, however, in order to permit an uninterrupted handling of the Bethel theophanies (chs. 28:10-22, JE, and 35:9-13, 15, P).

1. *Theophanic encounter with Isaac at Beersheba* (*Gen. 26:1-6, J,*[41] *and 23-25, J*). At the outset of ch. 26, Isaac plans to answer the problem of famine as Abraham had previously. He will go to Egypt. But before the plan can be pursued, Yahweh intervenes into Isaac's history. He appears (*wayyērāʾ*, v. 2) in a theophany to Isaac, and commands the patriarch to follow another course: "Sojourn in this land" (v. 3). The promise that incorporates supporting divine presence, general blessing, land, and an abundance of descendants is now

[41] Although Gen. 26:23-25 is almost consistently given to J, ch. 26:1-6 is attributed to J with less enthusiasm and confidence. Two traditions are apparent in the latter. In one, Isaac is instructed at an unmentioned site not to go down to Egypt (v. 2). In the other, the theophany comes to Isaac in the land of Gerar (v. 1). As Lindblom, *loc. cit.*, p. 99, suggests, the former tradition no doubt belongs either to Beer-lahai-roi (Gen. 24:62; 25:11) or Beersheba (Gen. 26:23; 46:1). Although the matter cannot be finally decided, we shall provisionally assume that both theophanies were thought to have occurred to Isaac at Beersheba.

mediated to Isaac as it previously had been to Abraham. At the end of the dominating *hieros logos* (v. 5), Yahweh takes a new step in patriarchal theophanic disclosure. He provides the *reason* for his extending such a promise — Abraham was obedient. The patriarch had kept the word with which he had been encharged. His exemplary obedience is thus instrumental in promoting the transfer of the divine promise to his son. This inaugural theophany to Isaac resembles the inaugural theophany to Abraham (ch. 12). Its descriptive phrase in v. 2, "Yahweh appeared to him and said," parallels ch. 12:7; many of the expressions pertaining to promise and blessing directly reflect the phrases of ch. 12:1-3; and the patriarchal energies in both are completely channeled into the hearing — the patriarch utters no word. Unlike ch. 12:7, however, there is no mention in ch. 26:6, in the concluding description, that Isaac built an altar to Yahweh who had appeared. We only learn that Isaac settled down. Thus we cannot confidently designate this as a foundation theophany. But perhaps it does not matter, for Yahweh's self-disclosure has affected a relationship between deity and patriarch and this, after all, is what patriarchal theophanies are about.

Because ch. 26:23-25 was the object of a close investigation in the second chapter, during our form-critical attempt to search out the theophanic form (*Gattung*) as it first blossomed in Israel's literature, we need not dwell now at length upon this passage. A few features not of a purely form-critical nature, however, should be noted. The deity's theophanic appearance is again signaled by the *terminus technicus,* "And he appeared . . ." (*wayyērā'*) in v. 24. There is an additional notation that the event took place at night. In v. 24 the divine speaking unfolds with brief notation of self-asseveration, injunction against fear, signal of divine presence, and the *hieros logos* pertaining to Isaac's concrete situation. The intent of this theophanic narrative duplicates the previous theophany to Isaac (ch. 26:1-6). It assures the transfer of blessing from Abraham to Isaac. Again Isaac is completely silent during theophanic engagement. Once that disclosure has run its course, Isaac does respond in the usual manner (although absent from ch. 26:1-6) of erecting an altar and invoking the divine name (v. 25). Thus the sanctity of Beersheba is understood as both established by impinging divine presence and acknowledged by

Isaac's deed. What is most unusual in this narrative is the self-asseveration which fails to include the name of Yahweh. It reads in full, "I am the God of Abraham your father." [42] The continuation of the divine speech plainly shows why Abraham is referred to. The deity's special concern for the descendants arises from the special relationship that he had established with the patriarchal ancestor. Thus negatively the theophany testifies that Yahweh is not bound to one locale, and positively it makes a vital connection between Abraham and Isaac. Divine purpose insures here that patriarchal generations which are horizontally linked, from father to son, become vertically linked, from son to the intervening deity, as well.[43]

2. *Theophanic encounter with Jacob at Bethel* (*Gen. 28:10-22, JE*).[44] In the redaction of this well-known theophany, the Elohist's account lost out somewhat to the Yahwist's. That the E remains contain no divine speaking whatever encourages the conclusion that it is scarcely complete in its present form. Yet this does not render the extant E version uninteresting or insignificant. Some colorful details persist. That account presents two phases, the dream that Jacob experienced, and his existential reaction. With some leisure, v. 11 depicts Jacob's settling down for the night. He is there by chance. He does not specifically stop at this place (*māqōm*) in order to establish a sanctuary.[45] Rather, the setting of the sun requires this sojourner to set up camp here. That he does found a sanctuary in v. 18 and makes a lengthy and quite honest vow (vs. 20-22) is solely the result of Jacob's appalling conviction that through this dream he has been made the object of a theophany.

All that E says of the dream itself is confined to v. 12: "a stairway

[42] Interestingly, the notation on the construction of the altar does mention Yahweh by name.

[43] In both form and content, this J theophany to Isaac at Beersheba closely resembles the (essentially) E theophany to Jacob at Beersheba in Gen. 46:1-5. The formal connections are especially impressive.

[44] While the source analysis is complex, almost without exception, vs. 10, 13-16, and 19 are assigned to J, leaving 11-12, 17-18, and 20-22 to E. So S. R. Driver, *An Introduction to the Literature of the Old Testament* (Meridian Books, The Meridian Library, 1956), p. 16; Oesterley and Robinson, *Introduction*, p. 35; and (essentially) von Rad, *Genesis*, p. 278.

[45] If *māqōm* here is to be thought of as a *holy* place, it is in *anticipation* of the revelation that follows.

[*sullām*] was set on the earth, with its top reaching to heaven; and behold, the angels of God [*mal'ᵃkē 'ᵉlōhīm*] were ascending and descending on it." If tradition conceives of Jacob's ladder, etymology requires a solid stairway.[46] The Mesopotamian ziggurats (temple towers) have been introduced into the discussion with good reason by many a commentator as the most illuminating parallel. These towers which were provided with stairs or ramps that led to the summit, were regarded as the vital link between heaven and earth. This was the route which the god was thought to travel as he passed from his heavenly residence to his earthly place of manifestation. The fear that overcomes Jacob is expressed quite openly in v. 17: "He was afraid and he said, 'How awesome is this place!'" The patriarch is amazed that this place, Bethel (literally "the house of God"), should take on this ziggurat function of linking heaven and earth.[47] If the presence of divinity overwhelmed Jacob by its immediacy, the next morning he erected and anointed the very object upon which he had slept as a commemorative stone. Jacob's vow which follows, with its explicit faith in divine presence, support, and blessing, suggests that prior to its redaction, this Elohistic theophany preserved crucial divine speaking. Jacob, too, has reason to believe that life's relationships include the august vertical aspect.

Although the J version of the Bethel theophany won ascendancy over that of E, some of its edges have been chipped off. The Yahwist's account also must have opened with mention that on one particular night of his sojourn (probably night since v. 16 begins, "When Jacob awoke from his sleep"), Jacob stopped near Luz (cf. v. 19b). Then without warning, "Yahweh stood beside him" (v. 13),[48] in

[46] Cf. KB, p. 660; von Rad, *Genesis,* p. 279; Holt, *op. cit.,* pp. 169 f.; Speiser, *op. cit.,* p. 218. Not every scholar, however, is willing to separate himself from the traditional treatment of this text. Cf. J. Gwyn Griffiths, "The Celestial Ladder and the Gate of Heaven (Genesis xxviii. 12 and 17)," *ET,* Vol. 76 (1965), pp. 229 f., who, in preferring to abandon Babylonian ziggurats for Egyptian Pyramid Texts (with explicit mention of ladders between sky and earth), believes the ladder idea to be quite tenable.

[47] Holt, *op. cit.,* p. 170, wonders how Jacob, who in the larger narrative context is on his way *to* Mesopotamia, should know about ziggurats that are not attested in Palestine. He suggests both textual misplacement and the influence of folk memory (with analogy to Gen., ch. 11, and the tower of Babel). Either is plausible.

[48] Not "Yahweh stood above him"; the idiomatic use of *'ālāw* must be appreciated here as in Gen. 29:2 (see Speiser, *op. cit.,* p. 218).

order to address the patriarch directly with what is for J a quite elaborate speech. With its dual promise of land and posterity, the narrative intends to link Jacob with Isaac, just as J in ch. 26 had linked Isaac with Abraham. Consequently the self-asseveration lengthens: " I am Yahweh, the God of Abraham your father and the God of Isaac " (v. 13), and thereby the original promise is once more solemnly transferred in the total J epic. The promise of land and descendants as well as the assurance of active divine presence are also drawn at length. But if the elaborate character of divine speaking reminds us of the P account of El Shaddai's manifestation to Abraham in ch. 17, the terminology in ch. 28 is understandably the Yahwist's. Jacob's response here is twofold. He registers amazement that he has been made to feel immediate theophanic presence at a place which he had previously regarded as profane, and appropriately he renames the place Bethel, an act clearly denoting Jacob's new knowledge about this site. But if the last word of J focuses upon the place of Yahweh's self-disclosure — and here also we confront a foundation theophany — the content of divine speech still reverberates impressively.

3. *Theophanic encounter with Jacob at Bethel in the P stratum (Gen. 35:9-13, 15).*[49] While the P stratum sparsely inhabits the Jacob traditions, we have in these verses the Priestly account of the Bethel theophany to Jacob. Two divine speeches exist here although they are not separated by any speech on Jacob's part. In the first, the patriarch is renamed Israel. In the second, the opening words are identical with the first component of divine speech in the Priestly theophany to Abraham in ch. 17: " I am El Shaddai." The self-asseveration is characteristically the deity's " opener " in P. This theophany also resembles ch. 17 in that the *how* of theophanic engagement is depicted in essentially the same inconcrete manner. At the head of the account we read that the deity " appeared " (*wayyērā'*) to Jacob, and near its close (v. 13) it is noted that God " went up " (*wayya'al*) from the particular site of his speaking. There is no more " how," but then P is making some concession to connect the deity with a specific place at all. Although the divine speech is much more terse than in ch. 17, the dual promise of land and posterity is adequately

[49] The priestly cast of the narrative is readily discerned. Moreover, the Bethel account of J and E is found elsewhere.

recorded and extended to Jacob. Then in its own way, P presents Jacob's naming the site Bethel, for this is, in the words of v. 15, " the place where God had *spoken* with him."

4. *Theophanic encounter with Jacob at Penuel (Gen. 32:22-32, J).*[50] In Jacob's unusual experience at the Jabbok, an anticipated night of solitude, which the patriarch must have regarded as most needful prior to his return to Esau, was turned into a drawn-out physical contest with a mysterious protagonist. One might wonder whether this is a theophanic narrative at all. Does the Yahwist really mean to imply that Jacob's mysterious assailant was Yahweh himself? How much weight can v. 30 be made to bear in which Jacob exclaims, " I have seen God face to face, and yet my life has been spared "? Could Israel have entertained the belief that the deity had once *pleaded* with her patriarch Jacob to release him since dawn was breaking and that would spell his undoing? And what are we to make of the interpretation of this episode in Hos. 12:4 where the confrontation is affirmed to be between patriarch and angel?

Since answers to such questions do not come easily, perhaps it is best to address the account somewhat indirectly. It seems that Israel was the recipient of a story that told of a man who was assailed by a river numen or demon at the Jabbok and that she felt some need to fix this to the person of Jacob who was thought to have forded that stream. The Yahwist who later received the tradition was at least willing to imply that just as Yahweh had operated in a real sense through " three men " whom Abraham once entertained (Gen., ch. 18), so also he was effectively present in Jacob's nocturnal bout. Certainly the unconnected tenor of many of the narrative elements here owes more to the deliberate design of the Yahwist than to dismal textual transmission. Its primitive features must not divert our attention from vs. 28-29, which along with v. 30, may stand out as the most revealing items. Jacob's comment in v. 30 that he has had a face-to-face encounter with the deity is buttressed by v. 28 which discloses that Jacob was given a new name, and by v. 29 which notes tersely,

[50] Following von Rad, *Genesis,* p. 315; Walter Harrelson, *Interpreting the Old Testament* (Holt, Rinehart and Winston, Inc., 1964), p. 488; and Speiser, *op. cit.,* p. 252, we hold that while the text has its literary problems, it belongs fundamentally and pervasively to J.

"And he blessed him there." The Genesis narratives regularly reserve both functions for deity. Both Priestly theophanies in Genesis, for example, indicate that in the context of theophanic disclosure, blessing and name change transpire. What happens here to Abraham in ch. 17 is duplicated in ch. 35 with Jacob, and P is no innovator here. Moreover, Jacob's naming of the place Peniel/Penuel resembles previous doings at Luz. Like J's theophanic report in ch. 18, the present account is endowed with what Lindblom has cogently called "pre-Yahwistic mythological motifs,"[51] but as Lindblom himself avers, this is not to discourage our deducing that Israel in J's day read the Jabbok-Penuel episode as a theophanic disclosure of her deity. Still what may most impress us here is the Yahwist's remarkable reticence in identifying Jacob's adversary. If we cannot argue that J conspicuously manifests theological scruple, we can observe that this articulate narrator does not tell all.[52]

Theophanic Texts in Genesis Employing the Angel of Yahweh/Elohim

Hopefully our knowledge of Biblical theophanies as they relate to Israel's patriarchs has expanded through our investigation of a cross section of relevant texts. Our selection of passages, which is basically defensible, does fail at one point. These texts together yield but one mention (ch. 28:12) of the angel or divine messenger (*mal'āḵ*) and that one is atypical — it is in the plural and attests moving but *silent* angels. Yet the use of this theologoumenon in The Book of Genesis to represent a real yet more indirect self-disclosure of the deity is indeed significant. In fact, H. Wheeler Robinson considers this as the second of two major types of Old Testament theophanies.[53] Some form of the noun *mal'āḵ* appears in seventeen verses of Genesis. If seven may be set aside as not truly pertaining to theophanic encoun-

[51] From *loc. cit.*, p. 98.

[52] Attention should be called to J. L. McKenzie's rather recent and instructive article, "Jacob at Peniel: Gn. 32:24-32," *CBQ*, Vol. 25 (1963), pp. 71–76.

[53] *The Religious Ideas of the Old Testament*, p. 106. On the other hand, Jeremias, *op. cit.*, p. 2, claims without sufficient argument that the "angel of Yahweh" (*mal'aḵ Yahweh*) does not in fact constitute an integral part of Old Testament theophany.

ter,[54] ten, in four separate contexts, do depict divine self-disclosure.[55] Some consideration of this pervasive phenomenon should ensure a more thorough study of patriarchal theophanies.

But how did this theologoumenon come into use? Its diverse employment in the Old Testament seems to have been motivated by the fact that Biblical writers and antecedent and contemporary oral transmitters alike found in this mechanism a means of referring to Yahweh's active extension of himself in many places and situations without casting doubt upon his unity and transcendence. The *mal'āḵ* is more prevalent in the relatively late Old Testament traditions.[56] In Gen. 32:22-32 (J), Jacob appears to be confronting Yahweh himself in his encounter at Penuel, yet the Hos. 12:4 allusion to this event introduces the *mal'āḵ*. Moreover, in the late Book of Daniel, the interpreting angel is prominent. If by Hosea's time there was some interest in this theologoumenon, Jeremiah's visions attest no such agent. Thus while we may recognize an emerging development, no arbitrary date may be suggested.

Use of this theologoumenon appears further as a way of countering what was now considered to be offensive anthropomorphic language that previously had been used in depicting divine disclosure. But Hermann Gunkel was careful to point out that whenever the theologoumenon arose to ascendancy, it was only employed sporadically.[57] Not only are anthropomorphic phrases left intact, but at times the narratives do not really distinguish between the appearance of the *mal'aḵ Yahweh* and the real appearance of Yahweh himself. This is especially true in patriarchal theophanies. Hence, the oscilla-

[54] In Gen. 32:3, 6, human messengers are referred to, and in chs. 19:1, 15; 24:7, 40; 48:16; theophanic events are not being recorded.

[55] Gen. 16:7, 9, 10, 11; 21:17; 22:11, 15; 28:12; 31:11; 32:1. The two references to the "angels of God" in chs. 28:12 and 32:1 will not be examined, however, since in neither does any speaking occur.

[56] See Walter Baumgartner, "Zum Problem des 'Jahwe-Engels,'" *Zum Alten Testament und seiner Umwelt* (Leiden: E. J. Brill, 1959), pp. 244 f. Yet as Barr, "Theophany and Anthropomorphism," pp. 33 f., argues, this figure is embedded in such an ancient and unsophisticated account as Gen., chs. 18 to 19.

[57] *Genesis,* p. 187. Barr, "Theophany and Anthropomorphism," pp. 33 f., who claims that the Biblical writers have left "too many fierce anthropomorphisms untouched," conceives of the *mal'āḵ* as an "accompaniment," not a dilution, of the deity's anthropomorphic self-disclosure. Barr has sounded an important note here.

tion of the presence and voice of the *mal'āḵ* with that of the deity precludes any facile assumption that the former is a full-fledged substitute functioning in the absence of the latter. That this replacement of Yahweh by the *mal'āḵ* was not carried out consistently did not, however, disturb the Semitic mentality. As Millar Burrows and Aubrey Johnson have suggested, in the Ancient Near East, the man who spoke through a messenger whom he sent was considered personally and actively present in him.[58] The messenger can thus become a veritable extension of the divine person. Also the *mal'aḵ Yahweh* and *mal'aḵ 'ᵉlōhīm* have been infused into aetiological accounts that could not, by their very nature, submit to a complete transformation. Personal and place names related aetiologically to the narrative occasionally contain the name of the deity. Thus to make any sense, the accompanying explanation had to preserve authentic divine presence.[59]

Total Old Testament usage of the *mal'āḵ* demonstrates that in any given case the *mal'āḵ* and the deity may be kept separate, partially merged, or fully merged. In all four Genesis contexts with which we are concerned, however, the merger is complete. The first two, chs. 16:7-14 and 21:15-19, respectively contain the J and E traditions about the theophany to Hagar. In the Yahwist's version, any indication of the physical appearance of the *mal'aḵ Yahweh* is wanting. We learn only that the divine messenger " found " Hagar (ch. 16:7). Perhaps Hagar immediately apprehended him as a divine being. Perhaps not. We do learn that it is through audition that Hagar comes to recognize the identity of this intervening agent. The promise which the *mal'aḵ Yahweh* utters is astonishing: " *I* will so greatly multiply your descendants that they will be too many to count " (v. 10). Here is an implicit identity between Yahweh and *mal'āḵ*. The deity himself must be addressing Hagar. The coalescence, however, is more openly confirmed in v. 13: " So she called the name of Yahweh *who had spoken to her,* ' Thou art a God of seeing.' " Hagar professes that she has been directly visited by Yahweh himself, who is " a God *of* see-

[58] Burrows, *An Outline of Biblical Theology,* p. 120; Johnson, *The One and the Many in the Israelite Conception of God,* pp. 4 f.

[59] Accordingly, Gen. 16:11 with mention of Ishmael and ch. 32:30 with mention of Peniel must attest the actuality of divine visitation. See Baumgartner, *loc. cit.,* p. 245.

ing," one who lets himself be seen. Imperceptibly, hearing and seeing have merged.

In the Elohist's version, the *hieros logos* which the *mal'āḵ* speaks to Hagar reads in part, " Arise, lift up the lad . . . for *I* will make of him [*'ᵃśīmennū*] a great nation " (ch. 21:18). The first-person declaration is only appropriate provided that it comes from the deity himself. Deity and messenger are fully identified. Indeed, the words of the *mal'āḵ* in v. 17, " God has heard the voice of the lad," need not detract from this judgment, since elsewhere in divine speech in the Old Testament (cf. Ex. 19:24; 23:25; Isa. 6:12), God also refers to himself in the third person.

Two other situations require a brief word. First, in the E narrative of Abraham's near sacrifice of Isaac (Gen., ch. 22), the *mal'āḵ* addresses the patriarch from heaven as if he were truly the deity; " for now I know that you fear God, in that you have not withheld your son, your only son, *from me* " (v. 12b). Finally, in Jacob's accounting of his theophanic experience (at the time the flocks conceived) to Rachel and Leah, he relates that in a dream the *mal'aḵ 'ᵉlōhīm* had revealed his identity through the self-asseveration, " I am the *God* of Bethel " (*'ānōḵī hā'ēl bēt-'ēl,* 31:13, E). The messenger further discloses that he is the one who had formerly received Jacob's vow at Bethel (v. 13), a vow that Jacob had made to the deity himself (cf., ch. 28:20-22). Again the speaker is not merely a servant of God to be sharply distinguished from him; rather there is full representation.

All the Genesis traditions here cited agree that behind and through the theophanic eruption of the *mal'āḵ,* Yahweh is there himself in his august presence. If this figure may once have assumed a more significant role, the Israelite belief in Yahweh's uncompromising uniqueness and effective power made change inevitable. Yahweh and his messenger alike became the subjects of such texts, thus causing whatever independence the *mal'āḵ* may have enjoyed to fade away.

The Significance of Patriarchal Theophanies

It has either been argued or implied on every page of this chapter that the deity's self-disclosure to Israel's patriarchs was vested with significance. Lest we think of the various encounters as quite separate events that are only casually related, a word may be permitted to suggest their significance as one of creative coherence. Israel viewed herself as a called people who had been chosen by the deity, charged with hearing a particular word, living by its explicit imperative, and rejoicing under its hope. While this is made most vivid in the Sinaitic theophany of Ex., chs. 19 to 24, this is not the sole locus of such thought. In diverse ways, the patriarchs of Genesis are presented as being individually called by the deity, called through theophanic engagement.

Perhaps the most dramatic and vital call that is recorded here lies in ch. 12. It is Yahweh's *inaugural* theophany with Hebrew man. And it is remarkable that this call to Abraham does not fade away. Even apart from multiple sources which would be expected to furnish several theophanic accounts, it must be said that Abraham hears the call more than once, and in more than one place — precisely because his God is not confined to one locale. According to the Yahwist, Isaac and Jacob also received more than one call. God continually promises the patriarchs that his presence will accompany them. The guiding hand of the deity in man's history is discerned throughout The Book of Genesis. Each patriarch is affected. Such guidance is made known through theophanic meeting in which words are spoken and promises renewed. The deity persists in declaring to the patriarchs, who seem so susceptible to theophanic engagement, that they will enjoy a host of descendants and that these will one day possess the land of present patriarchal sojourning. In this connection we may savor the words of H. J. Kraus which press into the vital core of the matter: "This was the great word that pointed to the future; it was fulfillment of this word in later times that gave to the patriarchs their immense significance for the life of Israel." [60] We would only add, "Yes, and that word was imparted through theophany."

[60] *The People of God in the Old Testament* (Association Press, 1958), p. 27.

CHAPTER V

Theophanies Surrounding Israel's Prophets

That susceptibility to divine disclosure which we have discovered is so characteristic of the Old Testament patriarchs becomes as well a primary identifying mark of Israel's prophets. Frequently theophanic encounter serves as the vehicle for inaugural prophetic call. We may observe that in Isa., ch. 6, and Ezek., chs. 1 to 3, the theophany in each case issues the first divine summons to the witnessing mortal in question to take upon himself the prophetic task.[1] The five visions

[1] Because of its interest and significance, we should not repress the question of the similarity and distinction between theophany as such and the visions of the prophets whereby divine proximity is mediated. Accordingly, several pertinent considerations will be set forth here as a minimal statement on the matter. (1) The theophany in its strictest sense and the prophetic vision are by no means mutually exclusive. Especially in the various accounts of the prophetic call, we may discover a real compatibility between theophany and prophetic vision. Thus the first-mentioned theophany to Abraham in Gen., ch. 12, gives the unmistakable impression of a call and vision (see v. 7 with "Then Yahweh appeared") that provides an analogue to what is experienced by Israel's prophets. (2) Because we are accustomed to think of the prophet's call as a charge to a particular task, it is significant that the first encounters of Abraham, Moses, and Gideon with the deity whereby they are called to a task are indeed theophanic in character. (3) Some difference in terminology and presentation is manifest, however, and must be recognized. The narrative of the vision and call of the prophet is usually more elaborate, and is cast in first-person style (*Ichform*), while the theophany per se stands with a marked consistency in the third-person (*Erform*). Moreover, the vision and call are mediated to the prophet in his *solitude*. Whether or not he is in the presence of others, he alone is recipient of the divine manifestation. The theophany, however, may be attended by one or several persons. If in Gen., ch. 12 (J), Abraham is alone engaged in theophanic meeting, in Gen., ch. 18 (J), he and Sarah are both involved, and in Ex., ch. 19, "all the people" (E) are to be favored and appalled with an experience of quite immediate divine presence. (4) Despite these differences, the Biblical evidence as a whole

to Amos may similarly influence this prophet of Tekoa. Moreover, in I Kings, ch. 19, Yahweh draws near Elijah at Mt. Horeb in such manner that the prophet feels acutely the impact of immediate presence, but this event is not presented among the Elijah traditions as an inaugural moment that initiated Elijah into the prophetic office. Rather, this divine self-disclosure presumably dates much later in the prophet's career. Another variation is found in the final chapter of The Book of Habakkuk (that portion conspicuously absent from the Habakkuk Commentary of Qumrān), which is in its entirety a hymn displaying ample theophanic nuance. With one poetic image piled upon another, the prophet depicts his vision of Yahweh's theophanic intervention in behalf of his people Israel. This chapter presents a marked contrast to both the inaugural theophanies to Isaiah of Jerusalem and to Ezekiel, and the noninaugural theophany to Elijah.

Another and still different witness to theophanic disclosure among the prophets may be discerned in the writings of the prophet-poet of the exile, Second Isaiah. With enthusiasm Ludwig Köhler has interpreted this prophet's writing in its entirety as constituting a single theophany.[2] We prefer, however, to submit that Isa., chs. 40 to 55, contains both that type of theophanic engagement which resembles the inaugural theophany and summons that we may grow accustomed to expect in the preexilic prophets (so ch. 40:1-11), and in addition a well-utilized and nearly ubiquitous theophanic *terminology* that appears in all but five of these chapters.[3] This pervasive terminology, which clearly demonstrates Second Isaiah's respect for, if not dependence upon, the theophanies to the patriarchs in Genesis, is thus not to be linked arbitrarily with one moment of the prophet's life, but rather is to be appreciated as a means whereby the entire substance of his message may be more dramatically articulated.

The diverse patterns of theophanic depiction that make their home

---

demonstrates that theophany and prophetic vision do overlap. Often a close inspection of unfolding prophetic visions and the terminology employed will assure us that we are confronting further attestations of Biblical theophany.

[2] *Deuterojesaja,* pp. 124–127.

[3] I have been unable to uncover such terminology in chs. 47; 50; 52; 53; and 55. Nevertheless, its extensive use throughout chs. 40 to 55 is most impressive.

in the prophetic traditions of the Old Testament are understandably awesome. Equally impressive, however, is the centrality of the theophany within these traditions, a centrality that has led Abraham J. Heschel to maintain, "Prophecy must be understood, not as an individual's venture to find God in ecstasy, but within the tradition of theophanies in which God approaches man in decisive moments of history."[4]

Granting their variation and vitality, how may these theophanies surrounding Israel's prophets be brought into a meaningful relation with our study of Biblical theophanies as it has evolved thus far? At the risk of appearing dictatorial, the program for this chapter may be set forth as follows: we shall examine in turn the Yahwist's account of the inaugural theophany to Moses in Ex., chs. 3 to 4, the theophany to Elijah at Horeb in I Kings, ch. 19, the inaugural theophany to Isaiah of Jerusalem in Isa., ch. 6, and finally, theophanic event and language as presented by Second Isaiah in Isa., chs. 40 to 55. Since spatial restrictions alone press us into being quite selective in the materials we handle in this chapter and the following, only a sampling of prophetic theophanies may be examined in any detail. A number of texts do not readily lend themselves to such spatial limitation. Thus the intricacies of the theophany to Ezekiel (chs. 1 to 3) and the often obscure poetry in the theophanic vision of Habakkuk (ch. 3) preclude consideration here. We believe, however, that we have before us a representative selection of pertinent texts.

By moving in reverse order through the list, we may draw our defense of this selection without difficulty. The prophet-poet Second Isaiah is too well acquainted with the theophany and too aware of its significance for the ancient mind for us to pass him by. With unusual freshness, he envisages Yahweh's final theophanic intervention in a great eschatological event that will terminate and transform time as it has hitherto been known. Moreover, he persists in spelling out the Yahweh-Israel relation in theophanic terms, and these become the essential vehicles of his theology and constitute the very ground of his hope — Yahweh will intervene magnificently! Now the inaugural theophanic meeting involving Isaiah of Jerusalem is presented in a text that is at once suggestive in symbol and familiar in content.

[4] *The Prophets* (Harper & Row, Publishers, Inc., 1962), p. 365.

This prophet, who makes the most of presenting deity as "the Holy One of Israel,"[5] was in the environs (at least!) of the Jerusalem Temple when he found himself confronted by the immediacy of Yahweh's august theophanic presence. That experience, which appears to have colored all subsequent experiences of the prophet, is artfully and deliberately narrated, which further speaks for its consideration here. Then the ability of the I Kings, ch. 19, description of the theophany to Elijah to present a new and more sophisticated mode of theophanic meeting and yet its similarity to, as well as contrast with, Pentateuchal traditions confer a significance upon this encounter that should not be ignored.

Finally, the inaugural theophany to Moses must be examined as the vital prelude to the other three. Although this divine self-disclosure should not be promoted as forming the *immediate* background for the others, by its very nature, the theophany to Moses goes some distance in authenticating all subsequent theophanic experiences that belong to the Old Testament prophets. To a considerable degree, the various prophetic theophanies enjoy a vitality because Moses as Israel's first prophet, as the prophet par excellence, was favored by Yahweh's theophanic disclosure of himself.[6] Hugo Gressmann attempted to distinguish briskly between the theophany to Moses in Ex. 3:1 to 4:17 and the various theophanies to the canonical prophets, by passing on the former as mythological occurrence, but this less than convincing approach has not won many admirers.[7] On the contrary, the inaugural theophany to Moses closely parallels other Biblical texts that center upon the prophets. The call account of Moses rather conspicuously foreshadows many other theophanically mediated calls to Hebrew man in the Old Testament. With his sense of sight and hearing acutely stimulated, man is confronted by the Holy and consequently is charged with a particular mission. Von

[5] Cf. Isa. 1:4; 5:19, 24; 10:20; 17:7; 29:19; 30:11, 12, 15; 31:1.

[6] No study of Old Testament prophecy can ignore for long the colossal figure of Moses. Pentateuchal tradition twice maintains that Moses was the greatest among the prophets. Num. 12:6-7 attests that the deity spoke indirectly to the prophets in dreams or visions, but that with Moses the communication was *direct;* and in the account of Moses' death, Deut. 34:10 reads, "Since then no prophet has ever arisen in Israel like Moses, whom Yahweh knew face to face."

[7] *Mose und seine Zeit* (Göttingen: Vandenhoeck & Ruprecht, 1913), p. 21.

Rad speaks a crucial word here on the character of the Yahwist's version of the call of Moses:

> It would . . . be utterly wrong if we were to understand Moses' call as an appointment to be Israel's leader, for in this source document the leadership of Israel is Jahweh's alone. It would be much nearer the mark, in view of his commission to announce what Jahweh was purposing in history, to talk of a kind of prophetic commission.[8]

New direction is thus given to the life of this man, and a pattern is thereby established which is in large measure realized in many of the subsequent theophanic calls to Israel's prophets. In short, a study of theophanic manifestations to the prophets is obliged to begin here.

The Yahwist's Account of the Inaugural Theophany to Moses

In Ex. 3:1 to 4:17 we have the JE account of Moses' decisive confrontation with the deity which may be appropriately designated as the inaugural theophany to Moses. Although there are several Elohistic elements that are of special interest (e.g., Moses' transparent expression of fear in ch. 3:6, God's assurance in ch. 3:12 that he will be *with* Moses, and the first-time [for E] disclosure of the divine name " Yahweh " with its subsequent phrases which link this deity to patriarchal life and worship in ch. 3:14 ff.), these will be tabled in order that we might focus directly upon the Yahwist's version of this event. Our procedure, which at first blush may appear arbitrary, is justifiable on several grounds. Not only does J seem to be the earlier version, but as Martin Noth cogently avers, in these opening chapters of The Book of Exodus, " J is preserved in a complete and continuous form, whereas only fragments of E have been incorporated into the combined narrative work to expand the variant given by J." [9] Even as we pursue the Yahwist's account, we are committed to examining only what may be conjectured as the original version of the J theophanic narrative. Hence in ch. 3 we shall not press beyond v. 17a*a*. Moreover, the conversation within the context of theo-

[8] *Old Testament Theology,* Vol. 1, p. 292.

[9] *Exodus,* p. 35.

phanic meeting in ch. 4, whereby Moses seeks for himself some power of self-authentication, will be treated summarily, for we are mainly concerned to scrutinize the way in which the Yahwist depicts the initial movements of theophanic engagement, to observe the pattern of presentation, and to keep this in mind as we turn to subsequent prophetic theophanies. In short, we are judging the call of Moses as the appropriate, even indispensable, Biblical introduction to all other prophetic theophanies.

Given the present state of the text in Ex., ch. 3, the original version of the Yahwist may have read as follows: [10]

> 1ab*a* Now Moses was tending the flock of his father-in-law, Jethro,[11] the priest of Midian; and he led the flock to the west side of the wilderness. 2 And the angel of Yahweh appeared to him in a flame of fire out of the midst of the bush; and he looked, and behold, the bush burned with fire, but the bush was not consumed. 3 So Moses said, "I will turn aside now, and see this great sight, why the bush is not burnt." 4a When Yahweh saw that he turned aside to see, 5 he said, "Do not draw near; take off your sandals from your feet, for the place on which you are standing is holy ground."
>
> 7 Then Yahweh said, "I have surely seen the affliction of my people who are in Egypt, and have heard their cry on account of their taskmasters; for I know their sufferings; 8a and I have come down to deliver them out of the hand of the Egyptians, and to bring them out of that land into a good and broad land. 16 Go, and assemble the elders of Israel and say to them, 'Yahweh, the God of your fathers, the God of Abraham, of Isaac and of Jacob, has appeared to me, saying, "I have

[10] The disentanglement of J and E cannot be accomplished with complete confidence. It is widely held, however, that most of the initial phases of the theophany belong to the Yahwist. But the mention of Horeb in v. 1, the formalistic call by *'elōhīm* and the answer, "Here am I" (*hinnēnī*), in v. 4b, and the divine self-asseveration and Mosaic response in v. 6 are ordinarily attributed to E. Since vs. 9-15 duplicate and expand upon vs. 7-8, and in so doing employ the name *'elōhīm,* they are given to E, thus leaving vs. 7-8 for J. The Yahwist's narrative is thought to resume briefly with vs. 16 and 17a*a*. In v. 17a*b*b, however, we confront a later stereotyped depiction of the land and in vs. 18-22 elaborations that seem dependent upon subsequent phases of the Exodus legend. See Noth, *Exodus,* p. 41. For a quite different view, cf. Buber, *Moses,* p. 39, who maintains that a "homogeneous picture" may be secured in chs. 3:1 to 4:17 merely through the removal of a few additions.

[11] An insertion into the J narrative which does not attest this name for Moses' father-in-law. See Noth, *Exodus,* pp. 37 f., for a more detailed discussion.

surely observed you, and what has been done to you in Egypt."' 17a*a* And I have said, 'I will bring you up out of the affliction of Egypt.'"

We need not doubt that the Yahwist intended his readers to understand this passage as a witness to veritable theophanic experience. The sudden inbreaking of divine presence, the mysterious phenomenon of fire, the overt recognition that this space which Moses treads is now sanctified, and the speaking of the deity itself provide ample indication that this is the case. As Israel has remembered this event, it is clear that Moses' encounter with Yahweh in theophanic meeting, with its pronounced visual and audible aspects, is above all immediate and spontaneous engagement. Of course the angel (*mal'āḵ*) of Yahweh is said to be present, there to be grasped (vaguely) by Moses' vision, but this theologoumenon assumes a minor role in the narrative as a whole. The *mal'āḵ* may be the initiator of the divine-human encounter, but the *hieros logos* is solely attributed to Yahweh himself. And as we have noted on previous occasions, and shall also have further opportunity to observe, it is most normative in the Old Testament traditions for theophanic engagement to commence on the visual level and then pass over, often subtly, into the audible.

The opening moments may thus foster curiosity and spectatorship, but these human responses do not endure. Rather, Hebrew man thus involved soon finds that he is being addressed by words which confront him in their immediacy and particularity. Formerly the detached observer of unusual and unexpected phenomena, presently he becomes involved with a divinely mediated word that is especially communicated to him. Suddenly and mysteriously he becomes a full-fledged participant in I-thou confrontation. This applies, to be sure, to the J theophany under consideration. True, Moses does not voice his own concerns until ch. 4, but voice them he will! Yet the imperative with which ch. 3:16 opens, "Go" (*lēḵ*), that immediately calls to mind the theophanic speech to Abraham in Gen. 12:1 (J) where the same command is divinely uttered, presses in mightily upon this man Moses. In short, the audition matters most of all.

A form-critical perusal of the text will disclose that although the turns in the narrative are neither coarse nor abrupt, the Yahwist's account is marked by specific movement. The narrative shifts from

Ex. 3:1 with its notation respecting Moses' situation to ch. 3:2-3 with mention of the visual elements of the confrontation. Then in ch. 3:4a, 5, the text is concerned with a momentary yet significant act of purification before it moves on to the *hieros logos* which begins in ch. 3:7 in which Yahweh's concern for the past and present are linked with his gracious design for the future. Finally in ch. 4, the narrative shifts once more to a vivid depiction of Moses' ardent desire for self-authentication, on the one hand, and exemption, on the other, and here Mosaic reluctance is matched by divine forbearance.

Thus the movement of the narrative may be readily discerned. Yet we must acknowledge at once that this theophany to Moses is a quite spontaneous affair. Consider its opening clauses. Moses was alone tending the flock that belonged to his Midianite father-in-law. The text in no way encourages us to assume that Moses guided the flock to this solitary place so that he might accomplish a dual purpose — pasture animals *and* consciously induce divine confrontation at a reputedly holy site. The Yahwist simply reports that Moses is on this occasion engaged in daily work that has drawn him apart from other men, and suddenly in that solitude he finds himself standing before the deity who has drawn near. The initiative belongs solely to Yahweh, and in the process, Moses enjoys no preliminary announcement of impending visitation. Neither is he instructed to engage in lengthy rubrics of preparation for the crucial moment of encounter, which we have observed in Chapter III constitutes a conspicuous element in the J portions of Ex., ch. 19, that narrate the commencement of the divine self-disclosure at Sinai before Moses and the people. In the present context, however, the Yahwist attests that the deity is *suddenly* present. Neither from the point of view of God nor of man is direct theophanic meeting here presented as the object of careful, long-range planning. While the divine speaking that takes place in Ex., chs. 3 to 4, does manifest some cultic overtone, the descriptive element at the head of the narrative is nevertheless marked by spontaneity.

The visual elements, which are mentioned first and belong only to the Yahwist in this particular theophany, merit closer inspection. Although the speaking that transpires between the deity and Moses is by far the most crucial component in the J account, it is, apart from

Moses' reverential gesture in ch. 3:6b, the *sole* component in the E version. But the Yahwist wishes to report that theophanic encounter between the deity and the man of his choice did originate on the visual level. If the seeing is soon to be eclipsed by hearing, it is nevertheless real to the Yahwist. Our interest understandably centers upon v. 2 with its mention of the appearance of the angel of Yahweh and the mystifying burning bush that is not consumed.

Reference to the angel of Yahweh seems all too feeble. Heinrich Gross has tersely commented, "The angel of Yahweh appears — Yahweh sees and speaks."[12] Deity and theologoumenon are more closely connected here than in any of the related theophanic passages in The Book of Genesis. It may be doubted that the angel of Yahweh was in any sense the object of Moses' corporeal vision. P. van Imschoot focuses upon the verb *wayyērā'*, "and he appeared," a *terminus technicus* in the theophanies included in the J and P Pentateuchal strata, and reminds us that sometimes the Niph'al forms of the root *r'h* do not literally suggest corporeal vision, but rather give the notion of an appearance that is drawn "in a diminished sense" along nonanthropomorphic lines.[13] Hence, the text indicates that Moses was favored by an appearance of the angel of Yahweh, but it seems that he only saw the flaming bush. Martin Buber insists that Moses did not corporeally perceive any form as such, and does so on the basis of Moses' words in v. 3 — "I will turn aside now, and see this great sight, why the bush is not burnt." Buber quips, "Nobody who had seen a divine form in the fire could talk in that way."[14] This argument from common sense has its appeal.

We submit that it is quite possible that the Yahwist's line of reasoning ran somewhat as follows: The Yahwist realized that in his narrative of the patriarchs he had employed (although sparingly) the angel of Yahweh as a theologoumenon which had enabled him to depict real but not wholly immediate divine presence in the context of patriarchal theophanic encounter. In anticipation of his account of

[12] "Der Engel im Alten Testament," *Archiv für Liturgiewissenschaft*, Vol. 6 (1959), p. 32.

[13] *Theology of the Old Testament*, Vol. 1, p. 136, n. 2; van Imschoot alludes to Lev. 16:2 with Yahweh's appearing in the cloud, and Lev. 9:6, 23; Num. 16:19 with his presence in the congregation.

[14] *Op. cit.*, p. 41.

the great theophany at Sinai where tradition held that Yahweh had manifested himself in fire and smoke (Ex. 19:18), the Yahwist now wished to mention the appearance of fire in the present context. In fact, if this were the manner in which he had received the story from earlier times, he would have felt *obligated* in the matter. Then as a way of indicating to his audience that the fire, which he has not mentioned in any theophanic context since Gen. 15:17, is to be understood as an appropriate and real form of divine manifestation, J predicated the familiar angel of Yahweh to this fire phenomenon.

Whatever we are to make of the burning bush itself will be something less than what Biblical interpreters of an earlier era made of it, for they claimed that a hidden truth was to be discerned here. The bush was taken as a symbol of Israel in her profane state and the fire that did not consume the bush was thought to represent the holy Yahweh who dwelt among Israel without destroying her.[15] No grounds are available, however, for imputing this to the mind of the Yahwist whose main motivation was clearly to say that on the occasion of Moses' call, this was the way in which the deity chose to present himself. The only legitimate symbolic value that we may attach to the narrative lies in the threefold use of the word "bush" (*s^{e}ne*[*h*]) in v. 2 which does seem to suggest the name Sinai and thereby anticipate the great theophany to follow. The Yahwist may have understood that the theophany to Israel at Sinai, the theophany par excellence, was in a real sense previously actualized for Moses at the time of his call. If so, we may detect in the repeated mention of the bush J's deliberate design to suggest what lay ahead. Yet in the earliest oral transmission of this event, the word *s^{e}ne*[*h*] could not have borne any hidden allusion to the mountain. It is very likely, however, that the Yahwist and his more immediate predecessors did make the connection. This would also explain the mention of the fire phenomenon as well.[16] In any event, the bush is said to be aflame and we know that the presence of fire is repeatedly mentioned in the Old Testament as a physical yet mysterious manifestation of Yahweh.[17]

[15] For further comment, see von Rad, *Old Testament Theology,* Vol. 1, p. 181, n. 13, and *Moses* (London: Lutterworth Press, 1960), p. 18, who is confident that Israel had no interest in the spiritual decoding that is implied by such an approach.

[16] Following Noth, *Exodus,* p. 40.

[17] Cf. Gen. 15:17; Ex. 13:21; 19:18; 24:17; Judg. 6:21; Ezek. 1:27.

The peculiar nature of the fire in Ex. 3:2-3 evokes the curiosity of the beholder. He will turn aside and *see,* but Yahweh who *sees* this maneuver (the root *r'h* is employed in both instances) now addresses Moses, and from here on the speaking fully takes over.[18] Mosaic inquisitiveness is nowise promoted. Yahweh's words that Moses must keep his distance and remove his sandals, and the explicit reason for these imperatives (" for the place on which you are standing is holy ground ") ensure that his curiosity over the bush will not remain. Now Moses had not come to " the west side of the wilderness " as a hardy pilgrim arrives at the familiar haunts of a sacred site. Had this place enjoyed a well established and reputed sanctity, the tenor of surprise and spontaneity so transparent in the narrative would be lacking. An encounter with deity would be expected. But what unfolds here is unexpected. The place is holy by virtue of Yahweh's coming to Moses in theophanic meeting. Holiness is not static but relational; it has to do with I-thou confrontation.[19] Thus Moses who is so fully unprepared for theophanic encounter may now know that he is being confronted by deity, for he is instructed through divinely uttered imperatives that some space must be respected as out of bounds (cf. Ex. 19:11b-13, J). The holy must not be approached, and those areas which are directly adjacent to the locus of maximum sanctity may only be trodden by one who is barefoot. The removal of the sandals, which permits the feet to return to their natural condition, provides Moses a way of recognizing the holiness and sovereignty of the one who has come near. The J narrative lets us assume that Moses followed through on the command.

[18] J's use of the name " Yahweh " in Ex. 3:4a again betrays his belief that the deity who manifested himself to Moses not only was the one who had previously revealed himself to the patriarchs (a view shared by E and P), but also that all such disclosures were initiated by the deity under the same name by which he had been known from primeval times (cf. Gen. 4:26).

[19] Brevard S. Childs, *Myth and Reality in the Old Testament* (Studies in Biblical Theology, No. 27; London: SCM Press, Ltd., 1960), p. 91, provides the following incisive statement which readily lends itself to the present passage: " Holiness is not an impersonal force stemming from a primeval act, but that which belongs to the covenant God and shares his being. A place is never holy apart from its relation to Yahweh. It can possess no permanent quality of holiness. The content of space is determined by its relationship to Yahweh rather than an inherent quality of the sacred."

With this respectful and formal act now accomplished, the *hieros logos* may commence in v. 7. It is the sole justification for theophanic meeting. Yahweh discloses to Moses that he has witnessed the afflictions and heard the cries of persons, those whom he chooses to designate in sheer covenantal terminology by addressing them as "my people" (*'ammī*). His intention to "come down" (from the root *yrd,* a favorite term in the J version of the Sinaitic theophany for designating Yahweh's earthward approach) is not a conditioned response to the petitions of the enslaved Hebrews but rather an unconditioned act on the part of one who hears and knows before men call. It is further motivated by his desire to intervene in the concreteness of human history and fulfill a plan that has already been framed in the divine mind. Here the cumulative effect of the verbs is noteworthy: "I have surely seen . . . I have heard . . . I know . . . I have come down . . . ." Thus the promise of land that was mediated again and again to the patriarchs is indeed still to be realized.

Especially appropriate to the interests of this chapter is that portion of the *logos* contained in ch. 3:16-17a*a,* for there theophanic engagement decidedly assumes the tenor of a prophetic call. Many years before classical prophecy blossomed forth in Israel, the Yahwist depicted the call of Moses as the deity's summons to one who would serve as his messenger, who would publicly announce impending divine activity prior to its accomplishment. The man of God's choosing is thus entrusted with the word that he is to speak, a word that addresses past, present, and future alike, and once more Moses hears the voice of divine imperative: "*Go,* and *assemble* the elders of Israel and *say* to them . . . ." Through theophanic encounter the commissioning of a prophet, Israel's first and foremost prophet, has taken place.

Although the covenantal nuance of Yahweh's speaking, his dynamic concern for those whom he calls "my people," is impressive, the Yahwist's simple recognition that the deity confronted Moses *in order to speak with him* is itself significant. To be sure, the God whom the Yahwist portrays in theophanic encounter is not silent; he is represented on many occasions as speaking to the patriarchs. Yet the following judgment of Claus Westermann excellently grasps the importance of the speaking per se:

> Quite aside from the question of the historicity of Moses and his work, the significance of this event [the exodus] positively demands that it could not have happened wordlessly. It is unthinkable that this beginning occurred without words, as a more or less fortuitous happening which only subsequently was given the meaning that it has in the "historical credo." To this act of deliverance belongs necessarily some event of speaking (*Wortgeschehen*).[20]

The very climax of theophanic meeting is thus realized through divine speech. Despite the interest they evoke, the antecedent elements in the theophany pale in their significance.

That crucial "event of speaking" to which Westermann refers, however, is not an unbroken unit. In the J and E versions alike Yahweh has the dominant word, and the last word, but not the *only* word. Moses has his words to speak which ably convey that he is not at all enthusiastic about assuming the prophetic office. He asks that another be invited to accept the messenger's responsibility (ch. 4:13). Yahweh's commission appalls him. It is too awesome a thing for him to accept, but it is not too awesome a thing to raise a protest. Moses remonstrates that belief on the part of the people (ch. 4:1) and eloquence on his own part (ch. 4:10) are quite out of the question. Such protest in turn leads to further revelation. Because of Mosaic doubt and unwillingness, the *hieros logos* is extended.

Although the magical element in ch. 4:2-9 and the secondary link between Moses and Aaron in ch. 4:13-16 present problems which we shall deliberately ignore here, ch. 4:1-16 as a whole may be viewed as the Yahwist's attempt at portraying on the one hand a credible Moses who cringes from the prospects before him, and on the other, a persistent deity who is generous in further promise and forbearance. Again this theophany sets the pattern for many subsequent theophanies to the Old Testament prophets. Not only may we see it as possibly influencing the theophanic call to Jeremiah who is similarly given to objecting against divine intent, and whose objections are effectively answered by deity, but in ch. 4:11 we confront a vivid word that reminds us of the very nature of classical Hebrew proph-

[20] "The Way of the Promise through the Old Testament," tr. by Lloyd Gaston and Bernhard W. Anderson, *The Old Testament and Christian Faith,* ed. by Anderson (Harper & Row, Publishers, Inc., 1963), pp. 202 f.

ecy. Here Yahweh meets Mosaic protest with a battery of questions: "Who has made man's mouth? Who makes him dumb, or deaf, or seeing, or blind? Is it not I, Yahweh?" Thus Moses is told in this theophany that in the moment of crisis the word will come. Israel's other prophets who were also summoned to their tasks through theophanic meeting did not know the situation to be otherwise.

The Theophany to Elijah at Mt. Horeb

While an appreciative understanding of Yahweh's self-revelation to Elijah at Horeb cannot be achieved apart from an intelligent handling of the material in I Kings 19:9a, 11b-19a,[21] neither can it be secured without recollection of two antecedent passages. The first, Ex. 33:12-23 (J), depicts a theophany to Moses that is conceived along quite anthropomorphic lines, and against this tradition the theophany to Elijah emphatically reacts.[22] The other, I Kings 18:1 to 19:8, enables us to answer the crucial question, "Why is Elijah at Horeb and in what condition does he arrive?"

Now Ex. 33:12-23 is set against Ex., ch. 32, which depicts the orgy at the foot of Sinai/Horeb. Because "the people . . . rose up to play" (ch. 32:6), Yahweh informs Moses with appalling clarity that while he will send an angel (*mal'āk*) as a guide, he will not himself abide with this stiff-necked calf-worshiping people lest in his holiness he might consume them (ch. 33:2-3). After some conversational give-and-take, the protesting Moses asks that the deity show him his

[21] We follow the majority of scholars who see in I Kings 19:9b-11a an accident in textual transmission (cf. *inter alios*, John Skinner, *Kings* [Edinburgh: T. C. and E. C. Jack, 1904], p. 239; Norman H. Snaith, "Introduction and Exegesis to I and II Kings," *IB*, Vol. 3, p. 163, who also includes v. 9a; J. Mauchline, "I and II Kings," *Peake's Commentary on the Bible*, ed. by Matthew Black and H. H. Rowley [Thomas Nelson & Sons, 1962], p. 346). The retention of ch. 19:9b-11a only creates an insurmountable problem of needless repetition, while its excision allows for a smooth, well-structured narrative.

[22] Jeremias, *Theophanie*, p. 162, writes that in I Kings, ch. 19, "the influence of the literarily expanded Sinai tradition (Ex. 33:18 ff.) is most distinct." Actually we are faced with a choice of contrasting Elijah's reverence (I Kings 19:13) with Mosaic boldness in Ex. 33:12-23 (J), or paralleling it with Mosaic reverence in Ex. 3:6b (E). The whole tenor of this Elijah passage and its concern to depict a *new* form of theophanic disclosure make it obvious, however, that the former alternative was uppermost in the narrator's mind.

glory (*ḳābōd*). In his request, he boldly sets forth his desire to catch an unhindered glimpse of Yahweh's divine majesty. He seeks for himself the option of complete divine self-disclosure. In his response, Yahweh indicates that if divine denial need not be the order of the day, divine qualification surely is. The deity is unwilling to dissipate his holiness for the sake of Mosaic curiosity. Yahweh alone will take the lead in marshaling his act of self-disclosure. The strikingly concrete J narrative now proceeds to set forth the arrangements for the encounter. Close to Yahweh's abode is a rocky cleft and there Moses is to stand and await the passing of Yahweh's glory. Owing to the very danger of this moment of confrontation, Yahweh will protectively cover Moses with his anthropomorphic hand to ensure that Moses will not gaze at the divine glory from the front, into its face. Rather, Moses will eventually be permitted to look upon the glory from the stern — " . . . you shall see my back; but my face shall not be seen " (ch. 33:23). Thus the indiscreetly bold Moses is afforded theophanic experience and assurance, but solely on divine terms, for in ch. 33:20 the Yahwist gives expression to the pervasive Israelite belief that no man shall see the deity and live. That ominous observation, which is deliberately attributed to Yahweh himself, is considered to be quite essential, since Moses, who is caught midway between holy deity and unholy people, is vividly presented as forthright rather than hesitant, presumptuous rather than reverent.

We propose to set this interesting Exodus pericope aside momentarily and move on to brief consideration of I Kings 18:1 to 19:8, the other antecedent passage that is directly relevant to the theophany to Elijah. Although a summary of the Mt. Carmel episode and its dismal consequences is neither required nor welcome here, notice should be taken of the changing character of the prophet. It is important that we observe what Elijah brings to the Horeb theophany. To say this, of course, is to go on record that we regard ch. 19 as the original sequence to chs. 17 to 18. This can neither be emphatically proven nor disproven. The sequence of events in the text as it now stands, however, does provide an explanation for a change in the prophet's mood.[23] At Carmel (ch. 18) Elijah is a giant. With sobriety

[23] Contemporary scholarship is divided here. For example, Weiser, *The Old Testament: Its Formation and Development,* pp. 175 f., maintains, "The story . . . of

and excitement, he shows that he has the situation well in hand. He and his God triumph, while the Ba'al devotees fail miserably. They first lose face and then life.

But as ch. 19 opens, the situation changes radically. The zealous Jezebel is enraged upon hearing of the Ba'alistic debacle at Carmel. Through an ominous oath she threatens to make an end of the prophet. With great candor the text discloses, "Then he was afraid, and rose up and went for his life" (ch. 19:3a). Elijah is now terrified and uncertain, physically tired and terribly conscious of his failure (and perhaps Yahweh's, for Jezebel is forthrightly assuming the upper hand). In ch. 19:4-8 we follow him finally to Horeb, where he undoubtedly desired to grasp afresh divine presence and guidance.[24] He searched out the past and in this sought both to relate himself to the place of origin of the covenant faith *and* to the person of Moses who had ably implemented that faith into actual religious practice.

With ch. 19:9, divine confrontation is imminent. Our translation of that portion of the Hebrew text with which we are most concerned runs as follows:

9a Now he came there to the cave and spent the night there.
11b And behold, Yahweh passed by,
and a great and mighty wind rent the mountains,
and shattered the rocks before Yahweh,
but Yahweh was not in the wind;
and after the wind an earthquake,

God's appearance on Horeb . . . is set merely artificially into the whole context; . . . it is an original isolated narrative." But Otto Eissfeldt, *The Old Testament: An Introduction,* tr. by Peter R. Ackroyd (Harper & Row, Publishers, Inc., 1965), p. 291, holds that the language of I Kings 19:1-2 may well affect an original continuation from chs. 17 to 18.

[24] Although Israel was now settled in Canaan, perhaps Sinai/Horeb continued to be thought of as Yahweh's true residence under the influence of the Elohist, and thus taken to be the preeminent locus of divine self-disclosure (cf. Deut. 33:2; Judg. 5:5; Hab. 3:3; Ps. 68:8). Skinner, *op. cit.,* p. 238, conjectures that in his rebuttal against the prevailing mentality that caused Yahweh and the local *ba'alīm* to coalesce, "Elijah may have repudiated the notion that he was actually present in every Israelitish sanctuary, and have clung to the thought that he dwelt in awful majesty amid the thunder clouds of Sinai." See also Hans-Joachim Kraus, *Worship in Israel: A Cultic History of the Old Testament,* tr. by Geoffrey Buswell (John Knox Press, 1966), p. 171.

but Yahweh was not in the earthquake;
12 and after the earthquake a fire,
but Yahweh was not in the fire;
and after the fire,
a voice of a gentle stillness.

13 Now when Elijah heard it, he wrapped his face in his mantle and went out and stood at the entrance of the cave. Then behold, there came a voice to him and said, "What are you doing here, Elijah?" 14 He said, "I have been very jealous for Yahweh, the God of hosts; for the people of Israel have forsaken thy covenant, thrown down thy altars, and slain thy prophets with the sword; and I, even I only am left; and they are seeking my life, to take it away." 15 But Yahweh said to him, "Go, return on your way to the wilderness of Damascus; and upon your arrival, you shall anoint Hazael to be king over Syria; 16 and Jehu, the son of Nimshi, you shall anoint to be king over Israel; and Elisha, the son of Shaphat of Abel-meholah, you shall anoint to be prophet in your place. . . ."

19 So he departed from there, and found Elisha. . . .

Formally this theophanic passage is made up of three components. First in ch. 19:9a, 11b-13a, we have the decisive and radical introductory description of theophanic meeting. Secondly, in ch. 19:13b-18 we witness the conversation between deity and prophet which opens with an abrupt question from Yahweh, "What are you doing *here,* Elijah?" implying that he erred in retreating from the world to Horeb which was not the sole dwelling of the deity and whose history was not to be the present object of Elijah's seeking, and this is followed by Elijah's plaintive answer, and Yahweh's *hieros logos* for this particular occasion. Finally, in ch. 19:19a we meet the brief concluding description which indicates that the encounter has been completed and that the prophet is already engaged in the task with which he has been entrusted. Again the speaking and hearing are truly significant elements. In fact, Elijah *sees* nothing.[25] Yahweh has drawn near in order to speak, and the speaking takes on the form of

[25] Thus as has been suggested by Murray Newman, "The Prophetic Call of Samuel," *Israel's Prophetic Heritage,* ed. by Bernhard W. Anderson and Walter Harrelson (Harper & Brothers, 1962), p. 97, we have a parallel to the E version of Moses' theophanic call in Ex., chs. 3 to 4, where Yahweh is heard but nowise seen.

a prophetic commission. Like his predecessor Moses, Elijah hears the divine command, "Go . . ." (*lēk*, v. 15); Elijah, as Moses before him, is sent back into the world. Once more prophetic activity is to manifest its solid link with history. The sovereign covenant deity has again spoken in theophanic meeting to his messenger the prophet.

The specific content of the *hieros logos* is vital to the Elijah tradition, but we shall not enter into a discussion of that material. Rather, we choose to concentrate finally and in some detail upon the decisive introductory description, for it is here that the theophany with its *avant-garde* overtones evokes greatest interest. Three questions require an answer here: (1) How does the deity draw near? (2) How does Elijah respond? and (3) What is the meaning of these proceedings?

In answer to the first question, it must be said that the actuality of divine presence is stated in terms that at least attempt to be precise. I Kings 19:11b opens on a seemingly anthropomorphic note—"And behold, Yahweh passed by." The theophany to Moses in Ex., ch. 33, is obviously being recalled.[26] Then suddenly a new note is struck. We are informed that Yahweh is not to be found by Elijah in the wind, earthquake, and fire, all disruptive realities of nature which, according to the traditions of Ex., chs. 19 to 24, were the adjuncts of Yahweh's crucial self-manifestation at Sinai. Such stupendous spectacle does not disclose the deity to Elijah. But *after* these potentially catastrophic elements have passed into oblivion, there does come to Elijah a sure impression that the deity is present. He draws near in "a voice of gentle stillness." Yahweh's presence is perceived, and perceived surely, in the lull of eerie silence that presses in upon the prophet. R. B. Y. Scott rightly admonishes against interpreting this stillness as the voice of Elijah's conscience. That silence is rather, says he, "a silence that could be heard, as it is sometimes said that a darkness is so great that one can feel it." [27]

The translations that have been advanced for the Hebrew *qōl dᵉmāmā daqqā* are most varied. The RSV follows the traditional

[26] The root *'br* is used in both accounts (cf. Ex. 33:22; 34:6; and I Kings 19:11). Moreover, *hammᵉ'ārā*, "the cave," in ch. 19:9 suggests the rocky cleft perspective of the attendant Moses in Ex. 33:22.

[27] *The Relevance of the Prophets* (The Macmillan Company, 1944), p. 70.

rendering, "a still small voice," but John Skinner submits "a sound of thin silence."[28] Following C. F. Burney, James A. Montgomery renders "a sound of a light whisper,"[29] Norman H. Snaith provides "a sound of a gentle stillness,"[30] while Samuel Sandmel translates "stillness, and then a small voice."[31] We know that the modifier *daq* means "thin, scarce, fine, low," and the noun *d^e^māmā* denotes "motionlessness" or "calm,"[32] but unfortunately the two words are connected only in this one verse of the entire Old Testament, and they in turn linked adjectivally with the common noun *qōl* meaning "sound" or "voice." Yet if the preferred renderings vary, the underlying grammatical phenomenon may be confidently identified. We have here an oxymoron, a contradiction in terms. Silence and sound are curiously juxtaposed,[33] and apparently for the explicit purpose of suggesting that between the violent exhibit of nature and the articulate speaking of the deity, there was an eerie silence that Elijah truly felt and identified as Yahweh's very presence.

The inquiry, "How does Elijah respond?" may be answered more simply, for the text of ch. 19:13a rings clear: "Now when Elijah heard it, he wrapped [*wayyāleṭ*] his face in his mantle." Either the prophet had already been nurtured on the dogma that man cannot see God and live, or the narrator is concerned here to show the quite exceptional nature of Elijah's experience at Horeb.[34] By this gesture Elijah is vividly portrayed as consciously acknowledging the one who has drawn near. As in the theophany to Moses in Ex., ch. 33, an effective screen is raised up between divine and human ex-

[28] *Op. cit.*, p. 240.

[29] *A Critical and Exegetical Commentary on the Books of Kings* (ICC; Edinburgh: T. & T. Clark, 1951), pp. 313 f.

[30] *Loc. cit.*, p. 163.

[31] *The Hebrew Scriptures: An Introduction to Their Literature and Religious Ideas* (Alfred A. Knopf, Inc., 1963), p. 459, n. 2. Our translation agrees with B. W. Anderson, *Understanding the Old Testament* (2d ed., Prentice-Hall, Inc., 1966), p. 217.

[32] KB, pp. 216 and 214 respectively.

[33] Jeremias, *op. cit.*, p. 114, speaks of their resounding paradoxical nature. Cf. also Job 4:16, but there we confront a hendiadys, one idea expressed by two words that are joined by a conjunction: "A calm, then a voice I heard."

[34] Montgomery, *op. cit.*, p. 314, finds a close parallel in the traditions surrounding the call of Muhammed.

istence, but a distinction in the two accounts is more noteworthy than the parallel. In the self-disclosure in Ex., ch. 33, the erection of the barrier is a calculated divine act, while here it is the spontaneous and voluntary deed of the attending mortal. In the former situation Yahweh must work against indiscriminate Mosaic boldness. Here Elijah enters upon a reverential and life-saving action on his own.

Then what is the meaning of these proceedings? It would appear that the narrative is attempting to show that Yahweh's self-manifestation is no longer to be conceived in favored traditional terms, in symbols that belong to the established liturgy of the cult. Through the delightfully measured phrases that occur in vs. 11b-12, it is argued that the more ancient representation, which connected Yahweh's presence with the deafening display of nature, is now to be forthrightly set aside. Wind, fire, and earthquake do not offer God to man. Rather, his august presence is recognized in the audible stillness. It is the calm that plainly *follows* the storm which moves the prophet toward a reverential acknowledgment of divine presence. Theophany is now linked with what John Gray calls "intelligible communication."[35] Consequently, this narrative of Elijah's experience of immediate divine presence becomes a programmed attack against the conservative mentality of the cult that anticipates in its favored liturgy the stupendous inbreaking of Yahweh into human life, that judges the Sinaitic theophanic mode to be the sole manner open to deity for purposes of self-disclosure.

Although the Elijah cycle as a whole witnesses to the universality of Yahweh's power, at one level the present narrative argues for Yahweh's disassociation from the storm elements, and at another for a complete separation of Yahweh and his realm from Ba'al and his. Thus Elijah faces a *new type* of encounter with deity. Yahweh has come near, but the joint impact that is created by the manner of divine approach and speaking that transpires leads directly to the conclusion that the God who comes to Elijah is not the God whom man expects. Elijah has sought rational certitude. He has coveted for himself the experience of Moses. He has gone to Horeb and seized upon virtually nothing. Clearly, he has not seen a thing. The present Eli-

[35] *I and II Kings, A Commentary* (The Old Testament Library, The Westminster Press, 1963), p. 365.

jah narrative thus suggests that Yahweh's self-revelation will now assume another and more subtle form. The Mosaic theophanic mode is now thought to be past. As W. F. Albright suggests, the external aspects of Yahweh's self-revelation in nature become increasingly confined to poetic imagery.[36] Yet in poetic garb they are by no means consigned to some remote closet shelf. Although many of the poetically construed theophanies of the Old Testament are most difficult to date, some are younger than the present narrative and their influence is considerable. It is characteristic for Israel to remember, to rehearse past events. This foremost mark of the cult assured that the Mosaic theophanic mode was not to meet a sudden death.

The Inaugural Theophany to Isaiah of Jerusalem

As a way of introducing the inaugural theophany to Isaiah in Isa., ch. 6, we shall refer briefly to Ezek., ch. 1, a later pericope that offers several affinities with the Isaiah chapter.[37] Ezekiel attempted here a quite involved description of the deity who had confronted him in inaugural theophanic meeting. Ezekiel 1:28 concludes the visual phase of the encounter with the comment, " Such was the *appearance* of the *likeness* of the *glory* of Yahweh." Ezekiel speaks with obvious indirectness because he fully recognizes that he is describing the ineffable. Thus it would be erroneous to suggest that some neat equation should be constructed beside every descriptive component. Rather, the overall *intent* of the prophet must be grasped.

Although the earlier first-person description of the inaugural theophany to Isaiah of Jerusalem is less complex, the preceding comment applies here as well. The intent of the prophet bears probing.

[36] *From the Stone Age to Christianity,* p. 235.

[37] These include (1) joint use of the verb, *wā'er'e[h]* (" and I saw ") in Isa. 6:1 and Ezek. 1:1; (2) the seraphim mentioned explicitly in Isa. 6:2 and implicitly in Ezek. 1:11; (3) Yahweh's glory (*kābōd*) in Isa. 6:3 and Ezek. 1:28; and (4) the thunderous voice (*qōl*) of the deity in Isa. 6:4 and Ezek. 1:24-25. C. F. Whitley, " The Call and Mission of Isaiah," *JNES,* Vol. 18 (1959), p. 39, concludes that Isa., ch. 6, is postexilic and thus dependent upon The Book of Ezekiel or upon an emerging ideology from it. The school of Isaiah's disciples, however, could have reshaped many of it's master's original words. The traditio-historical position has its word to offer here.

No series of equations, no single formula can be imputed to Isa., ch. 6, that will fully explain all. It has been held that on this occasion of his prophetic call, Isaiah was either *in, before,* or *not near* the Temple.[38] That a New Year's Day ceremony is here in progress is a suggestion that has both been advanced and withheld. Yet all is not lost, for at least a few vital observations would receive rather widespread consent among interpreters: (1) Isa., ch. 6, is a classical statement of man's confrontation with the holy, (2) the prophet is undergoing something of a trance experience which affects a transfiguration of his physical surroundings,[39] and (3) the visual and the audible are both present, with the latter taking the more dominant role.

The Hebrew text of Isa. 6:1-12 may be rendered as follows:[40]

1 In the year of the death of King Uzziah, I saw the Lord seated upon a throne, high and lifted up, with his train filling the Temple. 2 The seraphim stood above him; each one having six wings: with two he covered his face, and with two he covered his feet, and with two he flew. 3 And one called to the other and said,

"Holy, holy, holy, is Yahweh of hosts;
the whole earth is full of his glory."

4 And the foundations of the thresholds shook at the voice of him who called, and the house was filled with smoke. 5 Then said I,

"Woe is me! for I am undone;
for I am a man of unclean lips,
And I dwell in the midst of a people of unclean lips;

[38] E.g., Ivan Engnell, *The Call of Isaiah: An Exegetical and Comparative Study* (Uppsala: A.–B. Lundequistska, 1949), p. 28; J. Philip Hyatt, *Prophetic Religion* (Abingdon Press, 1947), p. 32; and Edward J. Kissane, *The Book of Isaiah* (Dublin: Browne and Noland, 1941), Vol. 1, p. 74, respectively. As Engnell suggests, a final decision on the matter cannot be achieved.

[39] Although we do not believe that the phrase "trance experience" is inappropriate, we would recognize the wisdom behind the judgment of Norman C. Habel, "The Form and Significance of the Call Narratives," *ZAW,* Vol. 77 (1965), p. 310, that Isaiah's "experience is not depicted as an ecstatic trance in the proper sense of the term, for rational reflection and dialogue are possible during the encounter."

[40] Verse 13 is omitted. Its text and meaning are difficult to establish and it appears to be a later extension of vs. 11-12. Mention of a remaining tenth contradicts what precedes, and as R. B. Y. Scott, "Introduction and Exegesis to Isaiah, Chs. 1-39," *IB,* Vol. 5, p. 212, suggests, the conditional clause that introduces v. 13 itself indicates that an emendation of vs. 11-12 is intended. Georg Fohrer, *Das Buch Jesaja* (Zürcher Bibelkommentare, Zürich/Stuttgart: Zwingli-Verlag, 1960), p. 22, represents a second scholarly approach that also regards v. 12 as supplementary.

For my eyes have seen the king,
Yahweh of hosts! "

6 Then one of the seraphim flew to me with a fire-stone in his hand which he had taken with the tongs from the altar; 7 and he touched my mouth and said,

" Behold, this has touched your lips;
your guilt is removed,
and your sin is forgiven."

8 Then I heard the voice of the Lord saying,

" Whom shall I send,
and who will go for us? "

I answered, " Here am I; send me." 9 Then he said, " Go, and say to this people,

'Truly hear, but do not understand;
Truly see, but do not discern.'
10 Make the heart of this people fat,
make their ears heavy,
and shut their eyes,
Lest they see with their eyes,
and hear with their ears,
and understand with their heart,
and return and be healed."

11 But said I, " How long, O Lord? " And he said,

" Until cities lie waste without inhabitant,
And houses without man,
and the land be left a dismal desolation,
12 And Yahweh has removed men far away,
and many be the forsaken places in the
midst of the land."

We would agree with Ivan Engnell that we have here a " genuine psychic experience " *and* a perceptible literary form, that one does not compete with the other, since " It is a question of 'both — and', not 'either — or'." [41] The experiential dimension of the theophany, however, will be set aside for the moment so that the more noteworthy aspects of the formal structure of Isa., ch. 6, may be highlighted. A pressing of the inevitable relation between content and form evokes the conclusion that a tripartite structure is manifest.

[41] *Op. cit.*, p. 30.

Isaiah 6:1-4 deals with seeing, vs. 5-7 with purification, and vs. 8-12 with commission. But there is more. A closer inspection will disclose that in each succeeding portion, the poetic lines increase in number while the prose element diminishes. And there is a near perfect correlation between description and prose on the one hand, and speaking and poetry on the other. Only vs. 8 and 11 contain quite brief utterances which stand outside the poetic structure. Consequently, *the farther we move into the chapter, the further we witness audition as Isaiah's dominant experience.* Although this prophet's confrontation with deity may be justifiably contrasted with Elijah's in that the latter heard but saw nothing, while Isaiah heard *and* saw, the audition in Isa., ch. 6, is by far the prevailing element.

While the initial phase of the theophany (vs. 1-4) does not rule out speaking and hearing, the visual aspect is first and foremost. The imperfect first-person verb, " I saw " (*wā'er'e*[*h*]), immediately follows the introductory notation of date. Amid the cultic proceedings currently taking place in the Temple, Isaiah was granted a vision of God. In the process, the prophet does not suddenly lose touch with his physical surroundings, but they take on radically new meaning. The deity who is enthroned in majestic loftiness is surrounded by seraphim — apparently the transfigured cherubim. These fiery celestial beings are themselves incapable of looking comfortably upon the deity in whose court they enjoy a certain status, and they also take measures to assure that they are hidden from the deity's direct vision. Mention in v. 1 of the royal throne and train highlight the regal dimension of deity, and this is buttressed by the prophet's comment in v. 5 (in phase two), " For my eyes have seen the king, / Yahweh of hosts! " and by the divine speech in v. 8 (phase three) which indicates that it is the royal function of deity to commission another to speak in his name and in behalf of his imperial court.

Moreover, if this personal experience of Isaiah took place during Israel's New Year festival, a most significant cultic event whose existence has been rigorously argued and debated at length, then the prophet's language is even more accountable. For this festival achieved its climax with the epiphany of Yahweh as Israel's divine king whose presence was symbolized by the apparatus of Ark and cherubim. On this day Yahweh was especially regarded as invisibly enthroned upon the Ark. By the vision that comes to him, however, Isaiah is able to penetrate that invisibility.

The prophet posits the seeing although he qualifies it considerably. While only a fleeting glimpse is suggested, " the Lord " is the indisputable direct object of the verb " I saw " in v. 1. Yet after the pattern of Ex. 24:9-11, only the splendid surroundings of deity are depicted. Isaiah focuses upon Yahweh's royal robe and the surrounding seraphim. The prophet's reverence is clearly manifested. But why the seraphim? Granted that the specific noun form, *śᵉrāpīm,* is attested only in Isa., ch. 6, what are we to make of these winged creatures? The text discloses that they have six wings, stand beside Yahweh's throne, intone his praise, and function in the act of Isaiah's cleansing. As the attendants of the divine court and ministers (and perhaps guardians) of the heavenly sanctuary, the *symbolic* function of the seraphim may be easily fathomed. It is impossible, however, to reach a definite decision concerning precisely what is being transfigured. Is it the Temple priests (so B. W. Anderson),[42] or the cherubim under whose extended wings the Ark is located (so H. M. Buck),[43] or perhaps the visual motif of winged heavenly creatures that adorns the Temple walls (so Claus Westermann)? [44] Many interpreters have handled v. 2 in such manner so as to avoid either the question or a commitment to it. Buck's explanation appears to us as entirely reasonable:

> At the annual enthronement ceremony, the innermost chamber of the Temple containing the ark and the cherubim would be open to the view of those standing in the Temple, as Isaiah was. When the bright sun lighted on the images, they could appear to be on fire, and hence the meaning of *seraphim* would be " the burning ones," in this case the burning cherubim.[45]

Since we have already spoken against a methodology that provides an equation at every turn, we shall conclude with the somewhat bold

[42] *Understanding the Old Testament,* p. 265.

[43] *People of the Lord: The History, Scriptures, and Faith of Ancient Israel* (The Macmillan Company, 1966), p. 226.

[44] *A Thousand Years and a Day,* tr. by Stanley Rudman (Muhlenberg Press, 1962), p. 215.

[45] *Op. cit.,* p. 226.

suggestion that concrete settlement in the long run does not truly matter, for the prophet obviously intends to emphasize Yahweh's majestic, lofty, and regal character, and that alone. Allusion to the seraphim, then, is not a dead-end street, but rather a direct route to the more significant canticle that resounds in v. 3.

The account of the seeing, however, is also subjected to some sophisticated qualification that merits closer attention. We have already noted that the glimpse of deity is quite fleeting and that the surroundings, not the divine essence itself, are elaborated. In addition, a contradictory note is struck, one which betrays considerable theological sophistication. In v. 1a, Isaiah states that he *saw* the Lord, yet the circumstances of seeing that are introduced in the chapter seem downright impossible. Not only does the royal train of the deity fill the Temple (v. 1b), but in v. 4b the prophet remarks, " and the house was filled with smoke," and according to the Sinaitic tradition alone, the smoke would vouchsafe the hiddenness of divine awfulness. Of course it might be argued that the events of v. 4 *followed* those of v. 1, thus assuring that in the latter instance at least Isaiah had perceived the visual, and at the same time, conceding that the vision did not remain. Such an interpretation, however, cannot cope with the notation in v. 1b that Yahweh's train *filled* the Temple.

We would do well, then, to discern in Isaiah of Jerusalem the conscious artist who deliberately wishes to avoid objective portrayal. It is enough for the prophet simply *to suggest* that the visual element was present and real. He has deliberately shunned further demarcation. This, however, is not timidity at work. Indeed, v. 4 provides ample indication that the prophet is undergoing theophanic experience. Both the trembling and the smoke there mentioned effectively signal Yahweh's presence in a manner that calls to mind such passages as Ex. 19:18; 20:18; Lev. 16:13; Ps. 18:7-8; 97:2-6. Tradition held that at Yahweh's self-disclosure on Sinai the mountain quaked. Moreover, the smoke-filled Temple would offer an affinity to both the smoke and cloud accompaniments of the Sinaitic theophany. Hence, Isa. 6:1-2, 4, relates something more than a feeble hint of divine presence. Nevertheless the depiction of the visual equally manifests theological sophistication and studied artistry.

The impact of divine presence, however, is secured even more through the audible component in v. 3 which presents itself *experientially* as the initial audible element and *formally* as the first specimen of poetry in the chapter. Antiphonally the seraphim song is chanted:

> Holy, holy, holy is Yahweh of hosts;
> the whole earth is full of his glory.

Once more the familiar is transfigured. Sigmund Mowinckel avers that both in form and content, this seraphim utterance echoes the cultic hymn. He rightly holds that the basic ingredients of the hymn of praise are here contained "in the very shortest wording."[46] Thus the familiar anthem of cultic ritual was now heard by the entranced prophet as if sung by the supermundane seraphim.

In the second colon, the seraphim profess that Yahweh's radiating glory (*ḳābōd*) pervades all the earth. The *ḳābōd* is not confined to one particular place as had been the case with the Tent of Meeting in the wilderness period, when the *ḳābōd,* enveloped in a cloud, descended upon that sanctuary. The "glory" now denotes the manifestation of the deity in *all* terrestrial space. Ordinarily any thought of the whole earth becoming host to the divine *ḳābōd* was thought conceived upon a purely eschatological base.[47] In Isaiah's vision, however, this is the wondrous *present* state of affairs. But the nature of the *ḳābōd* is to be comprehended in relation to the superlative Trisagion in the first colon of the chant, which conveys the threefold repetition of "holy" (*qādōš*). Both elements, the *ḳābōd* and the *qādōš,* are encompassed by the deity. The *qādōš,* however, can only denote the separateness of Yahweh who stands entirely apart from the created world. While it may be interpreted as the other side of the *ḳābōd,* it is only the latter that fills the whole earth. Thus divine transcendence and imminence are both affirmed. Now for the first time Isaiah has been awakened to an awareness of the nearness of deity along *audible* lines. This sense of Yahweh's close proximity is

[46] *The Psalms in Israel's Worship,* Vol. 2, p. 147. See also Kraus, *Worship in Israel,* p. 214.

[47] So Rolf Rendtorff, "Die Offenbarungsvorstellungen im Alten Testament," *Offenbarung als Geschichte,* ed. by Wolfhart Pannenberg (Göttingen: Vandenhoeck & Ruprecht, 1961), p. 29.

then heightened by the attendant phenomena of v. 4 that have already been examined.

The second and third phases of the theophany may be treated more briefly. The second (vs. 5-7), which focuses upon the effective purification of the prophet, contains two speeches which are separated by the act of sanctification itself. The first speech, which is the prophet's, is from first to last a cry of awful exposure. In the face of holy divine being, Isaiah is appalled by his uncleanness, a defilement that he shares with his own people. His words are at least symbolically anticipated in phase one by the posture of the seraphim who stand reverently in Yahweh's presence.

The pronounced impact of the theophanic experience upon the prophet moves here in two directions. First, Isaiah recognizes that what is forbidden for the corporeal gaze of mortals has become the very object of *his* vision! If a privileged few have been afforded a glimpse of deity (cf. Gen. 16:13 and Ex. 24:9-11), it is by no means a commonplace event. Secondly, the prophet is brought to a new awareness of deity that sets in bold relief the immeasurable gulf between divine and human being, between one whose nature is radically ethical and holy and one whose nature is sinful and defiled. Isaiah's outburst, "Woe is me!" is perhaps more keenly motivated by this latter consideration which nurses as its corollary the thought that sin cannot prosper in such divine presence. "Either he must perish with his sin, or it must perish that he might live."[48] The latter is achieved not through Isaiah's cultic doing, but through the work of one of the seraphim who symbolically purifies Isaiah with fire from the (transfigured Temple) altar, and then announces to him that his sin and guilt have been put away.

Finally, the third and last phase of the theophany (vs. 8-12) presents an intensified I-thou encounter between the holy deity and the prophet who has been rendered holy. Isaiah who is now equipped to hear the proceedings taking place within the divine council, spontaneously volunteers for the task at hand (v. 8). This immediately evokes the *hieros logos* of prophetic commission which is only once briefly interrupted (v. 11) with Isaiah's plea of disbelief, "How long, O Lord?" Isaiah is here addressed the same way in

[48] Rowley, *The Faith of Israel,* p. 66.

theophanic meeting as was Abraham (Gen., ch. 12), Moses (Ex., ch. 3), and Elijah (I Kings, ch. 19). Time and again, the first word of divine summons to the attending mortal is "Go . . ." (*lēḵ*). As one who is sent, Isaiah is twice contrasted with Israel which is referred to as "this people" (cf. vs. 9-10). A careful reading of the *hieros logos* will convince anyone that the prophet was charged with a most ominous mission. His was the task to make the heart insensitive, the ears shut, and the eyes closed. It is likely that the charge is as authentic as it is grim. We may regard it as a conviction that was more supported by subsequent experience than colored by it. Those within Israel who were unworthy to be the people of the covenant deity were to be cast out from his holy presence. If the summons to Isaiah strikes us as a more adequate representation of result than purpose here, we are to be reminded that the ancient mind did not distinguish sharply between the two.[49]

A comparative conclusion is in order. Since the theophany to Elijah has nothing to do with his original call to prophecy, Isa., ch. 6, is more readily matched with Ex., chs. 3 to 4, than with I Kings, ch. 19. In the theophany to Moses, a suffering people was declared elect and on the verge of divine deliverance. In the theophany to Isaiah, an elect people is declared degenerate and on the verge of divine judgment. In response to the *hieros logos,* Moses uttered the protest of reluctance, Isaiah the cry of disbelief. Both were afforded an authentic confrontation with deity that evoked disturbance and challenge alike. Moses in the wilderness setting and Isaiah in the Temple precincts each knew a familiar environment and in the contexts of familiarity they were given to know firsthand a God who acts.

Theophanic Usage and Language in Second Isaiah

In each of the preceding chapters, a brief conclusion has been attempted as a way of summarizing the various theophanic texts or

[49] A slight modification of an idea advanced by T. H. Robinson, *The Decline and Fall of the Hebrew Kingdoms: Israel in the Eighth and Seventh Centuries B.C.* (The Clarendon Bible, Vol. 3; Oxford: Clarendon Press, 1930), p. 145.

data under consideration. In the present chapter, however, we intend to conclude with the investigation of a new area — Second Isaiah's employment of the theophany. This seems justifiable on two grounds: (1) chronologically, this prophet of the exile is the most recent of Israel's four prophets under consideration; (2) stylistically and theologically, the theophany attains a certain climax in the splendid poetry that Second Isaiah offers us. Notwithstanding his anonymity, it is safe to suggest that this Hebrew outdistanced his predecessors and successors alike in his cognition of theophanic manifestation. Moreover, his ability to depict the theophany and to use theophanic language is masterful. His success is attributable to both his readiness to use phrases that swarm with theophanic nuance and his eagerness to relate the theophany in eschatological manner to the lively prospects of a new beginning. In the former instance, he is fully dedicated to articulating the Yahweh-Israel relation, while in the latter he is concerned to offer trustworthy support and hope to his fellow exiles. In the former, he takes up and virtually improves upon those verbal elements that prospered in the theophanies to the patriarchs — "I am Yahweh," "fear not," "I am with you," "I will help you," etc. In the latter, he transcends the barriers of space and time and sets forth in the charming and stirring poetic line his glorious vision of the future which centers upon Yahweh's self-manifestation to "all flesh" in a theophany that encompasses the whole created order.[50]

An appreciative understanding of this talent and special interest of the prophet-poet is, of course, absolutely dependent upon a careful, straightforward reading of Isa., chs. 40 to 55, in its entirety. The selective considerations that follow must necessarily build upon that. Clearly, those verbal theophanic assurances that are so reminiscent of the Genesis theophanies are nearly ubiquitous in Second Isaiah's compositions. No other element in the various oracles of the deity is more pronounced than the self-asseverations which appear in one form or another on nearly two dozen separate occasions. They are to be found alike at the beginning, in the midst, and at the conclu-

[50] Muilenburg, "The Speech of Theophany," *HDB*, Vol. 28 (1964), p. 46, nowise overstates the case in writing, "the eschatological theophany receives its consummate and . . . its classical formulation in Second Isaiah."

sion of various strophes.[51] Moreover, the admonition "Fear not," although less frequent, is conspicuously present on nearly a dozen occasions within Isa., chs. 40 to 55.[52] In two instances it is accompanied by a direct assurance of divine presence. Thus the strophe ch. 43:3c-5a, which depicts Yahweh's act of ransoming Israel, concludes with "Fear not, for I am with you" (cf. also ch. 41:10). In three instances we may observe that the same three components of the theophanic *Gattung* appear together, namely, the divine self-asseveration, the admonition against fear, and the assurance of divine presence and promise. Thus the strophe ch. 41:11-13, which sets Israel over against the nations that are adversely judged, concludes with:

> For I am Yahweh your God
> who has hold of your right hand;
> who says to you, "Fear not,
> I will help you."[53]

Moreover, the *hieros logos,* Yahweh's special word of disclosure, resounds throughout these chapters. Only a few verses of the 333 in Isa., chs. 40 to 55, could be confidently excluded here! This has led Ludwig Köhler to submit that Second Isaiah has no use for random theophanic representations. Rather, he suggests that the prophet is preoccupied with the "foreshadowings of the one last great theophany which is the goal of all history," and devotes all of Isa., chs. 40 to 55 to this preoccupation.[54] It is true that Second Isaiah is quite uninterested in duplicating those theophanies that loom large within Israel's historical traditions. James Muilenburg rightly holds that

[51] In the present listing and the one that follows, an italicized reference indicates that the strophe in question commences with the self-asseveration; one with an asterisk shows that the self-asseveration is the concluding element of the strophe. The self-asseverations in Second Isaiah include chs. 41:4*, 10, 13; *42:6,* 8; 43:3*, *11,* 13, 15*, *25;* 44:6*, *24-28**; 45:5, 6, 7*, 18, 22; 46:9; *48:12,* 17*; 49:23, 26*; *51:15.* Significantly, in ch. 44:24-28, the entire strophe constitutes an extended self-asseveration in which one descriptive participial clause is piled upon another. Here we are in debt to the results of the incisive strophic analysis of Muilenburg, "Introduction and Exegesis to Isaiah, Chs. 40-66," *IB,* Vol. 5, pp. 415–418.

[52] Cf. Isa. 40:9; 41:10, 13*, *14; 43:1-2,* 5a*; 44:1-2, *8;* 51:7; *54:4-5.*

[53] Cf. also Isa. 41:10 in the preceding strophe and ch. 43:1-3b.

[54] *Old Testament Theology,* p. 104. In *Deuterojesaja,* p. 124, he avers: "This is the world theophany, the turningpoint of time, the fulfillment of salvation. Fundamentally it is the one and true principal theme in his whole writing."

"parallels to the old theophanies (e.g., Jacob's at Bethel in Gen. 35:9-15) are never present in a pure form."[55] Instead the prophet is persistently concerned to mate theophany and eschatology in an absolutely fresh and effective manner.

A few selections from the text, with their own drama and clarity, should establish the point with some adequacy. From a brief poem that makes definitive statements about the Yahweh-Israel relation we read:

> I, I am Yahweh
> and apart from me there is no savior . . . .
> I am God, and also henceforth I am he;
> there is none who can deliver out of my hand;
> when I work who can hinder it?
> (Isa. 43:11, 13.)

In a poem that treats the downfall of Babylon's gods and Israel's salvation that is to be divinely wrought, the deity says:

> Remember the former things of old;
> for I am God, and there is no other;
> God, and there is none like me,
> who makes known the end from the beginning
> and from antiquity things yet undone . . . .
> (Isa. 46:9-10b.)

While the strophe Isa. 44:24-28, which is exclusively devoted to Yahweh's self-asseveration, is too long to cite in full, its ability to link the name-giving of the deity with his eschatological design is impressive:

> Thus says Yahweh, your Redeemer,
> who formed you from the womb:
> "I am Yahweh, who made all things,
> who stretched out the heavens alone,
> who spread out the earth — who was with me? . . .
> who confirms the word of his servant,
> and fulfills the counsel of his messengers;
> who says of Jerusalem, 'She shall be inhabited,'
> and of the cities of Judah, 'They shall be built,

[55] "The Speech of Theophany," p. 390.

and their ruins I will raise up'; . . .
who says of Cyrus, 'My shepherd
and all my purpose he shall fulfill'. . . ."
(Isa. 44:24, 26, 28ab.)

Finally, in a poem that speaks of the anticipated conversion of the nations we read:

Turn to me, and be saved
all the ends of the earth!
For I am God, and there is no other.
(Isa. 45:22.)

The list could be readily extended, but perhaps this particular selection of passages can denote what is in part at least on the mind of the poet and reflect as well his capacity to communicate it. Yahweh is one. He has acted in Israel's past. He is speaking to Israel's present. He will act in Israel's future. Theophanic terminology is employed here, although it does not consume every verse. It is strengthened at every instance, however, by the fact that the marvelous poem of Isa. 40:1-11, which eschatologically envisions Yahweh's final and world-sweeping self-revelation, stands at the head of Second Isaiah's poetry and infuses all the rest with unusual significance.

We thus terminate our study of the theophanies surrounding Israel's prophets with a brief consideration of Isa. 40:1-11 as it bears upon our subject. Despite the numerous voices that resound here, it is beyond question that with a sensitive eschatological perspective, Second Isaiah is communicating his understanding of Yahweh's imminent return, a return that he fully expects to manifest itself in a resplendent act of self-revelation. The eloquent anticipations of Yahweh's coming in vs. 3-4 are climaxed in the final verse of that strophe:

And the glory of Yahweh shall be revealed,
and all flesh shall see it together,
for the mouth of Yahweh has spoken.
(Isa. 40:5.)

As one who has had the opportunity of listening to the proceedings of the heavenly council (ch. 40:1-2), Second Isaiah boldly declares that Yahweh will appear in a self-revelation of unique proportions.

He who has manifested himself to Israel in significant past moments will now appear in theophany before all humanity. In Ex. 24:15b-18a, the Priestly stratum represented the glory of Yahweh (*kᵉbōd Yahweh*) as appearing to Israel at Sinai; in Isa., ch. 40, Second Isaiah now declares that it will occupy all space and time, that "all flesh" will behold it. All darkness will be dispelled and all challenges to Yahweh's universal sovereignty obliterated. A full and perfect disclosure of this mysterious theologoumenon is expected. The prevailing Old Testament belief that man's beholding the deity will cost him his life is to be rendered invalid. For in this eschatological context an absolutely new event will occur. Nature will be majestically transformed, and by virtue of its finality, universality, and decisiveness, the divine self-manifestation will inaugurate a new age in which Yahweh will rule supremely as king.[56]

Accordingly, Second Isaiah lives in the hope that this will one day take place. But that is not all. In the second strophe (vs. 6-8), the prophet picks up the phrase "all flesh" from the preceding strophe, and pessimistically and momentarily comments upon the passing human condition. His life resembles the ephemeral grass and the flower of the field. In v. 8, however, another climax is reached:

> The grass withers, the flower fades,
> but the word of our God shall stand forever.

The grass, the flower, and man himself will not triumph over inevitable deterioration. But it is affirmed that the word of God which is both in and above history so triumphs. Transient humanity is matched against eternal deity. The theological point is plain. What interpreters have been less open to discerning is the noteworthy and uncontested *sequence* of divine manifestation. The "glory of Yahweh" will be seen, the visual disclosure is anticipated, but no less impressively the word of Yahweh will be heard resounding against the flux and confusion of history. Although there is much that is new here, the traditional theophanic pattern with its distinct sequence of seeing and hearing has not been disturbed. The complete

[56] This analysis also depends upon v. 10 in which the portrayal of v. 5 is extended — "Behold, the Lord Yahweh comes with power, / and his arm rules for him."

manifestation of the divine glory, which the Israelite may have regarded as the most excellent of the theologoumena, is dramatically linked with the eternal manifestation of the word. Thus if the fashioning of Second Isaiah's eschatology could not abide a bland duplication of theophany as it hitherto had been known, neither could it turn full circle. Although this judgment is not intended to detract from the radically fresh vision that is communicated here, perhaps it can speak for the potency of past traditions. The new is not totally divorced from the old.

CHAPTER VI

Theophany and The Book of Psalms

Having subjected various portions of the Pentateuchal and prophetic literature of the Old Testament to a somewhat thorough examination, we are ready to investigate the theophany as it emerges in The Book of Psalms. At the outset it must be admitted that theophanic passages and allusions in the Psalter enjoy a quite significant role within the total expression of Israelite faith. On occasion, however, that significance appears to be defiantly exceeded by the mysterious image that is projected. No other Old Testament book delivers the self-revelation of God with greater puzzlement. The underlying reasons for this state of affairs have been tersely but ably expressed by J. H. Eaton in a recent article:

> One is puzzled by the confusing mixture of Hebrew perfects and imperfects, the lack of historical data, the difficulties of relating the theophany to its context, and above all the problem of tracing a meaningful sequence of thought throughout such psalms.[1]

Despite these problems which we shall come to know firsthand, the theophany in the Psalter does present itself as quite a compelling element that merits serious study.

Allusions in The Book of Psalms to divine self-disclosure are numerous, artful, and dramatic. And while it is by no means normative for the poetic description of Yahweh's decisive self-manifestation to constitute the sole component of a given psalm composition,

[1] From "The Origin and Meaning of Habakkuk 3," *ZAW*, Vol. 76 (1964), p. 163.

the theophany can at times be quite elaborately presented. Our inquiry will not seek for its own satisfaction to discern just how many psalm passages might legitimately be incorporated into the ensuing discussion, but will rather deal with a limited number of spacious and studied compositions that clearly display theophanic terminology, and do so at some length. This should prevent both a merely surface treatment of a plethora of selections [2] and a too cavalier and frequent identification of theophanic texts as if to suggest that the Psalter does not concern itself with other matters as well! Nevertheless we shall openly recognize here that we are not attempting a comprehensive treatment of the subject.

But before embarking upon a form-critical and exegetical scrutiny of several important psalm theophanies that will evoke our sustained attention, we would do well to state our overall position concerning the material at hand. We are motivated here not by a desire to peddle conclusions prior to a presentation of the evidence, but rather by a need to set forth a brief word of orientation. We affirm, then, that as it is totally represented in The Book of Psalms, the theophany partakes of all those qualities incorporated into our previously formulated definition of the theophany (see p. 45), but that through its predilection for metaphor, it lays a peculiar stress upon the *description* of the august approach of the deity. In so doing, it regularly employs, and at times with considerable elaboration, imagery that is reminiscent of the antecedent theophany — sometimes referred to by scholars as the *Urtheophanie* — on Sinai. Along with Jeremias we would hold that the *memory* of the Sinaitic event as it must have manifested itself in Israel's oral traditions is indeed at work here; in addition, we would say — and Jeremias denies this — that the *language* of the actual written narratives of the Sinaitic event in Ex., chs. 19 to 24, has also exerted an influence.[3] Now it

[2] For example, the essay by José M. González Ruiz, "Las teofanías en los salmos," *EB,* Vol. 13 (1954), pp. 267–287, suffers from a diffusion resulting from too hasty an examination of too many passages.

[3] Cf. Jeremias, *Theophanie,* pp. 101, 105–111, and *passim.* We would agree with Jeremias that it is too much to claim that the Ex., chs. 19 to 24, representations of the Sinaitic theophany provide us with the prototype for *all other* theophanic descriptions in the Old Testament. We would further affirm with him that a complete harmonizing of the prose materials from Ex., chs. 19 to 24, with the poetic theophanic descriptions that are common in Israel's hymns cannot be argued. Yet this

further appears that the theophanic representation within the Psalter attests a readily perceivable, although not necessarily complete, emancipation from the strict canons of the theophanic *Gattung* customarily employed in the early narratives of the Old Testament, so concerned is it with the marvel and impact of divine nearness. Finally, that description in the theophany is not grounded upon an aesthetic principle, but exists instead as part of the possession of the cult of Israel that eloquently testifies to the oneness, sovereignty, and intervention of Israel's Lord as the one who directs the course of man's salvation.

By scrutinizing selected theophanic passages in The Book of Psalms, reflecting upon the essential motifs there advanced, and inquiring briefly in the next chapter into the place of the theophany within the cultic enterprise of Israel, we hope to elaborate upon and defend the preceding assertions. On the connection between theophany and cult we must acknowledge our debt to Artur Weiser for his treatment of the theophany in the introduction to and throughout his Psalms commentary, and in his illuminating essay in the Alfred Bertholet *Festschrift*.[4] No other scholar has endeavored to draw attention to the Old Testament theophany as it is related to the Israelite cult so consistently and insistently as he. However hypothetical the annual Covenant Festival of Yahweh that he posits may appear,[5] and however extensive may be the materials from the Psalter

surely does not necessitate any automatic conclusion that the former has not influenced the latter. Rather, is it not highly probable that the poetic constructions are *intensifications* of their prose antecedents? Thus to mention but one example, whereas for Jeremias the mention of lightning in the Elohist's Sinaitic account as an accompanying phenomenon to Yahweh's presence (Ex. 19:16), and the representation of lightnings as dangerous arrows which Yahweh shoots in such a poetic theophany as Ps. 18 (see v. 14) are to be rigorously contrasted (p. 108), we would simply urge that the latter passage intensifies the former. Moreover, such a poetic intensification seems geared to appreciate rather than to contradict its antecedent. If Jeremias' reasoning that the Pentateuchal depictions of the Sinaitic event cannot be viewed as offering the prototype for all other Old Testament theophanies presses upon the present volume a useful word of caution, some of his statements do seem to be rather forced.

[4] "Zur Frage nach den Beziehungen der Psalmen zum Kult: Die Darstellung der Theophanie in den Psalmen und im Festkult," pp. 513–531.

[5] See especially, "The Place of the Psalms in the Cult of the Covenant Festival (Fragments of Liturgy)," *The Psalms*, pp. 35–52.

that he relates to that festival,[6] through his cult-functional approach, Weiser has, on the whole, convincingly presented the theophany as a living actuality that evoked Israel's cultic participation. Moreover, we shall follow his lead in underlining illustrative elements within the theophany in the Psalter that testify to the pervasive influence exerted by the Sinaitic theophany upon the language of the Psalter and upon the cultic appropriation of respective theophanic contexts.[7]

What apparently has *not* existed as a primary concern for Weiser but does so exist for us, however, is a direct confrontation with the vast majority of poetic verse units in the exegesis of a given theophanic passage. It may not rest upon spatial considerations alone that Weiser comments rather generally upon the theophany as depicted in the Psalter, that he sometimes moves at a noticeable distance from the Biblical text. True, a rationale for each image employed in the theophany cannot be provided, for the "poetical

[6] That Weiser brings an inordinate number of psalms and a diversity of traditions to a festival whose actuality is never asserted by specific statement within the Old Testament is the criticism of Hermann C. Büchers, "Zur Verwertung der Sinaitraditionen in den Psalmen," *Biblica,* Vol. 32 (1951), pp. 401–422, and more recently that of J. A. Sanders in his review of Weiser's Psalms commentary, *JBL,* Vol. 82 (1963), p. 127, who declares, "The argument from silence, broken only by begging the question, does not inspire great confidence." Weiser relates his festival to that of Tabernacles (or Booths or Ingathering) which on the basis of its being mentioned under the simple designation "the feast," *heḥāg* (cf. I Kings 8:2, 65; Isa. 30:29; Ezek. 45:23, 25; Neh. 8:14; II Chron. 7:8) partly demonstrates its singular importance for Israel. Against Büchers' objection (p. 406) that the framework of this festival is unable to accommodate all the traditions of the *Heilsgeschichte* that Weiser appropriates to it, Weiser (*The Psalms,* p. 31, n. 1) argues for the unusual receptivity of the Semitic people to an existing *seven* day festival where there was ample time to rehearse before an interested assembly the traditions of their sacred history (and the theophany?) prior to the actual renewal of the covenant (cf. Neh. 8:18). Moreover, Büchers' contribution is designed only to dislodge from its foundations a hypothesis he seriously questions and as such suffers under its own limitations. Nevertheless, the annual Covenant Festival of Yahweh is Weiser's particular interpretation of the Biblical witness, and remains subject to criticism as a hypothetical construct, although we believe it to be an intelligible approach to the Biblical materials. What is most disturbing and least convincing, however, is the ubiquity of the festival in Weiser's commentary where it is presented as the single answer to a multitude of situations.

[7] For criticisms of Weiser's position on this issue, see González Ruiz, *loc. cit.,* pp. 283 ff., and especially Westermann, *The Praise of God in the Psalms,* pp. 98–101.

language with bizarre figures and symbols far removed from reality "[8] that characterizes the prophetic oracle dominates equally in the theophanic descriptions within The Book of Psalms. Still a circumspect attempt to interpret the specific words and phrases employed is in order. We believe that this is to be attained through that kind of study of specific pericopes which allows for attention to literary and exegetical detail without losing sight of the overall purpose and effect of theophanic presence.

We shall focus in turn upon Ps. 18, 50, and 97 as excellent representations of the theophany in the Psalter. While the order of their examination is fortuitously numerical, it is actually based upon a theological consideration, namely, the relation of divine theophanic presence to, and its impact upon, the individual within the community of Yahweh (Ps. 18), Israel as Yahweh's own congregation (Ps. 50), and all peoples in relation to Yahweh's special people (Ps. 97). Although rigid lines cannot be drawn, we witness in turn the mediation of divine presence to the individual, to an elect people, and to the world. Psalm 18 conveys the most detailed description, but Ps. 50 is perhaps the truly classic example of theophany in the Psalter with its inclusion of the self-asseveration of the deity and an extensive and a compelling *hieros logos*. Climactically, it may belong last, but the sequence of Ps. 18-50-97 appears as more intelligible theologically.

Individual Deliverance: The Theophanic Representation of Psalm 18

In Ps. 18, one of the longest compositions in the Psalter, some scholars have discovered two psalms. Thus Hans Schmidt identified them as separate types of prayers of thanksgiving, the one appearing in Ps. 18:1-30 as spoken by the individual, and the other as a prayer in Ps. 18:31-50 uttered by the king.[9] Although any strophic analysis

[8] The phrase belongs to Johannes Lindblom, *Prophecy in Ancient Israel* (Oxford: Basil Blackwell, 1962), p. 317.

[9] *Die Psalmen* (*HAT;* Tübingen: J. C. B. Mohr, 1934), pp. 27, 29. As is the case throughout this book, we are following the RSV rather than the MT verse numbering.

must allow for a distinct break between vs. 30 and 31, a certain unity does lie beneath the entire psalm. For example, the dispersion of the enemies is celebrated in the first portion of the psalm (v. 14), but only in the second (vs. 37 ff.) is the victory over them mentioned as realized. Moreover, it is the joint testimony of both halves that produces the impressive and combined impact created by an eloquent witness to Yahweh's sovereignty on the one hand and the charming and unmitigated expression of human trust on the other.[10]

Although Hermann Gunkel's classification of the entire composition as an Individual Song of Thanksgiving is basically correct,[11] this designation requires amplification on two counts. First, the individual who utters the thanksgiving for divine help in battle which accomplished ensuing victory and the one to whom the psalm refers is the king.[12] Secondly, this royal personage stands *within the cult* that is witness both to the present narration of Yahweh's saving deed and to the individual response of thanksgiving, and here the unity between the cult as a corporate body of worshipers and the king as its representative before Yahweh must be acknowledged. Thus the individual in this case is not just any person, but rather the one who is truly *the* representative of the entire Israelite community.

The crucial theophanic element in the psalm is contained in vs. 7-15 where forceful and colorful description readily evokes our attention. The majestic style and graphic vocabulary mediate something of the reality and splendor of effective divine presence that operated in behalf of the king, who now testifies in the cult that theophanic divine intervention was truly realized. Now it has been conjectured that since a reading of vs. 16 ff. immediately following v. 6 would still convey the sense of royal praise and thanksgiving for divine deliverance, the theophany in vs. 7-15 with its forceful

[10] See Weiser, *The Psalms,* p. 187.

[11] *Die Psalmen,* p. 62.

[12] Notwithstanding the superscription, it is impossible to establish with any certainty the identity of the psalm's royal figure. Although Gunkel, Kittel, Oesterley, and Leslie suggest Josiah, they are challenged by F. M. Cross, Jr., and D. N. Freedman, "A Royal Song of Thanksgiving: II Samuel 22 = Psalm 18," *JBL,* Vol. 72 (1953), p. 20, who argue that on the basis of textual peculiarities, the psalm dates much earlier (to the ninth or eighth century B.C.). Davidic authorship is challenged by Mowinckel, who insists on a later date, and is accepted as a possibility by Eissfeldt, Weiser, and Dahood.

and exciting language is only the skillfully wrought insertion of an ancient Israelite poem dating to the time of the Judges or early Monarchy.[13] If the Canaanite associations of vs. 7-15 might warrant that judgment, still there may be no absolutely compelling reason to think that these verses constitute an addition to an ancient composition. We should like to argue that they may be viewed as the work of the original poet who introduced into his creation a body of known terminology, for indeed, these verses do not play havoc with the overall strophic structure of the psalm which might be expected were they a later insertion.[14] Moreover, an excision of vs. 7-15 would considerably diminish the sheer grandeur of the total composition. Thus we may tentatively conclude that vs. 7-15 may have belonged to the poem from the first and that notwithstanding the borrowed imagery employed, may be attributed to the genius of the poet.

Those portions of Ps. 18 in which we are most interested may be rendered as follows:[15]

The Desperate Peril of the King
4 The waves of death encompassed me,[16]
the floods of Belial assailed me;
5 The cords of Sheol entangled me,
the snares of death confronted me.

[13] So Cross and Freedman, *loc. cit.*, p. 21. Moreover, Jeremias, *op. cit.*, pp. 35 f., cites and himself joins a list of four scholars (Eberhard Baumann, Bernhard Duhm, Hermann Gunkel, and Rudolf Kittel) who view vs. 7-15 as a later insertion. But it is not unlikely that the following claim of Westermann, *The Praise of God in the Psalms*, p. 93, is quite relevant here: "It is . . . reasonable to assume that the epiphanics were originally parts of Psalms, and do not represent independent Psalms."

[14] The strophic structure of vs. 1-30 may be designated as follows: (1) the introductory hymnic lines of praise, vs. 1-3; (2) the desperate peril of the king, vs. 4-6; (3-5) the theophany, vs. 7-10, 11-12, 13-15; (6) the accomplishment of divine deliverance, vs. 16-19; (7) the declaration of the king's righteousness, vs. 20-24; and (8) the proclamation of Yahweh's faithful dealings with mankind, vs. 25-30.

[15] However instructive a comparison of Ps. 18 with its parallel in II Sam., ch. 22, may be, and however pertinent may be the dual rendering of the poem for the study of Old Testament textual transmission in general, we are not undertaking any rigorous and systematic comparison of the two. However, the brilliant treatment by Cross and Freedman, *loc. cit.*, pp. 15–34, may be profitably examined.

[16] Reading, with II Sam., ch. 22, *mišbᵉrē*, for MT *ḥeblē* which itself occurs in the succeeding bicolon and was likely introduced here into the text from that point.

6 In my distress I called upon Yahweh,
to my God I cried for help;
From his temple he heard my voice,
and my cry for help came into his ears.[17]

The Theophany

7 Then the earth did shake and quake,
the foundations of the hills trembled,
they were shaken, for he was wroth.
8 Smoke arose from his nostrils,[18]
and fire from his mouth devoured;
coals flamed forth from him.
9 Then he bowed the heavens and descended;
darkness was under his feet.
10 He rode upon a cherub, and flew,
he swooped down upon the wings of the wind.

11 He set darkness round about him,[19]
his pavilion was the rain cloud.[20]

[17] Until now, a 3 + 3 meter has prevailed in the MT. The problem of four beats may be solved by a deletion of *l^e^pānāw* which may be defended on three counts. (1) The plainly overburdened colon shows that either an explanatory gloss or alternative reading has been added; (2) if as Cross and Freedman, *loc. cit.*, p. 23, contend, the original consonantal spelling of the colon were *šw't* [*tb'*] *b'znw*, the loss of an original *tb'* could easily be accounted for as a triple haplography; (3) granting the original presence of *tb'*, *l^e^pānāw* may have been inserted in reaction to the anthropomorphic tone of the verse.

[18] With *b^e^'appō* the archaic prepositional meaning "from" is preserved. Cf. Patton, *Canaanite Parallels in the Book of Psalms*, p. 34; Cross and Freedman, *loc. cit.*, pp. 17, 24; Keith R. Crim, *The Royal Psalms* (John Knox Press, 1962), p. 77, n. 6; and Gordon, *UT*, pp. 95 f., 370.

[19] From the extant corrupted Hebrew text it is difficult to ascertain whether or not the original words in the verse have been rearranged, and if so, which ones. Three consecutive words start with the letter *Sāmek* which might betray dittography, but we cannot be certain. Since 3 + 3 meter dominates in the strophe, perhaps it should also be sought here. This has been achieved through a deletion of *sitrō* which, due to its absence from II Samuel, may be viewed as an alternative reading for *ḥōšek* at the beginning of the verse.

[20] On the basis of Ugaritic *ḥṯr* meaning "sieve," Samuel I. Feigin, "The Heavenly Sieve," *JNES*, Vol. 9 (1950), p. 41, discovers in *ḥašrat* the Hebrew cognate.

12 Thick clouds were before him OR before him his clouds passed by,[21]
hail and coals of fire.

13 Yahweh also thundered from the heavens,[22]
and the Most High uttered his voice; [23]
14 And he sent forth arrows, and scattered them; [24]
he flashed lightnings, and discomfited them.[25]
15 The channels of the sea then appeared,[26]
and the earth's foundations were laid bare,

With the earlier mention of *ḥōšeḵ* in this verse, the misreading of *ḥašrat* (which appears correctly in II Samuel) as *ḥešḵat* is readily conceivable. Since the former is far less common than the latter, it would be unlikely that an original *ḥešḵat* was miscopied and retained in II Samuel as *ḥašrat.*

21 We follow the provocative and not overly radical suggestion of Cross and Freedman, *loc. cit.,* p. 25, that through *'ābē šeḥāqīm minnōgah* and *negdō 'ābāw 'āberū* a dual reading has been provided. The pivot of their argument lies in the dittography that appears to exist between the final *Mēm* in *šeḥāqīm* and the initial *Mēm* in *minnōgah* that immediately follows. Upon a deletion of the latter, the close resemblance between consonantal *ngh* and *ngdw* is quite evident; probably both words should read *ngdw* (originally spelled *ngdh*), and if so, the phrase yields our chosen translation. The alternative reading requires no tampering whatever.

22 The prepositional prefix on *baššāmayim* is to be read "from" according to its archaic meaning.

23 Following II Samuel and the LXX version of Ps. 18, the third colon has been deleted as an obvious dittography from the preceding verse.

24 Reading *ḥiṣṣīm,* with II Samuel and the LXX version of Ps. 18, for MT *ḥiṣṣāw* so as to achieve the plural welcomed by the following colon.

25 Reading, with II Samuel, *bārāq* for MT *rāb;* perhaps after an unexplained loss of the *Qōph,* the remaining two Hebrew consonants were transposed to render a meaningful colon, "and he shot."

26 Reading *yām,* with II Samuel, for MT *mayim;* the initial *Mēm* appears originally to have been an enclitic *Mēm* belonging to the preceding word with the two words constituting a construct chain. The intervening *Mēm* within a construct chain between the *regens* and the *rectum,* which is common in Ugaritic, has been rigorously identified as a feature of early Hebrew poetry. Cf. Gordon, *UT,* pp. 104, 129; W. F. Albright, "The Old Testament and Canaanite Language and Literature," *CBQ,* Vol. 7 (1945), pp. 23 f.; and Patton, *op. cit.,* p. 12.

At thy menacing rebuke, O Yahweh,
at the blast of the breath of thy nostrils.

The Accomplishment of Divine Deliverance

16 He sent from on high, he took me;
he drew me out of many waters.
17 He delivered me from my strong enemies,[27]
from my foes for they were stronger than I;
18 They confronted me in the day of my calamity;
but Yahweh became a support for me.
19 He brought me forth into a roomy place;
he delivered me, for he delighted in me.

Some form-critical comment concerning structure and movement is in order prior to our exegesis of the theophany itself. The indigenous theophanic description (vs. 7-15) has its own framework. It is preceded by an opening strophe that swarms with hymnic lines of praise (vs. 1-3), and a second strophe which conveys in metaphorical detail the perilous situation confronting the king that provoked him to entreat the deity to intervene in his behalf (vs. 4-6). Both strophes which are set in the first person are recited by the king, the leading figure and representative par excellence of the people of God. They constitute the vital prelude to the ensuing theophany. In the first strophe (vs. 1-3) it is the king's declaration that Yahweh is his "rock" (*sal'ī* and *ṣūrī* both appear), "fortress," "deliverer," "shield," "horn of salvation," and "stronghold" (v. 2). Through the first-person singular suffixes that abound, Yahweh is praised as the source of unchangeable and irresistible strength, as the one who overwhelms the king's enemies and assures the royal triumph.

[27] Reading *mē'ōyᵉbay,* with LXX, Syriac, Targum, and Jerome, for MT *mē'ōyᵉbī* so as to achieve the plural welcomed by the following colon.

At once the anguished situation of the king is set forth in the second strophe (vs. 4-6) with its noticeable alternation of perfect and imperfect tenses. In vs. 4-5 we meet a series of four plural construct chains and four plural verbs with first-person singular suffixes whereby the peril of death is described. This is followed by the tetracolon of v. 6 with its mention of the king's cry for help that is divinely heard and responded to in the theophanic act itself. The remainder of the framework to the theophany per se lies in the two strophes that immediately follow it (vs. 16-19 and 20-24). In fact in the former the actual deliverance of the king is realized. Here the last stages of the theophany unfold and the rescue of the king is mentioned as accomplished. But it is only in the next strophe (vs. 20-24) that a fundamental *reason* for Yahweh's advent and his deliverance of the king is enumerated, which truly brings the theophanic impact and reflection upon it to a close. The theophany can be properly viewed only with this framework in mind.

But what of the structure and movement within those strophes (vs. 7-15) that depict the theophany itself? These verses confront us with a quite diverse terminology. A most minimal repetition of nouns and verbs alike would indicate that an indirect if not intentionally allusive element is at play in the theophanic description. One metaphor is laid upon another in such fashion that a note of splendor, rather than coherence, is achieved. The advent of Yahweh is recounted through necessarily indirect modes of speaking. Yet what is lacking in straightforward statement is compensated in the awesome impact of Yahweh's theophanic intervention which is achieved through the force of poetic phrase that does obtain. This impact thus derives primarily from the aggregation of carefully aligned descriptive components. Their own formation is worth examination.

Theophanic engagement is first depicted through the tricolon of v. 7 that alludes to the reverberations of the earth which indicate that Yahweh's visitation is imminent. The short Hebrew rhyme achieved by the introductory *wattig'aš wattir'aš,* and retained in our translation, " did shake and quake," appears as the premeditated expression for denoting the movement of the earth that is evoked even prior to Yahweh's appearance. This image is then reinforced by the two remaining cola of v. 7. In the tricolon that immediately follows (v. 8), the description begins, and for some verses will continue, to center upon the unfolding manifestation of Yahweh himself. In a pair of bicola (vs. 9-10) that conclude this first of three strophes depicting the theophany per se, Yahweh's arrival from the high heavens is portrayed with due emphasis upon the verbs employed — "bowed," "descended," "rode," "flew," and "swooped down." The next brief strophe (vs. 11-12), however, which testifies that Yahweh's essence is ever veiled places several nouns in prominent position. Mention is made of the darkness that Yahweh sets about himself, the pavilion of rain cloud that protects him, and the cloud bank that stages itself before him. Now without warning in a new strophe that commences with v. 13, the heavens are portrayed. This third theophanic strophe now moves with some deliberation towards its finish through its reference to the effects of the theophany upon the king's enemies, and indeed, upon the created order itself. The concluding thought on the theophany in v. 15 returns to the impact of Yahweh's theophanic visitation upon all terrestrial creation which was of primary concern at the beginning. As the earth is reported to have responded with its agitations immediately prior to Yahweh's coming (v. 7), its very bases are now revealed (v. 15). Thus sheer theophany and ireful intervention merge in the mind of the poet.

Obviously, in its formal aspects, the theophany here depicted resembles very little those theophanies we have previously encountered in the books of Genesis and Exodus where a regular theophanic *Gattung* with its various formal elements was often transparent. The literary evidence presented by this psalm is of another sort. Yet an alternative theophanic *Gattung* need not be posited. Rather the Pentateuchal narrative theophanic form has been extensively revised. Of course, owing to the probable antiquity of the poem, we cannot legitimately assume a slow evolution of an original theophanic form. Instead it appears that almost from its genesis, the theophanic *Gattung* was transmitted with a certain spontaneity. Thus we detect in Ps. 18 neither the transmission of the divine name through the self-asseveration of the deity nor the injunction against fear, let alone the assertion of divine presence or a *hieros logos* befitting the particular occasion. Instead, in vs. 7-15 the interest of the psalm converges solely around the *description* of Yahweh's theophanic manifestation. Those previously identified elements of the theophany that we have designated as " Introductory Description " and " Concluding Description " have in effect bridged themselves into one continuous whole, and in the process other components have been transformed. While Yahweh's voice is heard in the thunder (v. 13), the content of his speaking is not perceived. All creation is overawed by Yahweh's visitation, yet the words from the deity, " Fear not! " and " I will be with you " are conspicuously absent. The *manner* of Yahweh's appearing occupies all our attention, yet, as always the answer to the question, " How? " is necessarily imprecise, for in Ps. 18 as elsewhere, the theophany has to do with the ineffable.

Although form-critical and exegetical issues cannot and should not be fully divorced, it is now our design to sharpen and amplify some of the preceding comment through a straightforward exegesis of our passage. The poetic statement of the anguished condition of the king prior to Yahweh's intervention and actual presence must first occupy our attention. So hazardous were the dangers threatening the king's existence that he metaphorically represents himself here as already having descended to the underworld where he was overcome by the encroaching advance of the floods of Belial, the cords of Sheol, and the waves and snares of death. Impending annihilation is made quite vivid. The floods or rivers of Belial are understood by T. H. Gaster as denoting " currents of adversity, which bring neither benefit nor blessing and are likened to the streams of the nether world." [28] In the Hebrew *bᵉliyyaʿal,* we seem to have a compound derived from (1) the particle *bᵉlī* suggesting absence or lack and (2) the verbal root *yʿl* meaning " to profit, avail, benefit." [29] The worthless, base, and even destructive are hereby denoted. Thus the pernicious waters of the deep are metaphorically depicted as en-

[28] " Belial," *IDB,* Vol. 1, p. 377.

[29] Cf. KB, p. 389; BDB, p. 418. Other etymologies are advanced by G. E. Wright, " Introduction and Exegesis to the Book of Deuteronomy," *IB,* Vol. 2, p. 420, and Mitchell Dahood, *Psalms I (1-50): Introduction, Translation, and Notes* (The Anchor Bible, Vol. 16; Doubleday & Company, Inc., 1966), p. 105. Contemporary mention of this pictorial noun was made by *Time* magazine (February 11, 1966, p. 22) in its assessment of a recent and most extensive snowstorm as " a Belial of a blizzard! "

gulfing floods that assailed the king. Finally, the gravity of the situation is further enhanced by succeeding figures in v. 5 which personify death as a huntsman setting his traps for the prey.

In the tetracolon of v. 6 that balances the two bicola of vs. 4-5, the king states that in death's grip he cried to Yahweh for help and from the heavens where Yahweh sits enthroned his entreaty was heard. The witness of Isa. 6:1; Micah 1:2; Hab. 2:20; Ps. 11:4; and 29:9 induces the judgment that this *hēḵāl* is the *heavenly* temple, the site of Yahweh's dwelling and the worship of the heavenly hosts. This is supported by subsequent disclosures in v. 6d and vs. 7 ff. that the prayer of the king was heard by Yahweh in the heavens and that it was from the celestial realm that the deity, to whom the king covenantally refers with " my God " (Ps. 18:6b), descended for the deliverance of his suppliant. Then in v. 6cd where the fact of divine listening is emphasized, the circumstances are established for the imminent intervention of the deity.

In vs. 7-15 Yahweh's inbreaking is portrayed in incontestable grandeur as a theophany that (1) evokes a response from the whole terrestrial order to the splendid reality of divine presence, and (2) accomplishes the king's deliverance. Throughout divine omnipotence and hiddenness alike are defended. Although the bank of clouds and mantle of darkness that surround the deity may indicate his presence, they effectively conceal him from human gaze. As the *Deus revelatus,* Yahweh remains the *Deus absconditus.* Diverse natural elements relating to a severe storm on the one hand and an earthquake or a volcanic outbreak on the other are gathered as suitable figures of speech for representing the awesome and real advent of the deity for the purpose of salvation. This rich imagery, then, is to be studied in the light of the purpose which it serves, namely, a powerful communication within the cult of the divine majesty and power that are operative and readily perceived in the theophany.

Through the terrestrial agitations depicted by synonymous verbs in v. 7, the impending appearance of deity is signaled.[30] If the tremor depicted here and in v. 15 is to be understood solely as earthly convulsion, lucid reference in both instances to the deity's anger precludes our minimizing this terrestrial reaction to theophanic visita-

[30] Cf. Ex. 19:18; Judg. 5:4-5; Hab. 3:6; Isa. 24:18-20; and especially Job 26:11.

tion. In v. 8 the awful manifestation of divine wrath is represented by bold figures of speech. Yet this portrayal of Yahweh's angry approach does not lay bare the divine form. Although many parts of Yahweh's body are here enumerated—his nostrils (v. 8a), mouth (v. 8b), and feet (v. 9b), a concrete image of the deity is not fabricated. Weiser has fully appreciated this feature in the following comment:

> The nearness and the greatness of God, hidden behind the brightness of fire and behind dark clouds . . . , can be recognized only by means of the impression produced by his appearance—which has the proportions of cosmic catastrophes; and even within these limits they can only be surmised.[31]

As a visual manifestation of Yahweh's wrath, smoke ascends from his nostrils, but his essence is not openly revealed. The fire of divine anger is represented as flaming forth from Yahweh's mouth, consuming whatever it touches, yet he is not seen. Since within the tricolon of v. 8, notation of "smoke," "fire," and "coals" each precedes mention of its respective source, the emphasis falls more naturally upon the phenomena themselves than upon their points of origin. Together the images poignantly portray what is both ireful approach and theophanic intervention.

Depiction of the actual divine descent is given to vs. 9-10. Yahweh bows or bends (*wayyēṭ*) the heavens and comes down (*wayyērad*). As the *terminus technicus* of Yahweh's theophanic descent, the latter verb especially affirms the actuality of the deity's approach.[32] Yet his concealment is at once assured—"darkness was under his feet" (v. 9b). Although the one who is enthroned high in the heavens condescends to the king's urgent invocation, he is enveloped by a protective covering that is first perceived as a darkness (*ᵃrāpel*) "under his feet." That last expression, to be sure, calls to mind the expe-

[31] *The Psalms,* p. 190; see also Boman, *Hebrew Thought Compared with Greek,* p. 102, who avers that a uniform picture does not emerge here. In this connection, Jeremias, *op. cit.,* p. 38, is quite right in his judgment of the cumulative imagery involved: "Neither is a single nature phenomenon in itself a theophany of Yahweh, nor is Yahweh in his theophany bound to a single phenomenon."

[32] We have already recognized the significance of this verb for Biblical theophany. Cf. the similar expression in Isa. 64:1.

rience of the elders of Israel narrated in Ex. 24:10, and there too the anthropomorphic language does not attempt a full description of divine form. The darkness that dominates in this psalm, however, sharply contrasts the clear sapphire expanse that the Israelite delegation is reported to have viewed in the J Sinaitic account. Perhaps we may infer that through a quite conscious choice of imagery, the difference between Yahweh's theophanic disclosure in wrath and his self-manifestation for the establishment of the covenant is here successfully maintained.

Between the allusions of v. 9b and 11a to the darkness that envelops the deity, divine movement is further disclosed. In his downward flight Yahweh " rode upon a cherub " (v. 10a), and " swooped down upon the wings of the wind " (v. 10b). We meet in *ḵ^{e}rūb* a collective singular noun that replaces the customary plural *ḵ^{e}rūbīm.* The cherubim function in several capacities in the Old Testament, as guardians located " at the east of the garden of Eden " (Gen. 3:24), as winged creatures overshadowing the cover (*ḵappōret*) of the Ark of the Covenant (Ex. 25:18-22), and thus as the objects that comprise the divine throne itself (I Sam. 4:4; II Sam. 6:2; II Kings 19:15 [Isa. 37:16]). In the psalm, however, Yahweh is represented not as sitting upon a cherubim throne, but as *riding* (*rḵb*) in some manner upon a cherub as he draws near in the theophany. Mowinckel cogently claims that Yahweh is not depicted as riding or standing upon the back of the cherub, but rather is thought to have been transported by " the cherub chariot." [33]

The imagery is far from clear, however, since v. 10 in its entirety

[33] " Drive and/or Ride in O.T.," *VT,* Vol. 12 (1962), p. 299. This meshes well with the efforts of M. Haran, " The Ark and the Cherubim: Their Symbolic Significance in Biblical Ritual," *IEJ,* Vol. 9 (1959), p. 37, to explain on analogy with a phrase in Hab. 3:8de, " for thou didst ride upon thy horses, / upon thy chariots of victory," that Ps. 18:10 is declaring that Yahweh " rode in a chariot made up by a cherub." He avers that the implication is not that Yahweh rides upon either horse or cherub, but that his chariot is *harnessed* to the creature in question. However, Clements, *God and Temple,* p. 32, does not make a choice here when he concludes, " the cherubim were related to Yahweh, because he was the God of the skies, who came to his people from heaven, and . . . the cherubim were thought to draw, *or even to form,* his chariot " (italics mine). Concerning the wings of the wind, Jeremias, *op. cit.,* p. 37, n. 1, calls attention to the presence of this phenomenon in the Akkadian Adapa myth (cf. *ANET,* p. 101).

manifests a synonymous parallelism between "cherub" and "the wings of the wind" upon which Yahweh is said to have "swooped down" (*wayyēde'*). No consistent and lucid portrayal is drawn here. Moreover, it is rather surprising that the cloud itself is nowhere *specified* as the divine vehicle, for elsewhere it is understood as the divine chariot frequenting Biblical theophanies,[34] and is symbolized by the cherubim resting upon the *kappōret* of the Ark of the Covenant.[35] Again we may be certain that the psalm is dedicated to a portrayal of the grandeur and dynamic of theophanic presence, and not to an elucidation of an absolutely coherent sequence of thought.

At the outset of the second strophe (vs. 11-12), further mention is made of the impenetrable darkness that veils the deity, especially as it relates to the cloud phenomena that encompass him. The darkness (*ḥōšek*) indicated in v. 11a finds its parallel in v. 11b, "his pavilion was the rain cloud," which is further enhanced by the readings presented in v. 12a. The "coals of fire" at the close of v. 12 must in some way represent the lightning that is emitted through the rain cloud. Against any logical deduction that "coals of fire" (*gaḥ*ᵃ*lē 'ēš*) can only denote a steadily burning fire,[36] the context here necessitates our accepting the phrase as a unique expression standing for the flash of lightning which in its brightness resembles burning coals. Moreover, that the lightning flashes will be designated in the next strophe (v. 14a) as arrows shot forth by the deity does not argue against our interpretation, but rather witnesses again to the wealth of imagery employed by the poet.

The lightning is mentioned only momentarily. Now the third theophanic strophe commences (v. 13) with allusion to the manifestation of Yahweh's voice in the thunder prior to the detailed account of the lightning and its effects in v. 14. Apart from the brief and anticipatory mention at the close of v. 12, the extended reference to these storm phenomena amidst the theophany follows the same sequence as did the Elohist's narrative of the Sinaitic theophany: *thunder precedes lightning.*[37] The present strophe is also concerned to

[34] Cf. Ex. 16:10; 40:34-38; Num. 16:42; and implicitly in Ex. 19:9; 24:16.

[35] Cf. Ex. 25:18-22; Num. 7:89; I Sam. 4:4; II Sam. 6:2; Ezek. 1:4; I Chron. 28:18.

[36] So B. D. Eerdmans, *The Hebrew Book of Psalms* (Oudtestamentische Studiën, Vol. 4; Leiden: E. J. Brill, 1947), p. 156.

[37] Cf. Ex. 19:16; 20:18.

affirm Yahweh's heavenly residence. Curiously, the deity who has descended in the theophany, presumably drawing earthward while shrouded by the cloud, is still the deity whose voice is heard in the thunder originating in the heavens. Although a lack of coherence may be granted here, apparently its presence either was not perceived by, or was not disturbing to, the Semitic mind, because in v. 14 the psalmist mentions without embarrassment the flashes of lightning that also seem to have issued from the heavens. Prior to the more literal expression, "he flashed lightnings," of v. 14b, we confront the highly metaphorical phrase, "and he sent forth arrows," of v. 14a.[38] In the tumult that attends his theophanic manifestation, Yahweh causes the thunderbolt to hurl forth.

But what are we to make of the twofold reference to "them" in this verse? While out of context the four verbs of v. 14 may all be related to the lightnings provoked by the deity and to nothing more, we believe that when their full context is taken seriously, another interpretive route should be elected. The joint witness of vs. 3 and 17 suggests that the enemies of the king are being referred to. Certainly the opposition, from whose power the king is delivered by the display of divine might manifested in the theophany, stands in a direct connection with the theophany itself. The enemies are the very invokers of the divine wrath that persists throughout these verses.[39] Consequently, the king has come to know the miracle of Yahweh's saving historical intervention that can break into perilous earthly existence. Yet the effects of the intense tempest born of Yahweh's wrath are not confined to the flight of the enemies alone. The channels or bottom of the sea and the foundations or pillars of the earth (v. 15ab) are pictured as splendidly laid bare, so violent is the surging theophanic tempest.

One question remains: "What of the purpose and effect of the theophany?" Its answer is considerably influenced by one particular strophe (vs. 16-19) which eloquently declares the purpose of Yah-

[38] Cf. Ps. 144:6, which parallels Ps. 18:14 but reverses the cola and employs the imperative. The similar Canaanite motif is cited by Patton, *op. cit.*, pp. 22 f., and Jeremias, *op. cit.*, p. 87.

[39] Moreover, the verbal roots *pwṣ* and *hmm* employed here typically refer to the overthrow of the enemy; cf. Num. 10:35; I Sam. 11:11; and Ps. 68:1 with the former verb, and Ex. 14:24; Josh. 10:10; Judg. 4:15; and I Sam. 7:10 with the latter.

weh's presence as accomplished. The deity is represented in v. 16b as having reached down from on high and drawn (*mšh*) the king out of "many waters" (*mayim rabbīm*) which symbolize the enemies who had overpowered him.[40] In the day of his calamity (v. 18a) when adversity had not only confronted but had already overwhelmed him, Yahweh, who is the subject of all but two verbs in the entire strophe, delighted in the king (v. 19b) and acted in his behalf. Thus the psalm does not merely testify that Yahweh comes in a theophany because his efficacious presence has been invoked (v. 6); *also he comes to the one who is righteous in light of the covenant relation hitherto established.* The king declares, "Yahweh rewarded me according to my righteousness" (v. 20a). He announces that his hands are clean (v. 20b) and that he has respected Yahweh's ways (v. 21a), ordinances (v. 22a), and statutes (v. 22b). This is not a presumptuous statement of moral self-approval but rather a rigorous affirmation of the covenant relation between the king and his Lord. Yahweh is proclaimed as a God who displays a covenantal loyalty to individuals who obey his commandments (cf. vs. 25-27) and thus the psalm, like Judg. 5:4 ff. and Hab. 3:13, contends that this loyalty manifests itself in Yahweh's theophanic intervention before his own who call upon him. He favors his elect.

This strophe is significant for another reason. Through its use of the verb *mšh,* "to draw up," in v. 16, which occurs elsewhere in the Old Testament *only* in Ex. 2:10 in the naming of Moses, we may very cautiously assume a connection between the king and Moses. Both servants of the deity had experienced Yahweh's deliverance, and both had been favored by Yahweh's self-manifestation in the theophany. Both learned firsthand of the reality and efficacy of theophanic visitation. We are not saying that the presence of *mšh* in the psalm invites our identifying the king as a second Moses; rather we are merely submitting, that it would not be out of order to entertain the idea that the king is presented as standing within the same sacred-history framework of tradition as was Moses.

The overall purpose and effect of Yahweh's self-revelation is also to be considered in light of the traditional and cultic aspects of the

[40] See H. G. May, "Some Cosmic Connotations of *Mayim Rabbīm,* 'Many Waters,'" *JBL,* Vol. 74 (1955), p. 14.

psalm. Since balanced liturgical phraseology of the psalm demonstrates that it clearly existed as a cultic possession, its purpose and effect are necessarily influenced. Regardless of whether or not David was the king on the original occasion of the psalm, the king is represented as belonging to the Davidic dynasty (v. 50). With its sweep of imagery, the psalm calls to mind no single historical event centering upon the life of the king, but instead effectively combines into a singular portrayal numerous perils and effective acts of victory and deliverance which have been regarded as divinely wrought. The retrospection of the mercies that the king has enjoyed throughout his life is thereby actualized in the cult, and in particular it is affirmed that the king himself has experienced in his own person that marvelous power of divine salvation that Israel as a people of Yahweh has come to know. The deliverance of the king is thereby significantly taken up into the total framework of the *Heilsgeschichte* which presents itself as the most cherished property of the cult, that element around which cultic existence and ceremony revolve.

Moreover, the theophanic manifestation here depicted, while introducing *sui generis* phraseology, displays a conscious recollection of the Sinaitic event that historically occasioned Israel's becoming a people of Yahweh and was to anchor itself firmly in Israelite memory, thereby providing the very inspiration for much of her cultic activity. This is best realized by a perusal of the duplicate motifs and/or terminologies employed. The trembling of Mt. Sinai reported in Ex. 19:18 (J) may have some bearing upon v. 7 of the psalm. Just as fire (*'ēš*) and smoke (*'āšān*) indicate in the J Sinaitic narrative that Yahweh has descended (*yrd*) upon the mount (Ex. 19:18), so here in v. 8ab they signal Yahweh's advent, although they are linked with the mouth and nostrils of the deity. The *terminus technicus* for Yahweh's drawing near, *yrd,* freely employed in the J account of the Sinaitic theophany, occurs prominently in v. 9a of the psalm. The cloud motif that is present in both J (Ex. 19:9) and E (ch. 19:16) is met here in a more highly developed form in vs. 11-12. The thunderings (in Ex. 19:16 and 20:18 of the E account) and lightnings (in Ex. 19:16, also E) occur in the psalm in vs. 13-14, and we have already noticed the phrase " under his feet " that appears in both Ex. 24:10 (J) and Ps. 18:9b.

The equivalents between Ps. 18 and the Sinaitic accounts of J and

E must not be pressed beyond reason. If the theophany reported in the psalm has been influenced by the event at Sinai, there is much that is new. A more elaborate description is introduced that goes far beyond that attested in Ex., chs. 19 to 24. Still there is good reason for concluding that in Ps. 18 we also have a recollection of the theophany par excellence on Mt. Sinai, and that this treasured tradition of the cult has influenced the manner in which the psalm theophany has unfolded. Like Ex., chs. 19 to 24, Ps. 18 presents itself as a cultic witness to the operation of the grace of election and the august splendor of divine manifestation that Israel had come to know.

Judgment in the Cult: The Theophanic Representation of Psalm 50

A liturgical composition of remarkable, if disputed, dimensions appears in Ps. 50. Motifs of theophany and judgment are carefully blended together in such fashion that full weight is given to the awful splendor of theophanic intervention and to the sheer directness of divine rebuke. A powerful note of drama is produced. The immediate confrontation of deity within a cultic structure is compelling and decisive. Although not as extravagantly presented as in Ps. 18, the grandeur of the deity's august appearance is duly registered here through images that call to mind Israel's past encounter with divine presence on Sinai where the covenant relation was first affected. Yet the cosmic dimension of the event at hand is not ignored.

Yahweh comes for judgment that is witnessed by heaven and earth themselves. That judgment is actualized through the incisive rebuke voiced in all probability by the cultic prophet. He stands out here among the cult functionaries as the privileged and authorized speaker charged with the responsibility of expressing the divine will, and inspired by prophetic fervor and idea, he attempts through an utterance of the divine speech (*Gottesrede*) to instill in the people the proper mode and spirit of worship.[41] Through the judgment

[41] Cf. Hans-Joachim Kraus, *Psalmen* (2te Auflage, BKAT; Neukirchen: Verlag der Buchhandlung des Erziehungsvereins, 1961), p. 381. The prophetic tone of the psalm has been a favorite point of emphasis; cf., *inter alios,* Rudolf Kittel, *Die Psalmen* (4te Auflage, Kommentar zum Alten Testament; Leipzig: A. Deichert, 1922), pp. 184 f.; Gunkel, *Die Psalmen,* p. 215; W. O. E. Oesterley, *The Psalms* (London: S.P.C.K., 1939), p. 267; E. A. Leslie, *The Psalms* (Abingdon Press, 1949), pp. 205 f.; Harris Birkeland, *The Evildoers in the Book of Psalms* (Oslo: J. Dybwad,

conceived as instigated by God's theophanic visitation before his people, the inappropriate objects of cultic allegiance and concern resulting from misplaced religious zeal are subjected to rigorous attack. Although there is no outright denunciation of cultic ritual as such, and no injunction that the service of sacrifice must cease, the psalm forcefully condemns the too diligent esteem of external sacrifices that appear incessantly before the deity, and the blatant refusal to take seriously both the sacrifice of prayer that truly honors deity and those ethical precepts divinely instituted at Sinai through the Decalogue itself. Instead, that piety is enjoined which is wholly conditioned by the profound impact that is obtained through the theophanic manifestation of divine name, nature, and will.

Psalm 50 contains two decisive components, an opening descriptive account in the style of a hymn that depicts the awesome theophany of the deity that impresses itself upon the congregation assembled for cultic meeting, and the divine reprimand that issues from the *hieros logos* addressed to the cult. D. W. Caspari has rigorously emphasized that the divine speech voiced by the cultic prophet consumes the major portion and interest of the psalm (vs. 7-23).[42] Divine self-asseveration and rebuke stand at the very center of focus and as such are prefaced by a strophe of rather elaborate introduction (vs. 1-6). We do not discover here, however, a pale and subservient prologue. Possessing a significance of their own, vs. 1-6 depict both the manner and purpose of divine advent. Since the entire psalm is justifiably categorized as theophanic, it must be grasped as a unit. Yet while we cannot afford to ignore the content and thrust of divine speaking, our primary concern rests with the description of the theophany which occasions that speech.

Due to spatial considerations and the special relevance of vs. 1-7 for our study of the theophanic character of the psalm, only those verses will be rendered here:

1955), p. 63. The particular thrust of the prophetic polemic voiced in conjunction with the cultic theophany, however, must be kept in mind. Von Rad, *Old Testament Theology,* Vol. 1, p. 369, n. 30, rightly avers, "The observance of a cult is not at all called in question: only, the sacrifices are spiritualised."

[42] "Kultpsalm 50," *ZAW,* Vol. 45 (1927), pp. 257, 260. Caspari, however, assigns only vs. 8-21 to the divine speech proper, maintaining that in vs. 1-6, 7a, and 7b we have three distinct introductions (p. 263) and in vs. 22-23 a recapitulation of admonitions already issued (p. 257).

1 El, Elohim, Yahweh,[43]
he speaks and calls the earth,
from the rising of the sun to its going down.
2 From Zion, the perfection of beauty,
God shines forth.
3 Our God comes and he does not keep silence;
a fire devours before him,
round about him it is very stormy.
4 He calls to the heavens above,
and to the earth that he may judge his people.
5 " Gather to me my pious ones,
who made my covenant by sacrifice! "
6 The heavens declare his righteousness,
for God, he is judge.

7 " Hear, O my people, and I will speak,
O Israel and I will testify concerning you.
Yahweh, your God, am I . . . ."[44]

As essential preparation for our exegetical study of the theophany, several form-critical observations should be made. Clearly, one of the

[43] The curious situation created by three distinct divine names at the head of the psalm has invited various emendation. Gunkel, *Die Psalmen,* pp. 213, 219, and Oesterley, *op. cit.,* p. 268, wish to retain only the name " Yahweh " which would create a pleasant 2 + 2 meter in the opening bicolon. It can, of course, be conjectured that " Elohim " was the name given the deity at the time that the psalm was incorporated into the Elohistic Psalter (Ps. 42 to 83) and that " El " was an ensuing dittography. On three grounds, however, the integrity of the MT can be defended: (1) this sequence of divine names *is* found in Josh. 22:22 although admittedly nowhere else in the Old Testament; (2) the names are dramatic — through an aggregation of different names of the deity, each of which appears in the absolute state, the audience is persuasively led to fix its attention upon the one who comes; (3) retention of the names naturally presents v. 1 as a tricolon which meshes nicely with vs. 7 and 16 which also are tricola that introduce their respective strophes. Thus the MT requires, and here has received, no emending. Without any emendation, however, Dahood, *op. cit.,* pp. 304–306, renders v. 1a as " The God of gods is Yahweh," and finds here an instance of Hebrew superlative. This is certainly plausible, but it is by no means unlikely that we have before us three distinct divine names.

[44] It seems quite evident that " Elohim," the first word in the statement of self-asseveration in the MT, betrays an Elohistic editorial revision of an original " Yahweh " which we maintain in our own translation.

virtues of Ps. 50 is its lucid overall structure. We discover there three strophes of nearly equal length (vs. 1-6, 7-15, 16-21) which are followed by a brief coda (vs. 22-23). In the first strophe, the appearance of the deity is depicted, in the second, the divine self-asseveration and reprimand of conditions within the sacrificial cult are given, and in the third, the deity's rebuke against the wicked within the community is delivered. In the coda, the salient points within the *hieros logos* are reiterated under the forms of admonition and threat (v. 22), and exhortation and promise (v. 23). Except for the first strophe, the first-person speaking of Yahweh in the form of prophetic speech dominates, and even in the first strophe it appears in v. 5.

Conspicuous also are those specific intervals in which the strophes commence and terminate. Not only does an emphasis fall upon the concluding colon of each strophe, but the colon that immediately follows in each instance functions as an introductory component that advances the movement within the whole range of the theophany. Moreover, climaxes may be identified within the strophes themselves. Thus with " God shines forth," " that he may judge his people," and " he is judge," in vs. 2, 4, and 6, respectively, climactic notes are struck. Each pair of verses appears as a smaller unit within the first strophe. It should be further noted that the initial strophe opens with an emphasis upon deity which is achieved through mention of three distinct divine names, and appropriately terminates with a colon that is introduced by the deictic particle *ḳī* where attention is once more fixed upon the one who confronts the cult in theophanic meeting: " for [*ḳī*] God, he is judge."

Although the second strophe has its own symmetry, a somewhat different situation obtains since v. 7 should be set apart as the introduction to the first formal speech of the deity with its exhortation to listen, declaration of divine intent to issue judgment, and disclosure of the divine name. The *hieros logos* on sacrifice may then be divided into two units, the first consisting of vs. 8-11 with their declaration of the divine ownership of the world and its goods, and refutation of the present situation of Israel's sacrificing, and the second including vs. 12-15 which develop the thought of divine ownership and self-sufficiency, and set forth what kind of sacrifice is most desirable. Finally, the subdivisions of the third strophe, which conveys the second speech of the deity, appear to be vs. 16-17 with a general accusation, vs. 18-20 with specific enumeration of offenses that indicate a breaking of the seventh, eighth, and ninth " words " of the Decalogue, and v. 21 with the conclusion of the rebuke and its prominent climax.

Again, we may wonder how this psalm compares with the theophanic *Gattung* that was projected in the second chapter. While no theophanic composition in The Book of Psalms contains in simple sequence all the basic components there set forth, Ps. 50 compares more favorably in this respect than does Ps. 18. There is nothing here to resemble the simple divine injunctions against fear and the direct affirmations of divine presence that frequent the Pentateuch, yet in the promise of v. 15b, " I will deliver you and you shall honor me," divine help is pledged and divine presence implied. Although no concluding third-person description appears in the psalm, the introductory description is extensive and well wrought. Especially prominent in the psalm are the divine self-asseveration (v. 7) and the *hieros logos* (vs. 8-23) that are more eloquently conveyed here than anywhere else in the Psalter. Moreover, the self-giving of the divine name *prefaces* the particular word that is the burden of the first speech of the deity. We conclude, then, that while the original *Gattung* is not reproduced here in its pristine form, many of its aspects are resolutely affirmed in the present composition.

With these formal considerations in mind, we may turn now to an exegesis of the specific contents that have been incorporated into poetic theophanic portrayal. Without any prefatory strophe or colon, Ps. 50 opens with the initial unfolding of the theophany. The prelude to and plea for divine intervention belonging to Ps. 18 and such invocations as " Come to save us," " Restore us, O God," and " Cause thy face to shine that we may be saved! " that appear in the introduction of Ps. 80, another theophanic composition, are conspicuously wanting here. As the psalm stands, the deity's self-manifestation before the cult is unconditioned. Yahweh comes of his own accord. The verbs " he speaks " (*dibber*) and " he calls " (*wayyiqrā'*) of v. 1 appropriately hint that hearing will dominate in this characteristically Israelite theophany. To offset any overemphasis, however, attention must at once be called to God's *appearing* that is denoted by a most significant verb, " to shine forth " (*yp*ʿ), in v. 2. The audible and visual are both attested at the outset. The former, however, is indeed the more vital in this psalm that testifies to the dynamic of the divine word that confronts Israel and Israel alone. Yet the expressed object of the divine summons in v. 1 is the whole earth, " from the rising of the sun to its going down." Thus in the setting and imagination of the Israelite cult, the sphere of auditors that are called to attend the imminent speech of divine judgment (*Gerichtsrede*) assumes gigantic proportions. The terrestrial realm is addressed in its totality and called to behold the deity's judgment of his covenant people.[45]

A most crucial note is struck at the beginning of the psalm through the explicit subject of the verbs of audition in v. 1. Kraus cogently declares, " Three designations of God announce the mystery of the epiphany in which Yahweh now permeates everything and is the primary reality." [46] Indubitably, an emphasis is created by the very selection and accumulation of divine names. A deliberate movement from the general to the specific may be discovered. The name that heads the list, *'ēl,* is the generic Semitic name for deity.[47] While the etymology of the name is not undisputed, it seems that the basic meaning is power or strength which is here substantiated by the strophe as a whole through its portrayal of the impingement of august theophanic presence. After submitting the various proposed derivations of the name, Eichrodt observes that all commonly

[45] For another interpretation, see Evode Beaucamp, " La Théophanie du Psalme 50 (49)," *NRT,* Vol. 81 (1959), pp. 900 ff. He argues that in the divine economy, the only thing that merits being known through all the earth is the saving power of the deity. He cites Isa. 45:6; 59:19-20; Mal. 1:11; and Ps. 113:3, and holds that although the expression " from the rising of the sun to its going down " is employed in these passages, in no instance do they relate to God's judgment against Israel. He avers that God comes to *deliver* Israel, not to judge her. Except (perhaps) for Ps. 113, however, we do not meet in his list any contexts that point to cultic theophanies. Thus a similarity of language is not matched by a similarity of situation.

[46] *Psalmen,* p. 374.

[47] Marvin H. Pope, *El in the Ugaritic Texts* (*VTS,* Vol. 2; Leiden: E. J. Brill, 1955), p. 1, writes, " The word *il*(*u*), West Semitic *'ēl,* is common to all the Semitic languages except Ethiopic, as the general appellative meaning ' god ' in the broadest sense."

affirm the *distance* between God and man: "What is of primary importance is not the feeling of kinship with the deity, but fear and trembling in the face of his overwhelming majesty."[48] If, with some anticipation of succeeding verses, the dreadful element attached to theophanic manifestation is to be ascertained through the first name, under the second, *'ᵉlōhīm,* all attributes of the deity are subsumed. Yet Israel's Lord has attached himself to Israel in a special manner that is not grasped by the "plural of excellence." Thus in the third name, Yahweh, Israel's special knowledge of the deity and her privileged position as his people in an unparalleled sense are denoted. That name consistently calls to mind both Yahweh's historical deeds in Israel's behalf and the divine expectation placed upon the people he has taken to himself. It is Israel's sovereign Lord who now comes in the cultic theophany in august self-manifestation and with instructive word that will put an end to the illusion that the deity she worships is either negotiating or silent (see v. 21), and will impress upon the cult his authentic name, nature, and will.

That divine word, however, is not immediately issued. Rather descriptive cola in vs. 2-3 emphatically indicate the cultic theophany at hand. The key words in v. 2 lie at the extremities: "*From Zion,* the perfection of beauty, God *shines forth.*" In contrast to those Biblical theophanies that represent the divine point of departure as Sinai-Seir (Deut. 33:2), Seir-Edom (Judg. 5:4), Teman-Paran (Hab. 3:3), and "from afar" (*mimmerḥāq,* Isa. 30:27), here Zion is mentioned. The significance of Jerusalem's holy hill as the place of special divine presence is affirmed. He is thought to manifest his resplendent presence from the inner recesses of the Temple where he is invisibly enthroned upon the Ark of the Covenant. As prophetic oracles of the Old Testament disclose from time to time, Zion achieved the distinction of becoming the seat of Yahweh's dynamic residence. Yahweh's sanctifying presence thus conferred upon Zion a marvelous holiness.[49]

[48] *Theology of the Old Testament,* Vol. 1, p. 179.

[49] Cf., *inter alios,* Martin Noth, "Jerusalem und die israelitische Tradition" (1950), *Gesammelte Studien zum Alten Testament,* pp. 172–187; Sigmund Mowinckel, *Religion und Kultus* (Göttingen: Vandenhoeck & Ruprecht, 1953), p. 57; and Childs, *Myth and Reality in the Old Testament,* pp. 88 f.

Zion's situation here is anything but static, for as Ps. 50 discloses, the Sinaitic theophanic tradition itself has been transferred to Zion. As the result of David's magnificent rise to power, his auspicious choice of Jerusalem as the site for his capital, and his transfer of the Ark to Jerusalem (II Sam., ch. 6), Zion came to be recognized as God's holy mountain. For the Israelite mind, Zion now replaced Sinai as the site of law and revelation.[50] This was a matter of no incidental significance. Moreover, in the full appropriation of the tradition, such natural accompaniments of Yahweh's theophany as the intruding radiance of the lightning and the formidable tempest were also taken over. [51] Finally, this transfer may be reinforced in our own thinking through the phrase "the perfection of beauty" which is predicated to Zion, itself an expression that does not so much denote a stative quality as it does the efficacy of divine benediction made known by Yahweh's impelling and acting presence.[52]

The dynamic impression already produced is now intensified by the statement that in his self-revelation, God "shines forth" (*hōpīaʿ*). Here we have another *terminus technicus* of Old Testament theophany which is rendered in KB (p. 392) as to "shine forth beaming," and in BDB (p. 422) as to "shine out, forth, display beams," and to "cause to shine." Notable Semitic cognates appear in Akkadian *šūpū* (causative) and Ugaritic *ypʿ*.[53] The verb is of inter-

[50] The following words from the floating oracle of Isa. 2:3 and Micah 4:2 should be noted: "For out of Zion shall go forth the law"; see also Amos 1:2 and Micah 1:2.

[51] This has been well appreciated by Sverre Aalen, *Die Begriffe "Licht" und "Finsternis" im Alten Testament, im Spätjudentum und im Rabbinismus* (Oslo: J. Dybwad, 1951), p. 79, and Weiser, *The Psalms,* p. 395.

[52] Von Rad, *Old Testament Theology,* Vol. 1, p. 368, rightly states that Israel interpreted beauty not as a state but rather as an event, for she related it to divine action, not to divine being.

[53] See Carl Bezold *et al., Babylonisch-Assyrisches Glossar* (Heidelberg: Carl Winter's Universitätsbuchhandlung, 1926), p. 54, and Gordon, *UT,* p. 413, who admits that all the examples within his entry may not be derived from the same root, yet solely renders the Ugaritic verb "to arise." Norman C. Habel, *Yahweh versus Baal: A Conflict of Religious Cultures* (Bookman Associates, 1964), p. 68, n. 30, provides three possible translations for Ugaritic *ypʿ* — to "rise up, challenge, be presumptuous." F. L. Moriarty, "A Note on the Root YPʿ," *CBQ,* Vol. 14 (1952), p. 62, believes that the rendering "to arise" is useful for Ps. 94:1, but with respect to the theophany in Deut. 33:2 where the verb is also attested he writes, "It is difficult to choose between 'arise' and 'shine forth,' presupposing that the latter is a legitimate

est to us in part due to its rather frequent use in the Dead Sea Scrolls.[54] True, it cannot be said to exist as a vital element within lengthy passages devoted to the portrayal of Yahweh's theophany which themselves have yet to be uncovered in the Qumrān materials. In Hodayoth 9:31, however, a link is established between Yahweh's self-revelation and the exercise of his judgment which is relevant to the present context and may be rendered, "And since my youth thou hast shown forth [*hwpʿth*] unto me in the insight of thy judgments."

Certainly the most instructive parallel to Ps. 50:2 comes from 20:25 in the Zadokite document which is translated by Chaim Rabin as follows: "But as for all those of the members of the covenant who have broken out of the boundary of the Law: when the glory of God will appear [*bhwpʿ*] unto Israel they shall be cut off 'from the [midst] of the camp,' and with them all the evildoers of Judah."[55] While the deity's self-manifestation in Ps. 50:2 is depicted as present event, and here we confront the *object* of present hope and expectation, in both texts the conduct of those who stand within the covenant is a matter of concern (cf. Ps. 50:5), in both the deity appears to the nation that has joined in cultic assembly, and in both the visitation of God is intimately connected with the judgment to be rendered.

Finally, it should be noted that the root *ypʿ* appears in seven other Old Testament contexts, and in five (Deut. 33:2; Ps. 80:3; 94:1; Job 10:3; 37:15) the deity is the subject. Among them, only Job 10:3 is nontheophanic. Thus as sovereign over nature, God is represented as causing his lightning to shine (Job 37:15), and as sovereign over mankind, Yahweh is portrayed as having come from afar to shine forth in his theophany (Deut. 33:2). The imperative form of the

---

semantic development from the original meaning." He does not address himself here to Ps. 50:2. We have the distinct impression that the last word has not been spoken on the matter.

[54] Karl Georg Kuhn, *Konkordanz zu den Qumrantexten* (Göttingen: Vandenhoeck & Ruprecht, 1960), p. 91, lists eighteen attestations: Hab. *pēšer* 11:7; Manual of Discipline 10:2; War Scroll 1:16; 12:13; 18:10; Hodayoth 4:6, 23; 5:32; 7:3, 24; 9:26, 31; 11:26; 18:16; "Recueil d'hymnes" 14:4; and Damascus Document 20:3, 6, 25.

[55] *The Zadokite Documents* (2d ed., Oxford: Clarendon Press, 1958), p. 42.

verb is employed cultically in Ps. 80:3 and 94:1 where Yahweh is invoked to shine forth, and there the affinities with Ps. 50:2 are the more intimate.

With this recognition that *hōpīaʿ* is a most significant verb within both Biblical and extra-Biblical materials for representing the dynamic of the deity's self-disclosure, we may now consider the remaining verses in the opening strophe of Ps. 50 whereby the august visitation of theophanic presence is further delineated. The deity whom the Jerusalem cult serves in a devious and an inappropriate manner — to anticipate the *hieros logos* for the moment — yet the one it addresses in its liturgy as " Our God " (v. 3a), draws even closer in his self-manifestation. That he can do no other than speak his corrective word is implied by the Hebrew jussive *weʾal yeḥeraš* which needs not but nevertheless could justifiably be rendered, " he *cannot* keep silence."[56] If his will already has been offended (cf. v. 21), his silence will suffer no longer. Now v. 3 moves on to denote the fire and violent storm that are thought to accompany Yahweh's appearing. Although nothing is said here of a protective cloud that envelopes the deity, the inaccessibility and holiness of Israel's Lord are adequately conveyed through the nature images employed. The fire may well symbolize both divine majesty and anger, for Yahweh's judgment is imminent. The ominous character of his appearance is then reinforced through reference to the marked intensity of the storm. While differences in vocabulary may well exist, clearly, by the impression that is created, the psalm portrayal may be said to recollect the theophany on Sinai. It is Israel's Lord who appeared at Sinai in the self-giving of his name, nature, and will who now draws near to the present generation in cultic assembly to issue anew these same divine aspects. Yet presently these are to be set forth in the context of their own, that of instructive judgment.

To that end, v. 4 indicates that the deity summons the heavens and the earth alike " that he may judge his people." But for what purpose are they called? Are they to be understood as accusers called to testify that Israel has acted unfaithfully in the covenantal context, but strangely never given the chance to speak that specific word

[56] On the use of the jussive to express that which cannot or should not take place, see Gesenius, *Hebrew Grammar,* #109-o, p. 322.

within the proceedings of the psalm? Are they possibly the tribunal of judges themselves that decide the outcome of the lawsuit? Are they perhaps the ones who are addressed with the command given in v. 5a, "Gather to me my pious ones?" The role that scholars have attributed to them ranges between two extremes, from their being "nothing more than silent and appalled listeners" [57] to their being the distinguished judges before whom Yahweh acts as a plaintiff bringing up the charge against the people.[58] Now on form-critical grounds alone it is difficult to accept the status of the heavens and the earth as judges, because the climactic conclusion of the first strophe testifies that God himself is judge (v. 6b). Everything in the first strophe leads up to that declaration and in the succeeding strophes the deity as Israel's judge speaks the necessary word of reproach. Moreover, the psalm's proceedings conclude with the divine speech. If Yahweh were not the judge it is unlikely that the last word would be his.[59] If the function of judging is not to be accorded to the heavens and the earth, neither is theirs the act of summoning the accused, for it is more likely that the imperative "gather" (*'ispū*) is not addressed to any definite object. Although the general cultic significance of this verb in the Old Testament is not to be underestimated, no specific reference seems to be intended. Rather in a mutuality of simplicity and effectiveness, we confront here the compelling request on the part of the deity that his *ḥ^asīdīm* ("pious ones"), those who are members of the established covenant, be gathered.

Yet if the heavens and earth are neither judges nor heralds, it is not simply on the basis of an elimination of all posited conjectures but one that we claim for them the function of witnesses. Instead, the analogies provided by Deut. 32:1; Isa. 1:2; and Micah 1:2 and 6:1, as well as the testimony of Ps. 50:6a in the present composition

[57] So Beaucamp, *loc. cit.*, p. 908.

[58] So Gunkel, *Die Psalmen,* p. 219. He is followed by Friedrich Nötscher, *Die Psalmen* (Würzburg: Echter-Verlag, 1947), p. 99; E. Podechard, *Le Psautier* (Lyon: Facultés catholiques, 1954), Vol. 1, p. 224; and Edward J. Kissane, *The Book of Psalms* (Dublin: Browne and Noland, 1953), Vol. 1, p. 222.

[59] As significant witnesses, heaven and earth have no judicial authority of their own, and as G. E. Wright, "The Lawsuit of God: A Form-Critical Study of Deuteronomy 32," *Israel's Prophetic Heritage,* p. 47, has rightly argued, they are not to be regarded as "holding or wielding power."

that the heavens themselves speak in behalf of Yahweh's righteousness, provide convincing support that the role of the heavens and the earth as divine witnesses rings clear. The act of witnessing is not merely a matter of silent consent, but at least for the heavens (since there is no parallel for the earth), this involves active declaration.[60]

From the beginning of the second strophe on, the deity who has been proclaimed as righteous (v. 6a) addresses the assembled cult. The actual divine presence having effectively imposed itself upon the cult, the theophany now proceeds quite naturally with extended speaking that is conveyed through the mouth of the cultic prophet which lays bare Yahweh's will and rebuke. The divine declaration opens with a solemn and rather extensive introduction, "Hear, O my people, and I will speak, / O Israel and I will testify concerning you" (v. 7ab). From the address, "my people" (*'ammī*), past and present have clearly merged in the cult. Those who already belong to Yahweh and are under special obligation by virtue of the covenant they have made and sealed by sacrifice at Mt. Sinai (cf. v. 5b and Ex. 24:4 ff.) are now called to listen, to attend carefully the awesome testimony of the deity who now draws near for their correction and edification. The divine charges are grave. Yahweh's words are words of judgment and his wrath is not flatly suppressed. Yet both divine teaching and admonition are combined in the psalm, for an instructive word on appropriate sacrifice and right moral conduct is also given. These aspects are thus anticipated by the cola of introduction in v. 7ab.

Between these cola and the specific *hieros logos,* however, there stands the vital self-asseveration of the deity who confronts his people: "Yahweh, your God, am I" (v. 7c). The name that is indissolubly tied to its bearer is declared before the cult. The name that characterizes fully the one to whom it belongs is uttered by the cul-

[60] Concerning the problem as a whole, we concur with the judgment of George E. Mendenhall, *Law and Covenant in Israel and the Ancient Near East* (The Presbyterian Board of Colportage of Western Pennsylvania, 1955), p. 40, on this verse: "The list of witnesses need cause no difficulty, for in the very nature of the case, it would be impossible to appeal to any other third party as a guarantor of this covenant between Yahweh and Israel." See also p. 34 in his monograph, where heaven and earth are mentioned as included among the witnesses incorporated in Hittite suzerainty treaties, *ANET,* pp. 205 f., and the detailed notation of Dahood, *op. cit.,* p. 306.

tic prophet and presents itself as another veritable token of the deity's presence. Those participants in the service of the cult were no doubt aware that the very climax of the theophanic encounter was achieved through the utterance of the holy name. To that name now spoken were tied the historical recollections of Yahweh's mighty acts of deliverance. Through the suffixed form, " your God " (*'elōhe*[*y*]*ḵā*), the particular relation between Yahweh and his people was aptly emphasized. As a varied and shortened form of the self-asseveration of the deity that prefaced the Decalogue, both the experience of and the obligation upon Israel that obtained from, the Sinaitic theophany were recalled. In such manner, the proper moment was created for the deliverance of the *hieros logos* to follow in the remainder of the composition.

In the second strophe (vs. 7-15), Yahweh does not reprove the congregation for offering sacrifices and burnt offerings (v. 8), but rather for thinking that he is a god who needs such food to subsist (vs. 9-13). Not only does Yahweh not require animal offering (v. 13), but he is the sovereign owner over all that is. Cultic zeal is to be stimulated in a new direction. To this end the deity offers a specific word of instruction: " Offer to God a sacrifice of thanksgiving, / and pay your vows to the Most High " (v. 14). Then in time of need Israel's Lord may be invoked for her deliverance and in turn she may honor him (v. 15). In the third strophe, the words of the deity are addressed to " the wicked " (v. 16a), a word that is best interpreted as a collective used to designate those within the Israelite community who persisted in disobeying the recognized norms.[61] Although they have given lip service to Yahweh's statutes (v. 16), their hatred for the law and its discipline has been clearly manifested (v. 17). That a specific norm is in mind is evident from vs. 18-20 where portions of the Decalogue are recalled. The charge is forcefully laid against the wicked in v. 21: in the lack of any immediate retribution, they have thought of God in human terms, as either a bargaining or silent being, and thus the strophe concludes, " I now reprove you, and I lay the cause before your eyes " (v. 21c). In the coda, those who in their misplaced cultic fervor or in their moral laxity have forgotten who their God really is are reminded, on the

[61] See Birkeland, *op. cit.*, p. 64.

threat of Yahweh's wrathful destruction, to take seriously both the "sacrifice of thanksgiving" that really honors God (v. 23a, and summarizing the second strophe) and the law that has been given (v. 23b, summarizing the third strophe). The psalm ends on a word of promise that to him who obeys the word thus issued will be shown Yahweh's salvation (v. 23c).

Having scrutinized the psalm to this extent, we may now set forth what we believe to be the purpose and effect of this theophany. Certainly v. 4 provides the surest indication: God comes "that he may judge his people." The judgment that obtains is executed through the *hieros logos* that is at once admonishing and instructive. That which is amiss in the cult is so declared as this touches upon both the corporate observance and ethical conduct of its members. Yet there is more. The deity confronts the cult in theophanic meeting in order that the proclamation of his name may be heard, his nature better understood, and his will revealed. Through the utterance of the divine name it is plain that he is the God of this people here assembled: "Yahweh, your God, am I" (v. 7c). But by virtue of the covenant relation that has previously been established (v. 5), the people are also his. In v. 7a with "my people" (*'ammī*) and in v. 5a with "my pious ones" (*ḥ^{a}sīdāy*), he addresses them with possessives. It is expected that they hearken to the Torah which was given through Moses at Sinai, and the obedience enjoined is to be genuine, not merely an exhibition of outward conformity. In this something of the divine nature and will is manifested. Then through his own word that is spoken by the cultic prophet another aspect of his nature is laid bare — he is not a numen who is forever silent (v. 21a, cf. v. 3a), but rather, he intervenes through the theophany to speak his corrective word of rebuke and to issue the promise of salvation to the faithful. In short, through this self-revelation it is the deity's purpose to grant Israel a fresh realization of his character and claim upon her.

In the psalm's reappropriation of the theophanic event on Sinai, another vital purpose is served. Past event is transformed into actual experience for the present generation. We have already observed that the theophanic imagery of the psalm is akin to that employed in Ex., chs. 19 to 24. The words of the God of Sinai to Moses prior to his theophanic manifestation, "for all the earth is mine" (Ex. 19:5), are expressed anew in the speech of the God of Zion to the cult, "for the world and everything in it is mine" (Ps. 50:12). Moreover, in the Sinaitic narrative, Israel had become the deity's special possession (Ex. 19:5), and in the psalm she is addressed as belonging to Yahweh (cf. vs. 4b, 5a, and 7a). Also in vs. 18-20, in which portions of the Decalogue are rephrased, we may discover a vital element in the psalm. Yet the best evidence of the cultic reappropriation of the Sinaitic *Urtheophanie* lies in the proclamation of the divine name. Israel had already experienced Yahweh's communication of his name in the glorious theophany on Sinai (Ex. 20:2), and through it she had been moved by the immediacy of the divine confrontation. In the reappropriation of that experience of the self-disclosure of the divine name through the cultic liturgy of Ps. 50, there was in the contemporary Israelite generation the re-presentation (*Vergegenwärtigung*) of that climatic moment on Mt. Sinai through which the presence of the deity was especially manifested. Zion had become the new Sinai.

Sovereignty and Judgment: The Theophanic Representation of Psalm 97

As an isolated composition, the psalm to which we now turn might be viewed along several significant and inseparable lines, any one of which might be chosen by the exegete as truly essential for a full understanding of its contents. Contemporary, eschatological, universal, and theophanic aspects are all present in addition to the prominent motif of Yahweh's enthronement. While the theophanic representation cannot be comprehended apart from a general awareness of the psalm as a whole, we are mainly concerned to inspect the psalm as it presents itself as an integral part of the total theophanic tradition attested in the Old Testament.[62]

This composition exhibits an unmistakable cultic character. Specific references to Zion and the cities of Judah as engaging *at present*

[62] Thus we shall not enter into any lengthy discussion of the enthronement aspect of Ps. 97, since this would draw us too far afield from a study of the composition as a noteworthy theophanic passage.

in the act of rejoicing over Yahweh's enthronement, theophany, and judgment appear in v. 8. Stereotyped liturgical phrases, which owe their preservation to the conservative tendency that is naturally operative in the cult, may be found throughout the psalm. Despite the employment of fixed and borrowed forms, these traditional phrases have been creatively gathered into a dynamic whole. Yet we cannot help but notice parallels between Ps. 50 and 97 and the influence that the former has exerted upon the latter. Apart from certain identical and similar single words that are employed in both psalms which could create at best a rather mild impression of agreement, some very close and significant phraseological affinities emerge. For example, both Ps. 97:6a and 50:6a are to be rendered, " The heavens declare his righteousness," and while the verbs differ, " a fire goes before him " (Ps. 97:3a) is reminiscent of " a fire devours before him " (Ps. 50:3b). Significant for cultic considerations is the emphatic use of the verb " to hear " (*šmʿ*) at the head of the tricolon in Ps. 97:8 — " Zion hears and is glad " — which reminds us of the prominence of that verb in the same position in Ps. 50:7 — " Hear, O my people . . . ." Thus the terminology in Ps. 97 is not entirely strange to us.

Nevertheless, the present composition certainly does not thoughtlessly mimic the theophanic presentation of Ps. 50. Rather, the former moves beyond the latter. The righteousness of Yahweh that is operative here through the dynamic and active character of the divine appearance is manifested not with reference to Israel alone, as was the case in Ps. 50, but in connection with all peoples. The one who comes in theophany and judgment is " the Lord of all the earth " (v. 5b). His self-manifestation, in penetrating the furthest reaches of the earth, matches the sphere of his sovereignty. The theophanic encounter is plainly universal in scope. All peoples confront both his glory (*ḵābōd*) and the exercise of his judgment (vs. 6b and 7). Thereby universality and eschatology are combined.[63] From the first, the psalm presents a dual portrayal of the advent of the deity

[63] On the eschatological nature of the psalm, see Hermann Gunkel, *Ausgewählte Psalmen* (Göttingen: Vandenhoeck & Ruprecht, 1904), pp. 158 ff.; *Die Psalmen*, p. 425; Kittel, *op. cit.*, p. 317; Kraus, *Psalmen*, pp. 671 f.; and Weiser, *The Psalms*, p. 635.

and the inauguration of his Kingdom. The remote coastlands exult in Yahweh's enthronement (v. 1). Here future invades upon the present. Yahweh's presence is celebrated in the cult as a contemporary reality (vs. 2 ff.). Moreover, the gladness that sweeps over Zion and the cities of Judah is invoked by Yahweh's present judgments. Yet the full realization of divine presence, rule, and judgment is alone the object of hope. In particular, this is substantiated near the end of the psalm (v. 11) through the metaphor that "light dawns for the righteous." Thus the composition plainly evidences traces of the cultic affirmation that Yahweh has been present in his self-revelation and will again draw near.

If present and future realities are related in the psalm, the past is not forgotten. In particular, past theophanic event is recalled in the depiction of the present and future self-disclosures of deity. The influence of the *Urtheophanie* of the deity on Sinai is once more exerted. Some of the same vocabulary is employed, but this is set into more elaborate descriptive phrases which both tenaciously preserve and incisively deepen the impression created by that prior theophany par excellence of Yahweh to Israel. Thus Ps. 97 recalls the *Heilsgeschichte* tradition of the cult, and those elements of nature that are conspicuous in the theophanic depiction are subordinated finally under the predominant impression, which is created by the cultic reappropriation of the past, that to the eyes of faith Yahweh's theophanic manifestation is ever at base a historical actuality.

The following translation of Ps. 97 is submitted:

The Theophany Itself

1 Yahweh reigns; let the earth rejoice;
let the many coastlands be glad.
2 Clouds and darkness are round about him;
righteousness and justice are the foundation of his throne.
3 A fire goes before him,
and burns up his adversaries round about.
4 His lightnings lighten up the world;
the earth sees and trembles.

5 The mountains melt like wax
at the presence of the Lord of all the earth.[64]
6 The heavens declare his righteousness,
and all the peoples behold his glory.

The Effects of the Theophany

7 All who serve images are shamed,
who boast themselves in things of nought;
all gods bow down before him.
8 Zion hears and is glad,
and the daughters of Judah rejoice,
because of thy judgments, O Yahweh.
9 For thou art most high above all the earth;[65]
thou art exalted far above all gods.
10 O you who love Yahweh, hate evil,
he preserves the lives of his pious,
he delivers them from the hand of the wicked.
11 Light dawns for the righteous,[66]
and gladness for the upright in heart.
12 Be glad in Yahweh, O you righteous,
and give thanks to his holy name!

A form-critical inspection of the psalm leads us at once to pondering its strophic structure. The composition appears to us to possess two strophes each of six verses. In the first, the actuality of Yahweh's advent is portrayed, and in the second, its effects are poetically drawn. More precise analysis, however, necessitates a further divi-

[64] Deleting MT *millipnē Yahweh,* which owing to its closer resemblance to the two words that immediately follow and the absence of tricola in the first strophe support our viewing it as either an inner textual variant or an addition.

[65] Correcting the metrical imbalance of MT, v. 9 by deleting the vocative *Yahweh* which has just previously been employed at the close of v. 8.

[66] Reading, with one Hebrew MS., LXX, Jerome, Syriac, and Targum, *zāraḥ* for MT *zārua'*; the MT emendation is justified by (1) the lack of any Old Testament parallel in which *zr'* and *'ōr* are connected, (2) the combination of *zrḥ* and *'ōr* being elsewhere attested in the Psalter (so Ps. 112:4), (3) the accumulation of textual evidence for this alternate reading, and (4) the felicitous image that *'ōr zāraḥ* creates with respect to its immediate context.

sion of the two strophes themselves which is by no means simple. Any preliminary inclination to discover portions of equal length in the first strophe is thwarted by the content. The proposal of three equal subdivisions of two verses each is unacceptable since the cloud and darkness mentioned in v. 2, as indicators of Yahweh's theophanic presence, are then separated from the fire referred to in v. 3. Moreover, the parallel imagery evident in the trembling of the earth (v. 4) and the melting of the mountains (v. 5) is awkwardly bifurcated. Similarly, any suggestion that we are to discover here two poetic sections of three verses each is useless, for this plays havoc with the parallel imagery of fire in v. 3 and lightning in v. 4.

That the problem has no ready solution is evident from H.-J. Kraus' own indecision in the matter. In *Die Königsherrschaft Gottes im Alten Testament,* he indicated that the first two of four basic parts of the psalm consist of v. 1 alone, with its summons to the praise of Yahweh who has become king, and vs. 2-6, with the theophany,[67] yet in his Psalms commentary a decade later he maintained that vs. 1-2 treat the enthroned king and vs. 3-6 the theophany.[68] Kraus' latter judgment that subdivides the strophe between vs. 2 and 3 is clearly the more agreeable. Its most cogent form-critical support lies in the emphatic and parallel extremities of vs. 1-2. The expression "Yahweh reigns" (*Yahweh mālāḳ*) that introduces the unit is effectively complemented by the phrase "the foundation of his throne" (*mᵉḳōn ḳis'ō*) at the end of v. 2. Thus the testimony of v. 2a, "Clouds and darkness are round about him," refers to the present status of the deity who is enthroned in the cultic theophany and, in addition, as a descriptive element of his theophanic advent, it points to the fuller depiction of his theophany undertaken by vs. 3-6.

In the second strophe, two subdivisions of equal length are discernible; vs. 7-9 record the direct effect of Yahweh's theophany both upon the Gentile world, and upon Zion and the neighboring cities of Judah, and vs. 10-12 contain an address to the Israelite cult. While this division necessitates the assignment of the second-person language of vs. 9-10 to two different strophic subdivisions, this presents

[67] (Tübingen: J. C. B. Mohr, 1951), p. 133. This agrees with Gunkel's strophic analysis, *Die Psalmen,* p. 424.

[68] *Psalmen,* p. 671.

no problem since v. 9 and v. 10 contain different speeches, with the former (singular) addressed to deity and the latter (plural) to Israel. Moreover, our analysis allows the imperatives addressed to the cult in v. 10a and v. 12 to fall within the same unit. In short, we aver that vs. 1-2, 3-6, 7-9, and 10-12, constitute the verse groupings within the two strophes of vs. 1-6 and 7-12.

Then what do the key words suggest in the way of emphasis and movement within the respective strophes? The universal character of Yahweh's enthronement and theophany is plainly stressed in both the initial and concluding cola of the first strophe. The exultation of many coastlands to Yahweh's enthronement, and the nature of the theophany as a divine self-disclosure to all peoples who glimpse Yahweh's glory are the respective assertions of vs. 1b and 6b. In cola slightly more distant from the extremities of the strophe, the righteousness of the one who has come near is testified (cf. vs. 2b and 6a). Several crucial verbs signal the movement and dynamic of Yahweh's appearance itself. They emphasize the coming of the fire (v. 3a), its burning and consuming force (v. 3b), and the ominous worldwide presence of Yahweh's lightning (v. 4a). That theophanic confrontation sets the earth astir is evident through the sequence of verbs employed: "sees . . . trembles . . . melt" (vs. 4b and 5a). The climactic note of the theophany is achieved in the balanced bicolon of v. 6 in which each colon contains the verb, then, the witnessing subject, and finally, the divine aspect.[69]

In the second strophe, we discover that the opening and concluding cola behave differently. Rather than complementing one another they form a contrast. Through Yahweh's judging presence, those who worship graven images are "shamed" (v. 7a), yet the righteous are enjoined to "be glad" (v. 12a) and "give thanks" (v. 12b). Moreover, the emphatic verbal movement in vs. 7-9 is unmistakable. The tricolon in v. 7 conveys the response of the Gentile world that is now threatened, while that in v. 8 portrays the contrasting response of joy on the part of Yahweh's own people. The basic ground for the responses of both the pagan and the faithful, however, is elaborated in v. 9, the verse in which the first climax of the second strophe is reached. Then the last verse unit of the psalm (vs. 10-12) also

[69] Of course in our translation it has seemed advisable to reverse the MT order of subject and verb.

has its conspicuous formal aspects. Three specific exhortations to the cult are separated by three promises that are based upon the efficacious activity of Israel's Lord who has appeared. At either end lie the injunctions consisting of imperative and object: " hate evil " (v. 10a), " be glad in Yahweh " (v. 12a), and " give thanks to his holy name! " (v. 12b). Between the first and second exhortations lie the divine assurance that Yahweh preserves his own (v. 10b), delivers them from the wicked (v. 10c), and has instituted in his coming the signs of his final salvation (v. 11). The second climax of the strophe is thus attained in v. 11 and sustained through v. 12. Finally, it may not be too much to claim for the joint impact created by " Yahweh reigns " in v. 1a and " his holy name " in v. 12b a unifying force that blends two strophes into one hymnic whole in praise of the deity who has made his presence known in cultic theophany.

Again we witness a free development of the theophanic *Gattung*. From first to last we discover here a hymnic *description* of Yahweh's appearance and the effects it evokes. The divine self-asseveration and the injunction against fear are both wanting, and the *hieros logos* is by no means overt. Yahweh's promises are elaborated in vs. 10-11, but we confront no direct first-person formulation. If many of the original components have been cast aside, however, the vivid and majestic quality of Yahweh's theophanic visitation has been retained through the selection and specific ordering of the descriptive elements included within an admittedly dramatic presentation.

A rather full recognition of the formal conditions in Ps. 97 has necessarily oriented us to the content of its message. Portions of the psalm, however, merit closer exegetical study. With the fervent acclamation of Yahweh as king and the invocation for joy that resounds, the psalm is properly marked as a hymn from the start.[70] Since its opening expression does not run full course until the end of v. 2, enthronement and theophanic motifs are clearly united at the outset. The divine rule in its universal dimension is celebrated in terms of its righteousness and justice (cf. Ps. 89:14). The judicial aspects of the theophany which are more fully developed in the sec-

[70] In agreement with Mowinckel, *The Psalms in Israel's Worship,* Vol. 1, p. 109, who maintains: "The enthronement psalms are principally hymns of praise with the usual character of such hymns, and with the free variations occasioned by their special theme."

ond strophe are already anticipated. Shrouded by clouds and darkness, Yahweh is represented in traditional Israelite terms as one who is at once revealed yet mysteriously hidden. The full mystery of divine being is never dissipated. The Israelite cult which celebrates the actuality of theophanic manifestation also knows something about divine concealment.

We would do well to note that in these opening verses Yahweh's enthroned presence is not asserted with some detachment as simple fact. Rather it is sung. Through an invitation addressed to the world at large — even to the distant coastlands — to exult over the actuality of divine reign, Yahweh's presence is affirmed in a *reactio hominum,* in a hymnic response of the witnessing cult to the *actio Dei* that has been achieved through the theophany.[71] The acclamation of Yahweh's invisible but actual presence and his enthronement constitute a cultic response that obviously must be classified as a *present* cultic event. But when is his reign understood to have begun? Through our rendering of *Yahweh mālāḵ* as "Yahweh reigns," we would side with both Kraus and Weiser in asserting that the event that is realized in the cult possesses definite historical ties *and* an eschatological import.[72] If the cult freshly reexperiences his becoming king,[73] this does not deny that Yahweh's kingship is understood by the assembled congregation as existing through the full duration of time itself.[74] Thus we are more impressed with Mowinckel's assertion that the Israelite cult understood the divine nature and activity as dynamic, than by his persistent translation of *Yahweh mlḵ* as "Yahweh has become king." [75] In any event, the composition under discussion would indicate that Yahweh's kingship is freshly realized through the cultic theophany in which both past and future invade upon, and lend significance to, the present.[76]

[71] To employ the terminology of Weiser, *The Psalms,* p. 29.

[72] Cf. Kraus, *Die Königsherrschaft Gottes,* pp. 134 f.; Weiser, *The Psalms,* p. 618.

[73] So Mowinckel, *The Psalms in Israel's Worship,* Vol. 1, p. 115.

[74] See A. R. Johnson, *Sacral Kingship in Ancient Israel,* p. 57, n. 2, and Kraus, *Worship in Israel,* pp. 206 f., who calls attention to Yahweh's "unchangeable and eternal kingship" that is posited in Ps. 93:2.

[75] See *Psalmenstudien II: Das Thronbesteigungsfest Jahwäs und der Ursprung der Eschatologie* (Kristiana: J. Dybwad, 1922), pp. 3 ff.

[76] Kraus, *Die Königsherrschaft Gottes,* p. 135, cogently avers that the eschatological element is not alone a future reality but is also presently actualized: "The final day already sends forth its first rays into the world."

The self-manifestation of Yahweh before the cult is thought to be no less his self-manifestation before all the earth. Through a rich body of imagery in vs. 2-6, the dynamic of Yahweh's theophany is vividly presented as a composite of tempestuous storm and volcanic eruption. Once more the convincing portrayal of the actuality of Yahweh's appearing forcefully overshadows any problem that might emerge from the mixed imagery employed. It is enough for the psalm to convey in no uncertain terms that the presence of Yahweh is received and celebrated by the cult as a felt reality. Yahweh's harbinger is a devouring fire that consumes all inferior enemies. At once the earth is illumined by the lightnings that apparently issue from the approaching nearness of divine visitation. We read of a highly personified mention of the quaking earth which is followed by allusion to the dissolving of the mountains. The most sturdy and ancient parts of the universe are conceived as melting before the sheer power of the presence of one who comes as sovereign over " all the earth " (v. 5). At the very height of the dynamic impact of theophanic presence, witness is made in v. 6 to Yahweh's righteousness, i.e., his judging yet saving purpose, and his glory (*ḳābōd*), the most outstanding theologoumenon at his disposal.

In this strophe, mention of fire (*'ēš*) stands out as a particularly real and an ominous token of active theophanic presence. It has appeared in the two previous psalms under examination (cf. Ps. 18:8, 12; 50:3) and constitutes a conspicuous element in both the J and P accounts of the Sinaitic theophany (cf. Ex. 19:18 and 24:17 respectively). The dreadful character of this holy fire is effectively depicted in v. 3b. Its devouring spells the undoing of Yahweh's opponents. Here the Sinaitic image enjoys an extension. True, on the grounds of v. 3 alone we could not effectively argue that the Sinaitic event is being recalled, but in light of the combined evidence of vs. 2 and 4 that surrounds it, this assertion seems warranted. In v. 2a the enthronement of the deity is portrayed in part by a phraseology that recalls the dynamic of Yahweh's theophanic presence on Sinai: " clouds and darkness are round about him." The " cloud " (*'ānān*) is employed by all three strata in their depiction of the Sinaitic theophany (cf. Ex. 19:9, J; 19:16, E; and 24:15-16, 18, P), and E also mentions the darkness (*'ᵃrāpel*) in Ex. 20:21. As the deity was once enthroned upon Mt. Sinai in awful majesty, so in the present cultic moment he is depicted as invisibly enthroned as judge over all the world. Moreover, in v. 4 both the J and E Sinaitic accounts may also be reflected. Allusion to Yahweh's lightnings here recalls the Elohist's mention of the phenomenon as one of the accompaniments of divine presence (cf. Ex. 19:16 with the same Hebrew noun and ch. 20:18 with its synonym). Then the trembling of the earth, as if writhing in the pangs of labor, intensifies the mention of the quaking of the mountain in Ex. 19:18 in the Yahwist's account. In v. 5 the mountains are not said to shake but to dissolve before the awful impingement of divine presence.

Again there is an intensification of the earlier Sinaitic portrayal. Thus the motifs of Sinai are not only recollected but are sharpened and expanded. We are not to conclude, however, that a deliberate exaggeration of earlier traditions was undertaken by the cult for the sheer purpose of arriving at a more dynamic portrayal that might dwarf the significance of the former, as if to suggest that the older traditions of Yahweh's theophany have been replaced by a new and improved rendition. Rather the intensification is suitable to the specific *purpose* of the cultic theophany, for in the present passage it is not Israel alone but *all peoples* who are imagined as witnesses to Yahweh's theophanic presence. To them is granted the perception of his glory.

Yet more must be affirmed with respect to the overall theophanic purpose and effect of Ps. 97 which are best ascertained from a direct inspection of and reflection upon the second strophe. According to v. 7, theophanic presence has broken the power of the heathen and wrought the defeat and near annihilation of its gods. To be sure, no divine combat is presented. Rather, Yahweh's sheer presence evokes the downfall of pagan deities wherein they appear utterly contemptible; Yahweh's august theophanic disclosure claims their acknowledgment of his sovereignty, and produces an authentic sense of shame in those who trust in the worship of images which are predicated here as "things of nought," as "mere nothings."[77] Although it is pre-

[77] Our understanding of the *'ᵉlīlīm,* "things of nought," concurs with that of von Rad (*Old Testament Theology,* Vol. 1, p. 212, n. 49) and Weiser (*The Psalms,* pp. 629, 634). Their existence is not truly repudiated, but their despicable character is emphatically affirmed.

sented as both, the sum of the effects in v. 7 is perhaps less forcefully registered as divine triumph than as a divine *judgment* of world significance. In response to both Yahweh's appearing per se and the judgment divinely wrought, the cultic congregation assembled in Zion breaks into joy and the *reactio hominum* is widened to include the exultation of the cities of Judah. The festive joy that sweeps over the cult comes in full knowledge that Yahweh's righteous judgments are implied by his appearance and enthronement. Thus through the hymnic cry of the cult, the affirmation reverberates that Yahweh is exalted "above all the earth" (v. 9a) and "far above all gods" (v. 9b). As vs. 7-9 speak as a whole, then, to the effects of theophanic presence, they affirm that just as all people have beheld the glory of Yahweh in his theophany in the cultic event where present and future merge, all are now convinced either to their undoing or to their sublime satisfaction and joy that Yahweh in his dynamic and energetic theophanic act has shown himself to be absolutely supreme.

The second major effect of Yahweh's appearing relates to the speech that is addressed to the celebrating congregation assembled on Zion's holy hill. This theophany of Yahweh evokes words of obligation and promise that issue within the cultic framework. Those who belong to Yahweh are referred to by four designations — as those who love Yahweh (v. 10a), are pious (v. 10b), are righteous (v. 11a), and as those whose conscious intent is upright (v. 11b). Weiser rightly reads in the first "the motive power that leads to moral obedience to his [Yahweh's] commandments," [78] and in the remaining three we may discern the effective adherence to the law by those who are so designated. Thus the impingement of Yahweh's theophanic presence requires a rigorous aversion of all that is antithetical to his purposes. Those who love Yahweh are directly confronted by the exhortation to hate evil. There is further counsel in v. 11 in behalf of righteousness and obedience. To those in whom these are exemplified is promised the full realization of the light of salvation that dawns in Yahweh's present theophany, and in them is planted the hope of his coming again into the concreteness of their history.[79]

[78] *The Psalms,* p. 635.

[79] The dominant historical tenor of this and other Old Testament theophanies

In sum, Ps. 97 permits the conclusion that through theophanic meeting, several of Yahweh's purposes are served. He has come that his glory (*ḳābōd*) might be manifested to all people, that his sovereignty might be asserted, his commandments made vivid, and his promise for salvation renewed.

Conclusion

If we have fulfilled our commitment to examine three lengthy and conspicuously theophanic passages that have found their way into The Book of Psalms, the subject of theophany and Psalter has not been and cannot be exhausted here. Some excellent material has gone unexplored. Theophanic representation in Ps. 29 emphasizes the role of Yahweh's voice and does so with considerable excitement. Portions of Ps. 68 depict Yahweh as manifested in theophanic meeting before the exultant assembly. Moreover, in Ps. 81 the integral relation between theophany and law, between divine self-manifestation and the word that places Israel under divine judgment, is writ large. The list could be extended. Instead, we shall issue a brief concluding word that is insufficient in itself yet is buttressed to some extent by the brief chapter that follows.

Granting the limits of our investigation, we have discovered that the theophany as it is represented in the Psalter confirms our previous definition of Old Testament theophany, yet it stands in a unique position through its partiality for metaphor and elaborate description, and by its persistent and free development away from a theophanic *Gattung* strictly understood. Moreover, the wondrous, even terrifying, aspect of the deity's theophanic intervention, the command of his compelling sovereignty, and the manifestation of his action in nature and history as intervening judge and deliverer that recalls the full range of the ancient theophany on Sinai are all testified with unusual eloquence and theological stimulus.

---

cannot be overemphasized. Westermann, *The Praise of God in the Psalms,* p. 96, rightly regards this as the unique feature of Israelite theophanies: "In the place of a cosmic-mythical occurrence in the Babylonian epiphanies there is in the O.T. a historical one: Yahweh appears in order to help his people and to destroy his foes."

CHAPTER VII

The Theophany as Cultic Experience

All three compositions that we have just investigated, several theophanic psalms that we have not, the account of the Temple call to Isaiah of Jerusalem, and the various testimonies to the Sinaitic theophany in Ex., chs. 19 to 24, alike bear incontestable marks of individuality. At the same time, they all relate to the Israelite cult in one way or another. At the outset of our investigation of the Sinaitic theophany in Chapter III, we acknowledged that the language there employed to depict this divine revelation par excellence had undergone a conventionalization through cultic usage, and recognized the inevitable refraction and reworking of historical tradition within the cult. We have also had rather ample occasion in the preceding chapter to link the theophany to the Israelite cult. It is fitting, then, that as a final consideration we deal somewhat further, although not at unwarranted length, with the nature of theophany in the Old Testament as cultic experience. While this concluding investigation will not permit our linking all previous considerations into a comprehensive whole,[1] it will promote the unification of a number of issues.

[1] For example, the patriarchal theophanic narratives that assume a quite conspicuous position in The Book of Genesis appear essentially to stand outside the range of interests to be embraced by the present chapter. To be sure, the convincing treatment of patriarch and cult within Arvid S. Kapelrud's essay, "The Role of the Cult in Old Israel," *The Bible in Modern Scholarship,* ed. by J. Philip Hyatt (Abingdon Press, 1965), pp. 44–56, and to a lesser extent our own approach in Chapter IV, show that patriarchal theophanic episodes are certainly not anticultic, but are in fact precisely the opposite. Even so, these narratives seem to relate to a different element

Certain dangers attend such an undertaking. Since specific definitions and interpretations of "cult" vary according to the predilections of their authors, we must necessarily deal with admittedly ambiguous considerations. Moreover, we have rather slight tangible evidence upon which to draw. Indirect allusions to the cultic proceedings outnumber the direct. Thus we may understandably have reservations about Weiser's portrayal of the cult-theophanic drama on the basis of incomplete allusions that undoubtedly were rich with meaning for the Israelite worshipers participating in the enterprise of the cult, but may very well mislead the present-day exegete or dull his sensitivity. On the whole, Weiser's presentation impresses us as one that sets forth exciting and compelling solutions, but on occasion he is admittedly bold in pushing a single theophanic reference to the extreme. For example, on the witness of Ps. 68:11a, "the Lord gives the command," Weiser enters into a lengthy discussion which begins, "That Yahweh speaks with a loud voice is also a permanent feature of the tradition of the theophany . . . , so that the brief allusion of v. 11 is to be understood as reflecting the cultic epiphany." [2] He links that verse with Ps. 29:3 and suggests that the psalmist here was reflecting upon the divine voice as resembling the sound of thunder. While the testimony of Ps. 68:33b, "lo, he sends forth his voice, a mighty voice," confirms this possibility, a certain lack of caution is evident. Moreover, upon asserting that Ps. 68 as a theophanic psalm is but "a reflex of the cultic drama of salvation of which it forms an intrinsic part," [3] Weiser rather freely posits the character of that drama. If we do not know all the rubrics of the liturgy involved in the theophany, then extreme caution must be exercised in interpreting the cultic event. We believe that Weiser is correct in maintaining that "scanty intimations" alone could lead the mind of the ancient to recall an entire panorama of cultic drama,[4] yet that does not take

within the total Israelite structure of faith than do many other Old Testament theophanic traditions that both reflect a vivid memory of the Sinaitic theophany and display in an overt manner vital cultic terminology.

[2] From *The Psalms,* p. 486.

[3] *Ibid.,* p. 483.

[4] *Ibid.,* p. 488, n. 1; "Zur Frage nach den Beziehungen der Psalmen zum Kult: Die Darstellung der Theophanie in den Psalmen und im Festkult," *Bertholet-Festschrift,* p. 523.

away from us some genuine disappointment that he neither raises nor answers the question concerning the criteria that may be employed by the modern critic in his interpretive tasks that will ensure that his own thinking does not run off track.

If Helmer Ringgren, who follows Weiser on this matter, avers that little is required for the cultic representation of a "mythological" event,[5] our reply must be that the critic should take pains not to foster its *misrepresentation*.[6] If for no other reason, caution must be urged since our modern perspective separates itself radically from that of the ancient world. Thus it is always difficult to ascertain the exact function that a given composition in the Psalter assumed in the Israelite cult, and Muilenburg rightly judges this to be our "grievous loss."[7] On the other hand, the theophany within the Old Testament, and especially in the Psalter, displays a vitality that points to a colorful and living actuality within the cult, and this justifiably touches both our analytical minds and our imaginations.[8] For the sake of

[5] *The Faith of the Psalmists* (Fortress Press, 1963), p. 2.

[6] Weiser himself admits that the specific rubrics which governed the cultic theophany are not readily discernible. In "Zur Frage nach den Beziehungen," p. 524, he writes, "The fact that the theophanic descriptions of the psalms appear in totally different hymnic forms (*Liedgattungen*) and the fact that throughout, the theophany is asserted and presupposed as the *actio dei,* prohibits our seeing in these psalms the particular ritual of the theophany in the *Festkult*." Kraus, *Psalmen,* p. 145, is more negative. He avers that the Old Testament sources do not enable us to trace exactly the actual proceedings of the Israelite cult, and that the notion of a dramatically represented theophany is to be regarded only as an experiment. He adds: "Nevertheless the question must be raised: How should such a representation of the theophany have been accomplished? Is it thinkable that Israel allowed herself to be carried away in the cult with manifestations possessing some actual form?" It is his suggestion that the theophany of Yahweh should be related to the procession of the Ark of the Covenant in a Royal Festival on Mt. Zion "in the style of a kerygmatic proclamation" that would signal divine coming and appearance. In *Worship in Israel,* p. 216, Kraus argues, "When we try to decide how to picture this event to ourselves, and how and where a divine manifestation was perceived, if we are not to let our imagination run away with us we must restrict ourselves to those passages in which an actual theophany is described." After alluding to I Kings 22:19-20; Isa., ch. 6; and Ps. 50, he states that even within a cultic *Sitz,* theophany ought not be interpreted by the modern critic as anything other than "prophetic visionary perception." While recognizing the value of some restraint, our present chapter obviously attempts to speak against the full necessity of such conservatism.

[7] *The Way of Israel,* p. 110.

[8] If Weiser's approach to the issues that center upon theophany and cult is, as

clarity, our comments here will be presented under three headings — basic assertions on the cult relative to a study of Biblical theophany, indications of the essential character of the cultic theophany, and the significance of the theophany of Yahweh for the Israelite cult.

Basic Assertions on the Cult Relative to a Study of Biblical Theophany

First, how is the cult as such to be understood? Certainly it is not to be seen in a vacuum.[9] Cultic enterprises do not stand at some distance from Israelite life and thought and from that vantage point

we have already observed, sometimes radical, it is expounded in an extremely thorough and consistent manner. Moreover, his student, Walter Beyerlin, in his able study, *Origins and History of the Oldest Sinaitic Traditions,* pp. 133–143, endorses the ensuing methodology and outcome with some rigor. Both scholars have been challenged rather recently, however, by Hans-Peter Müller in his article, "Die kultische Darstellung der Theophanie," *VT,* Vol. 14 (1964), pp. 183–191. Müller does not discover in Ex., chs. 19 to 24, the lucid cultic representation that Weiser and Beyerlin assume. His own approach is to relate Old Testament theophany to the Israelite institution of Holy War and to discern in Josh., ch. 6; Judg. 7:16-22; and I Sam. 4:4-8 a more authentic cultic representation of the theophany. He observes (p. 188) that (1) the shout (*t^erû'â*) of the congregation is an original element in all three passages, (2) a later tradition of the *šôpār* blast has been added to Josh., ch. 6, and Judg., ch. 7, (3) a stratum of Josh., ch. 6, and I Sam., ch. 4, witness to the prominence of the Ark of the Covenant, and (4) all three pericopes attest that the "fear of God" is induced in the ranks of the enemy. He argues (p. 191) that these Old Testament passages present important clues for properly discovering the ritualistic representation of the Sinaitic theophany within the amphictyonic cult.

Moreover, in maintaining (p. 191) that the cultic representation of the deity in the Holy War is not repeated at regular intervals, not geared to the maintenance and renewal of any major Israelite institution (such as the covenant), and not dedicated to a re-presentation (*Vergegenwärtigung*) of an original past experience of salvation, Müller presents quite a different understanding of theophany as cultic experience. We are not confident, however, that this is an especially viable solution to the problem. Müller's discussion is dependent upon a new set of passages which he believes are undisputedly theophanic in character, yet we have not treated a single one of them in our discussion thus far. To be sure, their theophanic nature is not to be outrightly denied; still, we have not been sufficiently convinced of their centrality to include them in our study. Consequently, direct communication with Müller's article appears here to be neither advisable nor even possible.

[9] In this connection the assertion of Martin J. Buss, "The Meaning of 'Cult' and the Interpretation of the Old Testament," *JBR,* Vol. 32 (1964), p. 318, rings clear: "The role of the cult can be no more understood by isolated observation than the role of a king can be described without reference to the rest of society."

offer some assessment; rather they are an integral part of Israelite life and thought. As far as a definition of cult is concerned, we have no favorite, although many have been set forth. If that offered by Gottfried Quell is terse, it is not erroneous: "Cult is the material form of expression and the social organization of religious experience."[10] As such, the Israelite cult should be appreciated as a relational entity. In this connection Martin J. Buss insists that "the concept of cult . . . provides a way in which one can recognize the nature of Israelite reality as a structure of existence."[11] It presents us with a complex yet meaningful pattern of phenomena and data that relates the participant effectively to the very object of worship. Accordingly, in their statements on the cult, both Mowinckel[12] and Vriezen[13] refer to the integration of the communion and/or communication between Yahweh and people that the cult exists to achieve. As it points up the operational character of religious life, the cult is geared to retain and prosper what is essential in the encounter between Yahweh and Israel, and this necessarily involves, on the one hand, the communication of the name, nature, and will of the deity, and on the other, the hymnic and faithful response of the people to the deity who has so revealed himself. Both the *actio Dei* and the *reactio hominum* are involved, and we would aver that both are subsumed by Israel under the form of the cultic theophany.

If this is, briefly stated, the manner in which we understand the nature of the cult, a second remark concerns the importance of recognizing the *centrality* of the cult in ancient Israel, and of acknowledging the usefulness of the cult-functional approach with respect to the hymnic possessions of the cult. Cultic events were not insignificant acts taking place in the Temple before a disinterested assembly. The cult was not a mere adjunct to the life of the people, and the very locale in which cultic proceedings transpired was not taken

[10] From "Das kultische Problem der Psalmen," *BWAT*, Neue Folge, Heft 11 (1926), p. 44. A useful and more elaborate defining of the cult has been undertaken by Mowinckel, *Religion und Kultus*, pp. 10–13. See also Mowinckel, *The Psalms in Israel's Worship*, Vol. 1, p. 16, and Kapelrud, "The Role of the Cult," p. 45, for the latter's reaction to Mowinckel as well as some suggestions of his own.

[11] From *loc. cit.*, p. 317.

[12] *The Psalms in Israel's Worship*, Vol. 1, p. 15.

[13] *An Outline of Old Testament Theology*, pp. 280 f.

lightly. Rather, as the locus of the cult, the Temple was the place where events of genuine significance concerning the deity and his elect took place.[14] Hebrew man repaired to the sanctuary in order to enter into sacred meeting, to stand in the presence of the Holy One of Israel. Ringgren rightly sets forth a clear notion of what the sanctuary meant to the loyal Yahwist when he declares, "there he met God, seeing him in his power and glory."[15] The study of theophany is most relevant in this very context, for in such cultic meeting, the encounter between God and man, between Yahweh and people, occurred. The *hieros logos* was enunciated, and the decisive soteriological and judicial acts of the deity were conducted. Whatever might have been the partially stereotyped forms that obtained, Yahweh's theophanic presence in cultic meeting was a dynamic presence that was confronted in both awe and trembling, on the one hand, and in exultation and enthusiasm, on the other.

Finally, through the speaking that took place in the cult, past event underwent a re-presentation (*Vergegenwärtigung*) for the present generation. The memorable events of the past, and more important, the memorable divine speeches with their climax in the self-asseveration, invaded upon the present and effected the future.[16] In this connection Muilenburg cogently maintains, "It is the function of the cult to bring past events and future events into the immediacy of the present hour by the vitality of the spoken words."[17] No example of this merger of chronologically diverse moments was more instructive than the reappropriation of the Sinaitic event for the contemporary congregation. Through the Sinaitic traditions maintained by the cult, the self-disclosure that was granted to the ancestors at the foot of the holy mount was accorded to the people presently assembled for cultic meeting. Thus intrinsically the theophanic Sinaitic tradi-

[14] The discussion by Arvid S. Kapelrud, "Cult and Prophetic Words," *Studia Theologica,* Vol. 4 (1951), p. 9, is useful here.

[15] From *The Faith of the Psalmists,* p. 2; cf. also *Israelite Religion,* pp. 153–155, 163 f.; and Kraus, *Worship in Israel,* pp. 209 f.

[16] Cf. Kapelrud, "The Role of the Cult," p. 49; Mowinckel, *Psalmenstudien II,* p. 21, and *Religion und Kultus,* p. 79; and G. E. Wright, "Cult and History: A Study of a Current Problem in Old Testament Interpretation," *Interpretation,* Vol. 16 (1962), p. 14.

[17] From *The Way of Israel,* p. 32.

tions of the Yahwist and Elohist had no special interest in narrative, in history as such, but in the appropriation of the saving events for a later generation.[18] This was notably achieved through the words spoken in the cult with the deliberate change of tenses between the perfect, that looked back upon an event as completed in the past, and the imperfect, that represented the same event as still projected into the present.[19] In this manner, through the re-presentation that took place in the Israelite cult, the cultic event in question was not merely similar to its antecedent; it *was* that event. The present congregation assembled in cultic meeting shared in the same theophanic occurrence as had its predecessors. Because this was the case, Yahweh was concomitantly affirmed in the cult to be the God of Sinai and the Holy One intimately present within contemporary Israel.[20]

Indications of the Essential Character of the Cultic Theophany

The emphasis must fall upon the first word of this heading, for at best we have only a series of inferences concerning the manner in which the cultic theophany was conducted. From an aggregation of theophanic passages both within and outside The Book of Psalms that clearly manifest a cultic character, however, it is indeed possible for us to posit a few statements with respect to the unfolding of the theophany before the congregation assembled in cultic meeting.

At the outset, we would do well to acknowledge the *place* of cultic meeting. Although we have no reason to restrict the cultic appropriation of divine self-revelation to the Jerusalem Temple alone, the situation is more amply represented in conjunction with that important edifice. It is there that we may become best acquainted with theophany as cultic experience. The Temple presented itself to the Israelite worshiper as the locus of historical reflection, contemporary blessing, and future hope. During the annual festivals that were conducted within its sacred precincts, the founding of the covenant between God and people was recalled, the effective dominion of the

[18] See Beyerlin, *op. cit.*, pp. 168 f.

[19] See Weiser, "Zur Frage nach den Beziehungen," pp. 515 f. This view, however, has been all too briefly challenged by Jeremias, *Theophanie*, p. 121, n. 1.

[20] Clements, *God and Temple*, p. 22.

deity over the entire created order was affirmed, and the self-awareness and destiny of nation and individual alike were grasped with greater understanding. That this highly meaningful reflection could be actualized in drama and word at all depended upon one particular tenet of faith that was tenaciously held by the individual Israelite — *Yahweh was truly present in the Temple.* In the following paragraph, R. E. Clements speaks incisively to this very issue:

> The entire ideology of the Jerusalem temple centred in the belief that, as his chosen dwelling-place, Yahweh's presence was to be found in it, and that from there he revealed his will and poured out his blessing upon his people. When we press to find out how this presence was conceived, we find that it was dominated by the idea of Yahweh as the God of the exodus and Mount Sinai.[21]

As we have already maintained with respect to Ps. 50, Mt. Zion had become the new Sinai and it was here especially that God and man could enter into effective meeting, that the divine and human could engage in authentic confrontation by means of a theophany drawn along obviously cultic lines.

If we thus affirm that there is a particular place for cultic theophanic meeting, are we permitted to take the next logical step and speak of a particular *time* of meeting? Any proposal to the effect that Israel knew *only* one moment in her annual festival calendar in which Yahweh's presence could be effectively made known and truly felt within the cult must be labeled as dubious. Israelite sensitivities were loath to imply that even one religious festival existed in Israel in which human attendance was matched by divine absence. Yahweh's visitation was affirmed at every Jerusalem festival. Moreover, in those lesser moments that filled the time *between* the major festivals, Yahweh's effective presence was also felt. The offerings of the people did not rot upon the altar during drawn out periods of time that existed as grim preludes anticipating eventual divine presence. Rather it was held that Yahweh was as regular in visiting the Temple in order to accept the offerings of his people as were the latter in presenting them. Indeed, cultic ritual may have been a daily affair.[22]

[21] *Ibid.*, p. 76.

[22] Cf. Buss, *loc. cit.*, p. 319, and Ringgren, *Israelite Religion*, p. 185.

Such observations cannot persuade us into thinking of theophany in the cult as only an annual event. Nevertheless, it is quite possible that during the span of the cultic year in Israel, one moment above all others may have been respected as capable of laying bare Yahweh's theophanic presence in a special way. Due to its concern for the covenant relationship between God and people and its interest in recalling the past crucial experience on Mt. Sinai, it is most likely that this special moment coincides with the annual Festival of Tabernacles which, with its historical reflection and projection of future hope, inaugurated the new year. On this occasion, divine kingship, presence, and judgment were all affirmed within the context of an ongoing covenant reality. Theophanic actuality and covenant renewal existed as two sides of the same coin. Consequently Yahweh confronted Israel in the present just as he had confronted her in the past. In fact it would be more accurate to suggest that past and present became indistinguishable realities.

Now that we have posited the preceding comment on time and place, it would be pleasant indeed if we could set forth the actual proceedings of theophanic actualization within the cult and do so on the basis of sturdy epigraphic testimony. Unfortunately no document, Biblical or otherwise, has yet been discovered that provides the Israelite analogue with the Akitu Festival at Uruk and the Babylonian New Year Festival with its specific instructions for the actual conduct of cultic proceedings. This admittedly dismal state of affairs is explained by Weiser as the result of a solely oral tradition that was handed down from one generation of priests to the next.[23] Then if instructions never achieved a written state, may they be inferred through a close scrutiny of Israelite literature, especially The Book of Psalms, that has made its home in the Israelite cult? Weiser, who confronts this question in the context of the Covenant Festival of Yahweh which he projects at length, comes forth with a rigorous affirmative reply. He believes that the fundamental elements and concepts attending such a celebration and even the basic order of the cultic proceedings can be apprehended with some assurance.[24] Although as Weiser points out, the liturgy of such a composition as

[23] *The Psalms*, p. 35.
[24] *Ibid.*, pp. 28 ff.

Ps. 50 is remarkably transparent,[25] we are not confident that he persistently walks on sure ground as he posits the details of the cultic program involved.

As we now move to a more direct analysis of the indications of the essential character of the cultic theophany within Israel, we shall acknowledge our debt to Weiser and at the same time state that we prefer to take a more conservative, although we trust not unexciting, position and speak in turn of cultic *apparatus* and cultic *articulation*. The former term has to do with the Temple equipment that was utilized in the cultic theophany, and the latter with particular words that are spoken authoritatively in the name of the deity. The two most important objects appear to be the Ark of the Covenant upon which Yahweh is conceived as invisibly enthroned, and the horn (*šōpār*) which represents the divine voice. They respectively stand as the crucial visual and audible element for signaling divine nearness.

Like any other material property belonging to the Israelite cult, the Ark was in no way regarded as sheer material representation of the deity, for that would have run counter to the fundamental Hebrew conception of Yahweh. Images of the deity were outrightly prohibited in Israel. Even so, cultic equipment such as the Ark was valued as having the capacity to *symbolize* divine nearness. Thus the Ark possessed an imaginative connection with invisible divine presence. That cultic apparatus was housed in the *d^{e}bīr,* the Holy of Holies, of the Temple. In Phoenician and Assyrian temples, the manufactured image of the god in question was located in this especially sacrosanct area.[26] The *d^{e}bīr* of the Jerusalem Temple, however, contained only the Ark and the cherubim. It did not presume to foster within the cultic mentality a simple materialistic view of deity.

Israel's sacred Ark is clearly to be appreciated as an implement that existed in a functional relation to the theophany, for it was understood as the throne of Yahweh who in his divine sovereignty confronted Israel with his real but invisible presence. Although many scholars in recent years have interpreted the Ark as the divine throne,[27] this approach has not gone unquestioned. Thus Clements

[25] *Ibid.,* pp. 35 f.

[26] Cf. Clements, *op. cit.,* p. 64.

[27] So Noth, *The History of Israel,* p. 91 and n. 1; Eichrodt, *Theology of the*

has argued that divine presence was thought to be more intimately connected with the *kappōret* or mercy seat atop the Ark between flanking cherubim than with the Ark itself. He has pointed out, as others have before him, that the name itself, *'ārōn,* implies " box," not " throne," and that it is the cherubim who make up the cloud-chariot of the deity that truly symbolize the divine presence.[28] He does admit, however, that as a container of the tablets of law, the Ark may have been considered as " a pedestal for the invisible deity who guarded the covenant-law at his feet." [29] Thus the Ark could have been thought of as the divine *footstool.* This is indeed borne out by Ps. 99:5; 132:7; Lam. 2:1; and I Chron. 28:2.[30]

It seems rather doubtful, however, that every worshiper in the Temple would have made a clear distinction in his own thinking between the divine enthronement *upon* the Ark and enthronement *over* (meaning " above ") the Ark. Moreover, Clements himself appears to be less precise at a later point in his study in his assertion, " When Yahweh came to be with his people he was believed to appear over the ark." [31] Indeed, for our own purposes, it may be enough to suggest that the Ark of the Covenant is clearly *associated* with actual but invisible divine enthronement, and as such is to be appreciated as a vital apparatus of the Temple for depicting the cultic theophany.

A number of traditions closely link the deity with the Ark. It was in conjunction with the Ark that Yahweh dwelt with his people in their sojourn (e.g., Num. 10:33), in war (e.g., Num. 10:35-36; Josh. 6:4 ff.), and in their cultic worship (e.g., II Sam. 6:2; Ps. 68:1). Through the verb *yšb,* meaning among other things, " to sit, dwell," Yahweh was designated as one invisibly enthroned over the cherub-throne. And the cherubim themselves served a dual purpose in transporting Yahweh to the sanctuary for cultic meeting and in protecting him from the inroads of curious and gaping human inspection.[32]

Old Testament, Vol. 1, p. 108; and de Vaux, *Ancient Israel: Its Life and Institutions,* p. 301.

[28] *Op. cit.,* pp. 30 f.

[29] *Ibid.,* p. 35.

[30] Cf. Weiser, " Zur Frage nach den Beziehungen," p. 522.

[31] From *op. cit.,* p. 63.

[32] Cf. Weiser, " Zur Frage nach den Beziehungen," pp. 520–522.

The one who dwelt upon Sinai, the site of his former residence, was also present over the cherub-throne. Moreover, in the Psalter's six attestations of " Arise, O Yahweh " (Ps. 3:7; 7:6; 9:19; 10:12; 17:13; and 132:8), which were employed in the cultic invocation of Yahweh's presence, we may discern further evidence of the intimate connection of Yahweh and the Ark.[33] Nor is it improbable that in the invocation that Yahweh " shine forth " (*hōpīʿā* in Ps. 80:1 and 94:1), the deity is also understood as the one enthroned over the Ark of the Covenant for the theophany.

Thus the Ark assumes a central role in cultic theophany. One further consideration requires mention. The contemporary practical mind might feel itself constrained to establish a sure distinction between divine presence and divine visitation. That such an invocation to the deity as " shine forth " was uttered by the assembled cult might suggest that Yahweh was conceived as present in the Temple *only* after such a cry had been divinely heard. It follows that at other moments, Yahweh would be thought of as absent from the Jerusalem edifice. If Yahweh were to come down to visit his people within the Temple, then he would have to enter from somewhere else. The ancient Hebrew, however, did not think in such fashion. He discerned no tension in his dual affirmation of *permanent* divine presence within the Temple which was creatively symbolized by enduring cultic objects and *temporary* divine presence that was felt during the course of time-bound theophanic meeting. The permanent attachment of the Ark of the Covenant to the Jerusalem Temple fostered an affirmation of continual divine presence, yet in the context of particular worship experiences that transpired in the Temple, Yahweh was thought to come to his people and favor them with a quite momentary disclosure of himself. For the Hebrew it was clearly a case of both-and, not either-or. And obviously the Ark stood at the center of such affirmations.

Before we pass over to the audible apparatus, a recognition of the cloud of smoke that was very likely part of the visual mechanism of the cultic theophany is in order. Yahweh's concealment in the cloud upon Sinai presents itself as an emphatic element in the J (Ex. 19:9,

[33] See the Song of the Ark, Num. 10:35-36, and Ps. 68:1 with its expression, " Let God arise . . . ."

18), E (Ex. 19:16; 20:18-19), and P (Ex. 24:15, 16, 18) narratives alike. In order to explain this feature, Beyerlin refers to the use of smoke in the theophany transpiring in the Israelite cult and calls attention to Lev. 16:12-13 which mentions the "censer pan full of coals of fire" that belong to Yahweh's sanctuary.[34] These verses along with v. 2 of Lev., ch. 16, introduce within the same cultic setting both the thought of real divine presence and the possibility of mortal extinction that may result from too close an association with that presence. This representation of the cloud of smoke assured that Yahweh would be thought to remain hidden from the encroachment of mortal gaze. Moreover, the sheer ubiquity of references to fire and smoke in conjunction with the cultic theophany would further argue for the actuality of this visual theophanic element.[35]

Equally striking in the theophany taking place in the cult is the blowing of the horn (*šōpār*) which as Israel's primary signaling instrument could readily function as the veritable indicator of the voice of the deity who had drawn near in cultic meeting.[36] Among the various accompanying phenomena cited in the Sinaitic narratives, it is the *šōpār* that is uniquely, and somewhat problematically, connected with the antiphon that takes place between Mosaic speech and Yahweh's voice in thunder. On the basis of the evidence presented by II Sam. 6:15; Ps. 47:5; 81:3; and 98:6, it is clear that the *šōpār* is comprehended not as that which answers the deity, but rather as the divine voice itself. Thus an audible sign resounded for all who attended the cultic theophany to hear, and thereby came the assurance that the deity who had spoken to Israel in the thunder at Sinai continued to speak in cultic theophanic meeting.

Yet just as the sound of thunder and imputed *šōpār* on Sinai represented inarticulate noise that was joined by meaningful divine speech which was addressed to Moses in a special manner and mediated by him to the people, so too, in the cultic theophany, there were particular words constituting the *hieros logos* that were imparted by a cultic prophet who acted as a mediator between God and people.

[34] *Op. cit.*, pp. 134 f. See also Weiser, "Zur Frage nach den Beziehungen," p. 523.

[35] Both occur, for example, in each of the three extensive theophanic passages from the Psalter examined in the previous chapter.

[36] See E. Werner, "Musical Instruments," *IDB*, Vol. 3, p. 473, who writes also of its aptness in making noise although not music.

Thus the cultic theophany is also to be considered as incorporating concrete and particular *articulation*. It was more than a matter of audible and visual pageantry. Although the apparatus just examined were valued as meaningful instruments that served the cultic theophany in their own way, the proclamation of the divine name, nature, and will was also understood as an absolutely essential component to the theophany that was experienced within the Israelite cult.

Of crucial importance in the cultic theophany was the deity's identification of himself as he drew near for self-revelation before his assembled people. Through the self-asseveration, the divine name (*šēm*) was proclaimed. Since its centrality in the Sinaitic theophany (Ex. 20:2) has already been considered in some detail, we may more suitably refer here to the use of the divine name within the Psalter especially as it relates to Yahweh's theophanic visitation. Whatever else it may have accomplished, thought or explicit mention of, the divine name in the Israelite cult assured that divine presence and saving strength were not simply the objects of empty hope.[37] The individual worshiper might entreat the deity by saying, " O God, by thy name deliver me, / and by thy might vindicate me " (Ps. 54:1), and the cult as a corporate body might solemnly affirm, " Our help is in the name of Yahweh, / who made the heavens and the earth " (Ps. 124:8). Yahweh's people regarded the name as both a guarantee and an instrument of salvation (cf. Ps. 20:1; 23:3; 25:11; 75:1; 83:16; and 143:11). In the cultic theophany per se, the name that was offered in the form of a divine self-asseveration (cf. " Be still, and know that I am God " in Ps. 46:10; " Yahweh, your God, am I " in Ps. 50:7; and " I am Yahweh your God " in Ps. 81:10) marked the very climax of divine encounter. As such this was no magical exercise. Rather, Israel knew from her history that Yahweh had previously given himself to her through the announcement of his name, that he chose not to keep that name a secret. Israel had already experienced Yahweh's communication of his name in the glorious theophany on Sinai (Ex. 20:2), and thereby she had been moved by the immediacy of the divine confrontation. Hence, in the reappropriation of that experience through cultic liturgy, in the re-presentation of that climactic moment of her history in which God had made his presence directly

[37] See Eichrodt, *Theologie des Alten Testaments,* Teil 2/3, p. 21.

known, the name of the deity confronted the cult as a recurring reality through which Yahweh's presence was affirmed as truly actualized.

The divine self-disclosure in the cult, however, did not limit itself to the utterance of the name. Something of the divine nature, through reference to his saving deeds, and something of his will, through the proclamation of concrete commands and exhortations, were also conveyed. Had these been lacking, Yahweh's self-revelation would have been quite incomplete. In a real sense, these elements interpreted the *meaning* of the name for Israel. Especially in our study of Ps. 50 we have had an opportunity to discern these items within the cultic theophany and to observe that they make unmistakable the divine presence in its instructing, purging, and judging aspects. In this context of cultic theophany, the will of the deity might be proclaimed in words reminiscent of the Decalogue. Unswerving loyalty to Yahweh was enjoined. Foreign gods were to be put away. Yet the dynamic expression of the divine will also verged upon judgment, as may be noted from Ps. 50:16 ff. where the wicked are rebuked. Moreover, in Ps. 68:1-3 an emphatic distinction is made between the righteous and the wicked. Thus Yahweh's theophanic presence was an effective presence that brought about the defeat of all that was antithetical to divine purpose and it evoked from the pious a response of gladness and thanksgiving.

THE SIGNIFICANCE OF THE THEOPHANY OF YAHWEH FOR THE ISRAELITE CULT

As is the case with many of its other aspects, our knowledge of the Israelite cult with its unusual interest in the theophany of Yahweh is admittedly limited. A sure awareness of the specific acts that were executed in the cultic appropriation of the theophany, as this must have been realized both in the annual celebration of the new year with its rigorous covenantal orientation and in plausibly less dramatic and emphatic contexts throughout the year, has not been, and perhaps may never be, within the reach of the so-called modern interpreter.[38] There is sufficient witness in the Old Testament, how-

[38] This is certainly one of the reasons why Jeremias, *op. cit.*, pp. 118–122, can raise the question, "Do the theophanic texts reflect a celebration of the Jerusalem

ever, to support the conclusion that the recurring moments of divine self-disclosure that transpired within the ongoing life of the Israelite cult were for those involved moments of a most decisive character. Indeed, we are aware of no good reason which demands that we divest ourselves of a staunch conviction that has grown from chapter to chapter that the self-revelation of the one whom Israel addressed as her God stood at the center of her traditions. The Pentateuchal narratives of the theophany of Yahweh on Mt. Sinai preserved in The Book of Exodus and those psalms that we have scrutinized present themselves as but a vivid portion of a much vaster body of Old Testament material that emphatically supports such a verdict.

Israel's awareness that she had been confronted by the deity in the concreteness of her historicity, and called to be a people holy unto Yahweh, and her propensity to reappropriate her traditions and impute fresh significance to them through cultic reenactment, gives us reason to infer that Israel discovered in the rehearsal of the *Urtheophanie* within the congregation an impetus for the renewal of her original commitment to deity, and a new insight into the nature of the divine claim upon her. The experience of past revelation became a model for present disclosure. Always it was more than a matter of vivid memory recollecting past facts. Rather the past was vested with new life itself as it merged with the present into a coherent and meaningful whole. The new reality that was called into existence in the cult, however, was ever historical in nature. In the reenactment of past theophanic event, Israelite worshipers did not submerge themselves into a great divine abyss and thereby lose identity of self. No, in the cultic theophanic act, the pronoun " thou " remained an authentic part of God's address to man and his to God. Whether we think of Isaiah of Jerusalem or instead of scores of Israelites who must necessarily remain anonymous, those who were favored by such a direct awareness of deity knew themselves to be confronted by the divine will, by legislation and instruction, that was a ready complement to Yahweh's name and nature. Decision and response

---

cult? " and answer it in the negative. Of course another and perhaps ultimately more crucial reason is that his working definition of theophany is narrower than many. Perhaps this is the point on which future discussions of the problem shall have to focus.

were the order of the day for Israel as they always had been. Presumably the regular theophanic enactment in the cult never lost sight of this truth for long. If the cultic apparatus and articulation alike became too familiar, we may assume that fresh insights were brought to bear upon the original Sinaitic event. Psalm 50 offers us some clues here.

Throughout her history, Israel knew herself to be a called people. With their frequent cultic nuances, the theophanic traditions that reverberate throughout the Old Testament were in large measure responsible for the perpetuation of this conviction.

Bibliography

Aalen, Sverre, *Die Begriffe "Licht" und "Finsternis" im Alten Testament, im Spätjudentum und im Rabbinismus.* Oslo: J. Dybwad, 1951.

Albright, W. F., *From the Stone Age to Christianity: Monotheism and the Historical Process.* The Johns Hopkins Press, 1946.

——— "The Old Testament and Canaanite Language and Literature," *CBQ,* Vol. 7 (1945), pp. 5–31.

Alt, Albrecht, "Der Gott der Väter" (1929), *Kleine Schriften zur Geschichte des Volkes Israel.* Munich: C. H. Beck, 1953, Vol. 1, pp. 1–78.

——— "Die Ursprünge des israelitischen Rechts" (1934), *Kleine Schriften zur Geschichte des Volkes Israel.* Munich: C. H. Beck, 1953, Vol. 1, pp. 278–332.

Anderson, Bernhard W., "Old Testament View of God," *The Interpreter's Dictionary of the Bible.* Abingdon Press, 1962, Vol. 2, pp. 417–430.

——— *Understanding the Old Testament,* 2d ed. Prentice-Hall, Inc., 1966.

Baillie, John, *The Idea of Revelation in Recent Thought.* Columbia University Press, 1956.

Barr, James, "Revelation," *Dictionary of the Bible,* ed. by James Hastings; rev. ed. by Frederick C. Grant and H. H. Rowley. Charles Scribner's Sons, 1963, pp. 847–849.

——— "Theophany and Anthropomorphism in the Old Testament." Congress Volume: Supplement to *Vetus Testamentum,* Vol. 7. Leiden: E. J. Brill, 1960, pp. 31–38.

Baumgartner, Walter, "Zum Problem des 'Jahwe-Engels,'" *Zum Alten Testament und seiner Umwelt.* Leiden: E. J. Brill, 1959, pp. 240–246.

Beaucamp, Evode, "La Théophanie du Psaume 50 (49): Sa Signification pour l'Interpretation du Psaume," *NRT,* Vol. 81 (1959), pp. 897–915.

Begrich, Joachim, "Das priesterliche Heilsorakel," *ZAW*, Vol. 52 (1934), pp. 81–92.

Beyerlin, Walter, *Origins and History of the Oldest Sinaitic Traditions*, tr. by S. Rudman. Oxford: Basil Blackwell, 1965.

Bezold, Carl, *et al., Babylonisch-Assyrisches Glossar*. Heidelberg: Carl Winter's Universitätsbuchhandlung, 1926.

Birkeland, Harris, *The Evildoers in the Book of Psalms*. Oslo: J. Dybwad, 1955.

Boman, Thorleif, *Hebrew Thought Compared with Greek*, tr. by Jules L. Moreau. The Westminster Press, 1960.

Bright, John, *Early Israel in Recent History Writing* (Studies in Biblical Theology, No. 19). London: SCM Press, Ltd., 1956.

——— *A History of Israel*. The Westminster Press, 1959.

——— "Modern Study of Old Testament Literature," *The Bible and the Ancient Near East* (W. F. Albright *Festschrift*), ed. by G. Ernest Wright. Doubleday & Company, Inc., 1961, pp. 13–31.

Brown, Francis, Driver, S. R., and Briggs, Charles A., *A Hebrew and English Lexicon of the Old Testament with an Appendix Containing the Biblical Aramaic*. Oxford: Clarendon Press, 1957.

Buber, Martin, *Moses: The Revelation and the Covenant*. Harper & Brothers, Torchbook edition, 1958.

Buck, Harry M., *People of the Lord: The History, Scriptures, and Faith of Ancient Israel*. The Macmillan Company, 1966.

Büchers, Hermann C., "Zur Verwertung der Sinaitraditionen in den Psalmen," *Biblica*, Vol. 32 (1951), pp. 401–422.

Burrows, Millar, *An Outline of Biblical Theology*. The Westminster Press, 1946.

Buss, Martin J., "The Meaning of 'Cult' and the Interpretation of the Old Testament," *JBR*, Vol. 32 (1964), pp. 317–325.

Carpenter, J. Estlin, and Harford-Battersby, G., *The Hexateuch According to the Revised Version*, Vol. 2. Longmans, Green & Co., Inc., 1900.

Caspari, D. W., "Kultpsalm 50," *ZAW*, Vol. 45 (1927), pp. 254–266.

Childs, Brevard S., *Myth and Reality in the Old Testament* (Studies in Biblical Theology, No. 27). London: SCM Press, Ltd., 1960.

Clements, R. E., *God and Temple*. Fortress Press, 1965.

Crim, Keith R., *The Royal Psalms*. John Knox Press, 1962.

Cross, F. M., Jr., "Yahweh and the God of the Patriarchs," *HTR*, Vol. 55 (1962), pp. 225–259.

Cross, F. M., Jr., and Freedman, D. N., "A Royal Song of Thanksgiving: II Samuel 22 = Psalm 18," *JBL*, Vol. 72 (1953), pp. 15–34.

Cumming, Charles G., *The Assyrian and Hebrew Hymns of Praise.* Columbia University Press, 1934.

Dahood, Mitchell, *Psalms I (1–50): Introduction, Translation, and Notes* (The Anchor Bible, Vol. 16). Doubleday & Company, Inc., 1966.

Davies, G. Henton, "Theophany," *The Interpreter's Dictionary of the Bible.* Abingdon Press, 1962, Vol. 4, pp. 619–620.

Dickinson, Emily, *Poems,* ed. by Mabel Loomis Todd and T. W. Higginson. Little, Brown and Company, 1890.

Driver, S. R., *The Book of Exodus.* Cambridge University Press, 1911.

——— *An Introduction to the Literature of the Old Testament.* Meridian Books, The Meridian Library, 1956; first published in 1891.

Eaton, J. H., "The Origin and Meaning of Habakkuk 3," *ZAW,* Vol. 76 (1964), pp. 144–171.

Eerdmans, B. D., *The Hebrew Book of Psalms* (Oudtestamentische Studiën, Vol. 4). Leiden: E. J. Brill, 1947.

Eichrodt, Walther, *Theologie des Alten Testaments,* Teil 2/3, 4te Auflage. Göttingen: Vandenhoeck & Ruprecht, 1961.

——— *Theology of the Old Testament,* Vol. 1, tr. by J. A. Baker (The Old Testament Library). The Westminster Press, 1961.

Eissfeldt, Otto, *Hexateuch-Synopse.* Leipzig: J. C. Hinrichs, 1922.

——— *The Old Testament: An Introduction,* tr. by Peter R. Ackroyd. Harper & Row, Publishers, Inc., 1965.

Elliger, Karl, "Ich bin der Herr—euer Gott," *Theologie als Glaubenswagnis* (Karl Heim *Festschrift*). Hamburg: Furche-Verlag, 1954, pp. 9–34.

Engnell, Ivan, *The Call of Isaiah: An Exegetical and Comparative Study.* Uppsala: A.-B. Lundequistska, 1949.

Feigin, Samuel I., "The Heavenly Sieve," *JNES,* Vol. 9 (1950), pp. 40–43.

Fohrer, Georg, *Das Buch Jesaja* (Zürcher Bibelkommentare). Zürich/Stuttgart: Zwingli-Verlag, 1960.

Gaster, T. H., "Belial," *The Interpreter's Dictionary of the Bible.* Abingdon Press, 1962, Vol. 1, p. 377.

Gesenius, Friedrich H. W., *Hebrew Grammar,* ed. and enlarged by E. Kautzsch; 2d English ed. by A. E. Cowley. Oxford: Clarendon Press, 1910.

González Ruiz, José M., "Las teofanías en los salmos," *EB,* Vol. 13 (1954), pp. 267–287.

Gordon, Cyrus H., *Introduction to Old Testament Times.* Ventnor Publishers, Inc., 1953.

——— "The Patriarchal Age," *JBR,* Vol. 21 (1953), pp. 238–243.

——— *Ugaritic Textbook*. Rome: Pontificium Institutum Biblicum, 1965.

Gove, Philip Babcock (editor in chief), *Webster's Third New International Dictionary of the English Language, Unabridged.* G. & C. Merriam Company, 1961.

Gray, G. Buchanan, "Theophany," *Encyclopaedia Biblica,* ed. by T. K. Cheyne and J. Sutherland Black. The Macmillan Company, 1903, Vol. 4, cols. 5033–5036.

Gray, John, *I and II Kings, A Commentary* (The Old Testament Library). The Westminster Press, 1963.

Greenberg, Moshe, "*Nsh* in Exodus 20:20 and the Purpose of the Sinaitic Theophany," *JBL,* Vol. 79 (1960), pp. 273–276.

Gressmann, Hugo, *Mose und seine Zeit: Ein Kommentar zu den Mose-Sagen.* Göttingen: Vandenhoeck & Ruprecht, 1913.

Griffiths, J. Gwyn, "The Celestial Ladder and the Gate of Heaven (Genesis xxviii. 12 and 17)," *ET,* Vol. 76 (1965), pp. 229 f.

Gross, Heinrich, "Der Engel im Alten Testament," *Archiv für Liturgiewissenschaft,* Vol. 6 (1959), pp. 28–42.

Gunkel, Hermann, *Ausgewählte Psalmen.* Göttingen: Vandenhoeck & Ruprecht, 1904.

——— *Genesis,* 6te Auflage (Handkommentar zum Alten Testament). Göttingen: Vandenhoeck & Ruprecht, 1964.

——— *The Legends of Genesis: The Biblical Saga and History,* tr. by W. H. Carruth. Schocken Books, 1964; first published in 1901.

——— *Die Psalmen* (Handkommentar zum Alten Testament). Göttingen: Vandenhoeck & Ruprecht, 1926.

——— "Theophanie," *Die Religion in Geschichte und Gegenwart,* 2te Auflage. Tübingen: J. C. B. Mohr, 1931, Vol. 5, cols. 1130–1132.

Habel, Norman C., "The Form and Significance of the Call Narratives," *ZAW,* Vol. 77 (1965), pp. 297–323.

——— *Yahweh versus Baal: A Conflict of Religious Cultures.* Bookman Associates, 1964.

Haran, M., "The Ark and the Cherubim: Their Symbolic Significance in Biblical Ritual," *IEJ,* Vol. 9 (1959), pp. 30–38, 89–94.

Harrelson, Walter, *Interpreting the Old Testament.* Holt, Rinehart and Winston, Inc., 1964.

——— "Worship in Early Israel," *Biblical Research: Papers of the Chicago Society of Biblical Research III.* Amsterdam: North-Holland Publishing Co., 1958, pp. 1–14.

Harris, Erdman, *God's Image and Man's Imagination.* Charles Scribner's Sons, 1959.

Hempel, Johannes, *Gott und Mensch im Alten Testament: Studie zur Geschichte der Frömmigkeit,* 2te Auflage. Stuttgart: W. Kohlhammer, 1936.

——— "Die Lichtsymbolik im Alten Testament," *Studium Generale,* Vol. 13 (1960), pp. 352–368.

Heschel, Abraham J., *The Prophets.* Harper & Row, Publishers, Inc., 1962.

Holt, John M., *The Patriarchs of Israel.* Vanderbilt University Press, 1964.

Hyatt, J. Philip, *Prophetic Religion.* Abingdon Press, 1947.

van Imschoot, P., *Theology of the Old Testament,* Vol. 1, *God,* tr. by Kathryn Sullivan and Fidelis Buck. Desclée Co., Inc., 1965.

James, E. O., *The Ancient Gods.* G. P. Putnam's Sons, 1960.

Jastrow, Morris, *The Religion of Babylonia and Assyria.* Ginn and Company, 1898.

Jeremias, Jörg, *Theophanie: Die Geschichte einer alttestamentlichen Gattung* (Wissenschaftliche Monographien zum Alten und Neuen Testament). Neukirchen-Vluyn: Neukirchener Verlag, 1965.

Johnson, Aubrey R., *The One and the Many in the Israelite Conception of God,* 2d ed. Cardiff: University of Wales Press, 1961.

——— "The Psalms," *The Old Testament and Modern Study,* ed. by H. H. Rowley. Oxford: Clarendon Press, 1951, pp. 162–209.

——— *Sacral Kingship in Ancient Israel.* Cardiff: University of Wales Press, 1955.

Kapelrud, Arvid S., "Cult and Prophetic Words," *Studia Theologica,* Vol. 4 (1951), pp. 5–12.

——— "The Role of the Cult in Old Israel," *The Bible in Modern Scholarship,* ed. by J. Philip Hyatt. Abingdon Press, 1965, pp. 44–56.

Kissane, Edward J., *The Book of Isaiah.* Dublin: Browne and Noland, 1941–1943.

——— *The Book of Psalms.* Dublin: Browne and Noland, 1953–1954.

Kittel, Rudolf, *Die Psalmen,* 4te Auflage (Kommentar zum Alten Testament). Leipzig: A. Deichert, 1922.

Knight, George A. F., *A Christian Theology of the Old Testament.* John Knox Press, 1959.

Köhler, Ludwig, *Deuterojesaja (Jesaja 40–55) stilkritisch untersucht.* Giessen: A. Töpelmann, 1923.

——— "Die Offenbarungsformel 'Fürchte dich nicht!' im Alten Testament," *STZ,* Vol. 36 (1919), pp. 33–39.

——— *Old Testament Theology,* tr. by A. S. Todd. The Westminster Press, 1957.

Köhler, Ludwig, and Baumgartner, Walter, *Lexicon in Veteris Testa-*

menti Libros, 2d ed. Leiden: E. J. Brill, 1958.

Kominiak, Benedict, *The Theophanies of the Old Testament in the Writings of St. Justin.* The Catholic University of America Press, 1948.

Kraus, Hans-Joachim, *Die Königsherrschaft Gottes im Alten Testament: Untersuchungen zu den Liedern von Jahwes Thronbesteigung.* Tübingen: J. C. B. Mohr, 1951.

——— *The People of God in the Old Testament.* Association Press, 1958.

——— *Psalmen,* 2te Auflage (Biblischer Kommentar Altes Testament). Neukirchen: Verlag der Buchhandlung des Erziehungsvereins, 1961.

——— *Worship in Israel: A Cultic History of the Old Testament,* tr. by Geoffrey Buswell. John Knox Press, 1966.

Kuhn, Karl Georg, *Konkordanz zu den Qumrantexten.* Göttingen: Vandenhoeck & Ruprecht, 1960.

Leslie, Elmer A., *The Psalms.* Abingdon Press, 1949.

Liddell, Henry George, Scott, Robert, and Jones, Henry Stuart, *A Greek-English Lexicon,* 9th ed. Oxford: Clarendon Press, 1940.

Lillie, William, " The Religious Significance of the Theophany in the Book of Job," *ET,* Vol. 68 (1957), pp. 355–358.

Lindblom, Johannes, *Prophecy in Ancient Israel.* Oxford: Basil Blackwell, 1962.

——— " Theophanies in Holy Places in Hebrew Religion," *HUCA,* Vol. 32 (1961), pp. 91–106.

McKenzie, John L., " God and Nature in the Old Testament," *CBQ,* Vol. 14 (1952), pp. 18–39, 124–145.

——— " Jacob at Peniel: Gn. 32:24-32," *CBQ,* Vol. 25 (1963), pp. 71–76.

Mauchline, J., " I and II Kings," *Peake's Commentary on the Bible,* ed. by Matthew Black and H. H. Rowley. Thomas Nelson & Sons, 1962, pp. 338–356.

May, Herbert G., " The Patriarchal Idea of God," *JBL,* Vol. 60 (1941), pp. 113–128.

——— " Some Cosmic Connotations of *Mayim Rabbīm,* ' Many Waters,' " *JBL,* Vol. 74 (1955), pp. 9–21.

Mendenhall, George E., *Law and Covenant in Israel and the Ancient Near East.* The Presbyterian Board of Colportage of Western Pennsylvania, 1955.

Montgomery, James A., *A Critical and Exegetical Commentary on the Books of Kings* (The International Critical Commentary). Edinburgh: T. & T. Clark, 1951.

Morgenstern, Julian, " Biblical Theophanies," *ZA,* Vol. 25 (1911), pp. 139–193; Vol. 28 (1913), pp. 15–60.

——— *The Book of Genesis: A Jewish Interpretation.* Schocken Books, 1965; first published in 1919.

Moriarty, Frederick L., " A Note on the Root YP‘," *CBQ,* Vol. 14 (1952), p. 62.

Moule, C. F. D., " Revelation," *The Interpreter's Dictionary of the Bible.* Abingdon Press, 1962, Vol. 4, pp. 54–58.

Mowinckel, Sigmund, " Drive and/or Ride in O.T.," *VT,* Vol. 12 (1962), pp. 278–299.

——— " The Name of the God of Moses," *HUCA,* Vol. 32 (1961), pp. 121–133.

——— *Psalmenstudien II: Das Thronbesteigungsfest Jahwäs und der Ursprung der Eschatologie.* Kristiania: J. Dybwad, 1922.

——— *The Psalms in Israel's Worship,* tr. by D. R. Ap-Thomas. Abingdon Press, 1962.

——— *Religion und Kultus.* Göttingen: Vandenhoeck & Ruprecht, 1953.

Müller, Hans-Peter, " Die kultische Darstellung der Theophanie," *VT,* Vol. 14 (1964), pp. 183–191.

Muilenburg, James, " Abraham and the Nations: Blessing and World History," *Interpretation,* Vol. 19 (1965), pp. 387–398.

——— " The Biblical View of Time," *HTR,* Vol. 54 (1961), pp. 225–252.

——— " The Form and Structure of the Covenantal Formulations," *VT,* Vol. 9 (1959), pp. 347–365.

——— " The History of the Religion of Israel," *The Interpreter's Bible.* Abingdon Press, 1952, Vol. 1, pp. 292–348.

——— " Introduction and Exegesis to Isaiah, Chs. 40–66," *The Interpreter's Bible.* Abingdon Press, 1956, Vol. 5, pp. 381–773.

——— " The Linguistic and Rhetorical Usages of the Particle *kī* in the Old Testament," *HUCA,* Vol. 32 (1961), pp. 135–160.

——— " Modern Issues in Biblical Studies: The Gains of Form Criticism in Old Testament Studies," *ET,* Vol. 71 (1960), pp. 229–233.

——— " Old Testament Scholarship: Fifty Years in Retrospect," *JBR,* Vol. 28 (1960), pp. 173–181.

——— " The Speech of Theophany," *HDB,* Vol. 28 (1964), pp. 35–47.

——— " A Study in Hebrew Rhetoric: Repetition and Style." Congress Volume: Supplement to *Vetus Testamentum,* Vol. 1. Leiden: E. J. Brill, 1953, pp. 97–111.

——— *The Way of Israel: Biblical Faith and Ethics.* Harper & Brothers, 1961.

Newman, Murray, *The People of the Covenant: A Study of Israel from Moses to the Monarchy.* Abingdon Press, 1962.

——— "The Prophetic Call of Samuel," *Israel's Prophetic Heritage* (James Muilenburg *Festschrift*), ed. by Bernhard W. Anderson and Walter Harrelson. Harper & Brothers, 1962, pp. 86–97.

Niebuhr, H. Richard, *The Meaning of Revelation*. The Macmillan Company, 1941.

Nötscher, Friedrich, *Die Psalmen*. Würzburg: Echter-Verlag, 1947.

Norden, Eduard, *Agnostos Theos: Untersuchungen zur formengeschichte religiöser Rede*. Leipzig/Berlin: B. G. Tuebner, 1913.

North, C. R., "Pentateuchal Criticism," *The Old Testament and Modern Study*, ed. by H. H. Rowley. Oxford: Clarendon Press, 1951, pp. 48–83.

Noth, Martin, *Exodus, A Commentary*, tr. by J. S. Bowden (The Old Testament Library). The Westminster Press, 1962.

——— "Die Gesetze im Pentateuch" (1940), *Gesammelte Studien zum Alten Testament*, 2te Auflage. Munich: Chr. Kaiser Verlag, 1960, pp. 9–141.

——— *The History of Israel*, 2d ed., tr. by Peter R. Ackroyd. Harper & Brothers, 1960.

——— "Jerusalem und die israelitische Tradition" (1950), *Gesammelte Studien zum Alten Testament*, 2te Auflage. Munich: Chr. Kaiser Verlag, 1960, pp. 172–187.

——— *Überlieferungsgeschichte des Pentateuch*, 2te Auflage. Stuttgart: W. Kohlhammer, 1948.

——— *Überlieferungsgeschichtliche Studien*, Teil I. Tübingen: Max Niemeyer, 1957.

Oepke, Albrecht, "Kaluptō," *Theological Dictionary of the New Testament*, ed. by Gerhard Kittel, tr. by Geoffrey W. Bromiley. Wm. B. Eerdmans Publishing Co., 1965, Vol. 3, pp. 556–592.

Oesterley, W. O. E., *The Psalms*. London: S.P.C.K., 1939.

Oesterley, W. O. E., and Robinson, Theodore H., *An Introduction to the Books of the Old Testament*. London: S.P.C.K., 1934.

Patton, John Hastings, *Canaanite Parallels in the Book of Psalms*. The Johns Hopkins Press, 1944.

Pedersen, Johs., *Israel: Its Life and Culture, I–II*. London: Oxford University Press, 1926.

Phythian-Adams, W. J., "The Volcanic Phenomena of the Exodus," *JPOS*, Vol. 12 (1932), pp. 86–103.

Podechard, E., *Le Psautier*. Lyon: Facultés catholiques, 1949–1954.

Pope, Marvin H., *El in the Ugaritic Texts*. Supplement to *Vetus Testamentum*, Vol. 2. Leiden: E. J. Brill, 1955.

Pritchard, James B. (ed.), *Ancient Near Eastern Texts Relating to the Old Testament,* 2d ed. Princeton University Press, 1955.

Quell, Gottfried, "Das kultische Problem der Psalmen," *Beiträge zur Wissenschaft vom Alten Testament,* Neue Folge Heft 11. Berlin/Stuttgart/Leipzig: W. Kohlhammer, 1926.

Rabin, Chaim (ed. and tr.), *The Zadokite Documents,* 2d ed. Oxford: Clarendon Press, 1958.

von Rad, Gerhard, *Genesis, A Commentary,* tr. by John H. Marks (The Old Testament Library). The Westminster Press, 1961.

——— *Moses* (World Christian Books, No. 32). London: Lutterworth Press, 1960.

——— *Old Testament Theology,* tr. by D. M. G. Stalker. Harper & Row, Publishers, Inc., Vol. 1, 1962; Vol. 2, 1965.

——— *The Problem of the Hexateuch and Other Essays,* tr. by E. W. Trueman Dicken. McGraw-Hill Book Company, 1966.

Rendtorff, Rolf, "'Offenbarung' im Alten Testament," *TLZ,* Vol. 85 (1960), cols. 833–838.

——— "Die Offenbarungsvorstellungen im Alten Israel," *Offenbarung als Geschichte,* ed. by Wolfhart Pannenberg. Göttingen: Vandenhoeck & Ruprecht, 1961, pp. 21–41.

Ringgren, Helmer, *The Faith of the Psalmists.* Fortress Press, 1963.

——— *Israelite Religion,* tr. by David E. Green. Fortress Press, 1966.

Robinson, H. Wheeler, *Inspiration and Revelation in the Old Testament.* Oxford: Clarendon Press, 1946.

——— *The Religious Ideas of the Old Testament,* 2d ed. London: Gerald Duckworth & Co., Ltd., 1956.

——— "The Theology of the Old Testament," *Record and Revelation,* ed. by Robinson. Oxford: Clarendon Press, 1938, pp. 303–348.

Robinson, T. H., *The Decline and Fall of the Hebrew Kingdoms: Israel in the Eighth and Seventh Centuries B.C.* (The Clarendon Bible, Vol. 3). Oxford: Clarendon Press, 1930.

Rowley, H. H., *The Faith of Israel: Aspects of Old Testament Thought.* The Westminster Press, 1956.

Rylaarsdam, J. Coert, "Introduction and Exegesis to the Book of Exodus," *The Interpreter's Bible.* Abingdon Press, 1952, Vol. 1, pp. 833–1099.

Sandmel, Samuel, *The Hebrew Scriptures: An Introduction to Their Literature and Religious Ideas.* Alfred A. Knopf, Inc., 1963.

Schmidt, Hans, *Die Psalmen* (Handbuch zum Alten Testament). Tübingen: J. C. B. Mohr, 1934.

Schubart, Wilhelm, "Die religiöse Haltung des frühen Hellenismus," *Der*

alte Orient, Vol. 35, No. 2, Leipzig: J. C. Hinrichs, 1937.
Scott, R. B. Y., "Introduction and Exegesis to Isaiah, Chs. 1–39," *The Interpreter's Bible.* Abingdon Press, 1956, Vol. 5, pp. 151–381.
——— *The Relevance of the Prophets.* The Macmillan Company, 1944.
Skinner, John, *Kings* (The Century Bible). Edinburgh: T. C. and E. C. Jack, 1904.
Smith, W. Robertson, *The Religion of the Semites: The Fundamental Institutions.* Meridian Books, The Meridian Library, 1957; first published in 1889.
Snaith, Norman H., "Introduction and Exegesis to I and II Kings," *The Interpreter's Bible.* Abingdon Press, 1954, Vol. 3, pp. 3–338.
Speiser, E. A., *Genesis: Introduction, Translation, and Notes* (The Anchor Bible, Vol. 1). Doubleday & Company, Inc., 1964.
Straus, Erwin W., "Aesthesiology and Hallucinations," *Existence: A New Dimension in Psychiatry and Psychology,* ed. by Rollo May, Ernest Angel, and Henri F. Ellenberger. Basic Books, 1958, pp. 139–169.
Terrien, Samuel L., "Fear," *The Interpreter's Dictionary of the Bible.* Abingdon Press, 1962, Vol. 2, pp. 256–260.
de Vaux, Roland, *Ancient Israel: Its Life and Institutions,* tr. by John McHugh. London: Darton, Longman & Todd, Ltd., 1961.
Volz, Paul, *Mose: Ein Beitrag zur Untersuchung über die Ursprünge der israelitischen Religion.* Tübingen: J. C. B. Mohr, 1907.
Vriezen, Th. C., *An Outline of Old Testament Theology.* Oxford: Basil Blackwell, 1958.
Weiser, Artur, "Zur Frage nach den Beziehungen der Psalmen zum Kult: Die Darstellung der Theophanie in den Psalmen und im Festkult," *Bertholet-Festschrift.* Tübingen: J. C. B. Mohr, 1950, pp. 513–531.
——— *The Old Testament: Its Formation and Development,* tr. by Dorothea M. Barton. Association Press, 1961.
——— *The Psalms, A Commentary,* tr. by Herbert Hartwell (The Old Testament Library). The Westminster Press, 1962.
Werner, E., "Musical Instruments," *The Interpreter's Dictionary of the Bible.* Abingdon Press, 1962, Vol. 3, pp. 469–476.
Westermann, Claus, *The Praise of God in the Psalms,* tr. by Keith R. Crim. John Knox Press, 1965.
——— *A Thousand Years and a Day: Our Time in the Old Testament,* tr. by Stanley Rudman. Muhlenberg Press, 1962.
——— "The Way of the Promise Through the Old Testament," tr. by Lloyd Gaston and Bernhard W. Anderson, *The Old Testament and Christian Faith: A Theological Discussion,* ed. by Anderson. Harper &

Row, Publishers, Inc., 1963, pp. 200–224.
Whitley, C. F., "The Call and Mission of Isaiah," *JNES*, Vol. 18 (1959), pp. 38–48.
Wright, G. Ernest, "Book of Exodus," *The Interpreter's Dictionary of the Bible*. Abingdon Press, 1962, Vol. 2, pp. 188–197.
——— "Cult and History: A Study of a Current Problem in Old Testament Interpretation," *Interpretation*, Vol. 16 (1962), pp. 3–20.
——— "Introduction and Exegesis to the Book of Deuteronomy," *The Interpreter's Bible*. Abingdon Press, 1953, Vol. 2, pp. 311–537.
——— "The Lawsuit of God: A Form-Critical Study of Deuteronomy 32," *Israel's Prophetic Heritage* (James Muilenburg *Festschrift*), ed. by Bernhard W. Anderson and Walter Harrelson. Harper & Brothers, 1962, pp. 26–67.
Zimmerli, Walther, "Ich bin Jahwe," *Geschichte und Altes Testament* (Albrecht Alt *Festschrift;* Beiträge zur historischen Theologie, No. 16). Tübingen: J. C. B. Mohr, 1953, pp. 179–209.
——— *The Law and the Prophets: A Study of the Meaning of the Old Testament,* tr. by R. E. Clements. Oxford: Basil Blackwell, 1965.

INDEX OF BIBLICAL CITATIONS

INDEX OF SUBJECTS AND AUTHORS